A treatise on the mechanic's lien law of the state of Illinois : as in force March 1, 1894, so far as the same relates to real estate.

Julius A. Coleman

A treatise on the mechanic's lien law of the state of Illinois : as in force March 1, 1894, so far as the same relates to real estate.
Coleman, Julius A. (Julius Archer)
collection ID ocm15671029
Reproduction from Harvard Law School Library
Includes index.
Chicago : Wait Pub. Co, 1894.
xxviii, 281 p. : forms ; 24 cm.

The Making of Modern Law collection of legal archives constitutes a genuine revolution in historical legal research because it opens up a wealth of rare and previously inaccessible sources in legal, constitutional, administrative, political, cultural, intellectual, and social history. This unique collection consists of three extensive archives that provide insight into more than 300 years of American and British history. These collections include:

Legal Treatises, 1800-1926: over 20,000 legal treatises provide a comprehensive collection in legal history, business and economics, politics and government.

Trials, 1600-1926: nearly 10,000 titles reveal the drama of famous, infamous, and obscure courtroom cases in America and the British Empire across three centuries.

Primary Sources, 1620-1926: includes reports, statutes and regulations in American history, including early state codes, municipal ordinances, constitutional conventions and compilations, and law dictionaries.

These archives provide a unique research tool for tracking the development of our modern legal system and how it has affected our culture, government, business – nearly every aspect of our everyday life. For the first time, these high-quality digital scans of original works are available via print-on-demand, making them readily accessible to libraries, students, independent scholars, and readers of all ages.

The BiblioLife Network

This project was made possible in part by the BiblioLife Network (BLN), a project aimed at addressing some of the huge challenges facing book preservationists around the world. The BLN includes libraries, library networks, archives, subject matter experts, online communities and library service providers. We believe every book ever published should be available as a high-quality print reproduction; printed on-demand anywhere in the world. This insures the ongoing accessibility of the content and helps generate sustainable revenue for the libraries and organizations that work to preserve these important materials.

The following book is in the "public domain" and represents an authentic reproduction of the text as printed by the original publisher. While we have attempted to accurately maintain the integrity of the original work, there are sometimes problems with the original work or the micro-film from which the books were digitized. This can result in minor errors in reproduction. Possible imperfections include missing and blurred pages, poor pictures, markings and other reproduction issues beyond our control. Because this work is culturally important, we have made it available as part of our commitment to protecting, preserving, and promoting the world's literature.

GUIDE TO FOLD-OUTS MAPS and OVERSIZED IMAGES

The book you are reading was digitized from microfilm captured over the past thirty to forty years. Years after the creation of the original microfilm, the book was converted to digital files and made available in an online database.

In an online database, page images do not need to conform to the size restrictions found in a printed book. When converting these images back into a printed bound book, the page sizes are standardized in ways that maintain the detail of the original. For large images, such as fold-out maps, the original page image is split into two or more pages

Guidelines used to determine how to split the page image follows:

• Some images are split vertically; large images require vertical and horizontal splits.
• For horizontal splits, the content is split left to right.
• For vertical splits, the content is split from top to bottom.
• For both vertical and horizontal splits, the image is processed from top left to bottom right.

A TREATISE

ON THE

MECHANIC'S LIEN LAW

OF THE

STATE OF ILLINOIS,

As in Force March 1, 1894,

SO FAR AS THE SAME RELATES TO

REAL ESTATE.

BY

J. A. COLEMAN,

COUNSELOR AT LAW

CHICAGO:
THE WAIT PUBLISHING CO.
1894

S
US
932 IL
COL

TO

𝕷𝖊𝖘𝖑𝖎𝖊 𝕯. 𝕿𝖍𝖔𝖒𝖆𝖘,

THE LAWYER, THE SCHOLAR, THE MAN,

THIS TREATISE

IS DEDICATED

BY

THE AUTHOR.

PREFACE.

The Mechanic's Lien Law of the State of Illinois concerns, not only every one furnishing materials, rendering services and performing labor in the improvement of real estate, but every owner thereof, every person who holds security thereon for deferred purchase money, money loaned, or other indebtedness.

This law was designed to promote the improvement of such property and secure the rights of labor, and under it the owner's title may be divested, the justly secured claim of the vendor for purchase, or the creditor for loaned money may be scaled down and impaired by the claim of one whom he has never seen, known, or contracted with, and whose right originated long subsequent to his.

It may burden the property of an innocent purchaser for value, with a lien, secret and unrecorded; yet enforceable after his acquisition and possession, when his vendor's insolvency would cause him irreparable loss.

The vast interests involved in this class of property in Illinois, as well as the security of materialmen, whose credited supplies, and the laborer, whose toil waiting payment, make such improvement possible, demand an accurate knowledge of this law on the part of all who own or deal with such property. For nothing in business life will supply the lack of prudence guided by comprehensive information, and carefulness born of a correct understanding of one's rights, duties, and liabilities; while on the other hand, negligence and irregularity, due to anxiety for work or trade, and inattention to, or disregard of that knowledge and information, will make energy uselesss, effort fruitless, and the tenure of property precarious.

This law has been much abused, either because it has not been understood, or because it has been unwisely applied. Its careful study and full comprehension disclose a law, in major part, wisely and fairly framed to serve and secure the rights of all, — owners, incumbrancers, and operators.

This treatise is not designed to do more than present this law, as the courts of this State have interpreted it, nor does it intend to be more than a time saving convenience for the profession in the grouping of topics, citation of cases, and collection of different statutes with respect to mechanic's liens for reference in examining decisions rendered under such statutes

Every case cited by our Supreme and Appellate Courts is given, and the decision in all, so far as applicable to the present law, are herein presented While the special aim and intent of the author has been to make the work serviceable to business, as well as to professional men, the extreme delicacy of certain questions arising under the law, the nicety of their legal distinctions, and the necessity of accurate legal steps, not only in the enforcement of claims, but in the making of contracts, will call for the aid of those whose training and occupation best fit them to properly frame and direct the conduct of such affairs

It is especially hoped that this work will furnish such an understanding of their rights, obligations and liabilities to owners of real estate and of securities thereon, and to contractors, materialmen and laborers, as will enable the former to hold, and the latter to contract with safety in respect to its improvement.

If it shall give this information in such manner as to save to some extent cost, time and trouble in remedial effort, the principal purpose of its preparation will have been accomplished

CHICAGO, ILL., *March 1, 1894.*

J. A. COLEMAN.

CONTENTS.

CHAPTER I.

THEORY — NATURE — CONSTRUCTION

CHAPTER II.

PERSONS ENTITLED TO LIEN

CHAPTER III

NECESSARY REQUISITES OF AN ORIGINAL CONTRACTOR'S LIEN.

b

x CONTENTS.

CHAPTER IV

PERFECTING THE ORIGINAL CONTRACTOR'S LIEN

CHAPTER V.

SUB-CONTRACTORS

CHAPTER VI.

PERFECTING LIEN OF SUB-CONTRACTOR

CHAPTER VII.

ARBITRATION ASSIGNMENT.

CHAPTER VIII

INCUMBRANCES

CHAPTER IX.

LIMITATIONS

CHAPTER X.

REDEMPTION SATISFYING LIEN PAID CIRCUIT COURT CLERK'S
DUTIES

CHAPTER XI.

WAIVER AND RELEASE.

CHAPTER XII.

PLEADING AND PRACTICE.

c

TABLE OF CASES

RELATING TO

MECHANIC'S LIENS,

DECIDED BY THE

Supreme and Appellate Courts of the State of Illinois.

---

d

THE MECHANIC'S LIEN LAW

OF

THE STATE OF ILLINOIS,

AS IT RELATES TO

REAL ESTATE.

CHAPTER I.

THEORY — NATURE — CONSTRUCTION.

SECTION 1. Nature of lien
    Reasons for special protection under the law.

    2 Is a secret lien
    Attaches when contract is made

    3 Is strictly statutory.
    Is in derogation of common law.
    Enforced by sale only
    No remedy by receiver

    4. The lien on real estate only.
    Attaches to personal property only when attached to real estate
    Attaches to movable machinery when part of a plant so attached

    5 Destruction of improvement does not release lien, except as to mortgagee
    Does not follow improvements when detached
    If wrongfully detached, court will follow proceeds.
    Mortgagee may insure for his own benefit

    6 Lien creditor may insure for his own benefit

    7 Remedy cumulative and concurrent
    Suit at law and to enforce lien may be prosecuted the same time

    8 Priority, none between lien claimants

    9 Is a chancery proceeding, *quasi in rem*
    Binds only parties and privies

    10. If a lien is defeated suit fails
    Owner cannot recover judgment except for costs
    Judgment for damages not allowed owner
    Suit against owner and contractor fails, unless right to lien is shown

    11. Lien covers owner's interest in land

SECTION 1. **Nature of the lien.**— It has been well said that landed improvement is at once the cause and consequence of civilization The private interests it relates to are a large part of public progress. They promote general development, and accomplish the proper use of land   The general public share in this benefit, and should compensate and encourage it by increased, unusual and special privileges to those whose labor and material, if not causing, contribute directly to it   Lien laws are predicated upon such theories; and judicial interpretation of a statute is largely influenced by the motive for and purpose of its enactment, always by the equity of the statute itself.

The labor and property of those whose payment they secure are put into a permanent, instead of transitory shape; in such noticeable manner as to challenge attention on the part of those interested in the property improved; which property is thereby subjected to claim for payment, but where prior liens of record exist, such claims for improvements take precedence only to the extent of the actual value they add to the property.[1]

The spirit of justice well unites with the letter of the law in securing such payment to the extent of that fixed, enduring and enhanced value which is of their own creation.

---

[1] Sec 17, act 1874, as amended, Gaty v Casey, 15 Ill. 190, Croskey v N W Mfg Co, 48 id. 481, Clark v. Moore, 64 id. 273.

§ 2. **Is a secret lien.**— Yet the services of others who labor, the property of the merchant who clothes, of the grocer who feeds, are as sacred, their claims for payment are supported by equal justice, and, when it is practicable, should have equal recognition. Such party may extend credit on the faith of security in the real estate to one whose property is covered by this secret, unrecorded lien, which will prevent the collection of his debt; may even have taken and recorded a mortgage thereon to secure such debt, and still find this lien, resting on a verbal contract, has taken precedence of his and rendered it worthless [1]

The man who loans his money, the *bona fide* purchaser for value may get no warning from the public records of its existence, yet be forced to pay it off to save his security, or clear his title For this lien attaches the day the contract is made, and any incumbrance by trust deed or mortgage placed thereon, any lien by judgment, any sale thereafter is subject to it [1]

§ 3. **Is strictly statutory.**— Hence it is that our courts hold that the mechanic's lien does not spring from, but it is in derogation of the common law, [2] is opposed to common right, is a privileged remedy to a particular class; [3] is not a matter of right, but of statutory grace. [4]

It is a statutory mortgage on real estate that draws its life solely from the statute creating it, and must fulfill every requirement of that statute to gain and maintain its existence, comply with every provision of it to complete and accomplish the purpose of that creation. [5]

It gives no right to withhold the owner or deny him possession of his property, or in any way molest him in that possession, or to interfere with his use thereof, unless such use tends to impair its value as a security, as for instance, when an injunction could be properly invoked to prevent such injurious use. It gives no right of ejectment, no right to ask for a receiver for rents and profits; no right but to enforce the sale of the property as the statute prescribes to satisfy the debts that it secures

---

[1] Clark v Moore, 64 Ill 273, Thielman v Carr, 75 id 385, Paddock v Stout, 121 id 571, Franklin Savings Bank v Taylor, 131 id 376, Stout v Sower, 22 App 65, Freeman v Arnold, 39 App. 216.
[2] McLurken v Logan, 23 Ill 77, Canisius v Merrill, 65 id 67, Carney v Tully, 74 id 375, Belanger v Hersey, 90 id 70, Butler & McCracken v Gain, 128 id 23, Williams v Vanderbilt, 145 id. 238, C & St L R R v Cauble, 4 Bradw 133.
[3] Gaty v Casey, 15 Ill 190, Cook v Heald, 21 id. 425, Smith v Moore, 26 id 392, Croskey v. N W. Mfg Co, 48 id 481, Clark v Moore, 64 id 273
[4] Haines v Chandler, 26 App 400
[5] Underhill v Corwin, 15 Ill 556, Swift v Martin, 20 Bradw 515, Martin v. Swift, 120 Ill. 488.

§ 4 **The lien on real estate only** — The lien under this statute secures solely debts for that which becomes attached to, and a part of, and which thus merges into real estate   An eminent member of our appellate court dissented from the opinion that held this lien to cover those absolutely necessary parts of one common system of machinery, that were not attached to the land, and the majority of the court so held only because the improvement as a whole fixed the character of the property, and it required each and every part to make one entire and complete system.[1]

When work is done or materials are furnished under the provisions of this law, they become a part of the land, and together with the ground upon which the improvement is made, form one entire thing, that is real estate ; and however many interests there may be in the land, and by whatever names they may be known, all together constitute the land [2]

The lien created by the law is not against the specific thing furnished, nor necessarily against the interest alone in the land of the party for whom they are furnished, but against the land in this comprehensive sense.[2]

As a rich oriental perfume pervades every vacant space of the loftiest chamber, so does this lien, like a subtle essence, insinuate itself into every fibre of the material put upon and constituting that particular parcel of land ; into every stroke of the architect's pen in preparation of plans and specifications therefor; into every effort of superintendent, mechanic or laborer whose skill directs or toil fastens the material to its permanent place.[2]

§ 5 **Destruction of improvement does not release lien, except as to mortgagee** — Although the entire materials, buildings and improvements, on account of which the lien accrued, are removed, rendered worthless or destroyed by accident, the lien still continues against the land.[3]

The lien being against the land does not follow the materials furnished from place to place. When severed from the land they become personal property, and must be governed by the rules relating to such property until united with or merged in the land [3]

Yet, if wrongfully removed and sold, the court will treat the pro-

---

[1] Curran v Smith, 37 App 69
[2] Gaty v Casey, 15 Ill 190, Steigleman v McBride, 17 id, 300, Sontag v. Brennan, 75 id 279
[3] Underhill v Corwin, 15 Ill 556.

ceeds as real estate still, and will pursue it into the hands of the party so converting it and subject it to the lien [1]

As between owner and lien claimant, destruction of the improvements by fire does not release the lien upon the land [2] It does, so far as prior incumbrances are concerned [3] The proceeds of materials severed by fire and sold are subject to the lien, so the insurance money.[4] But where a prior mortgagee had the property insured in the owner's name, loss, if any, for the mortgagee's benefit, and paid for the insurance, it was held his right thereto was superior to the lien Had the owner paid for this insurance, the case would have been different [5]

§ 6 **Lien creditor may insure for his own benefit.**—It is an insurable interest which the lien creditor can protect; and where policies of insurance provide that liability of the company insuring ceases if the property is encumbered, without the written consent of such company, notice of such liens should be given to the company by the owner

§ 7 **Remedy. Cumulative and concurrent.**—It is a cumulative remedy.[6] To the ordinary remedy for debt is added that of the lien as an appropriation of a specific thing It the lien be defeated, the ordinary action of assumpsit will lie, or case, in event of fraud [7] If the property affected fails to satisfy the decree, a general execution can be issued against the owner to satisfy the balance unpaid to the original, and, under certain conditions, to the sub-contractor or sub-claimant [8]

It is concurrent ; the creditor can sue for his claim in ordinary action of assumpsit, by attachment, or on the case, and to enforce his lien at the same time, and in the same or different courts, and maintain his different actions, until his debt is satisfied by one or the other, but only one satisfaction can be had.[9]

§ 8 **Priority, none between lien claimants.**—There is no pri-

[1] Gaty v Casey, 15 Ill 190, Ellett v Tyler, 41 id 449
[2] Gaty v Casey, 15 Ill 190, Sontag v Brennan, 75 id 279, Elgin Lumber Co v Langman, 23 App 250, Paddock v Stout, 121 Ill 571
[3] Conduct v Flower, 106 Ill 105
[4] Gaty v Casey, 15 Ill 190 Sontag v Brennan, 75 id 279, Elgin Lumber Co v Langman, 23 App 250, Paddock v Stout, 121 Ill 571
[5] Elgin Lumber Co v Langman, 23 App 250
[6] Delahay v Clement 3 Scam 203, Templeton v Horne 82 Ill 191
[7] Geary v Bangs, 37 App 301
[8] Bouton v McDonough Co 84 Ill 384 Baptist Church v Andrews, 87 id 172, Green v Sprague 120 id 416, adv , 18 Bradw 476 Race v Sullivan, 1 id 94, sec 25, act 1874, as amended
[9] West v Flemming 18 Ill 248 Cook v Heald, 21 id 425, Culver v Elwell, 73 id. 536, Geary v Bangs, 37 App 301

ority between lien claimants on account of the times when they made their contracts, performed services, or furnished materials, nor can any one reap the preference of diligence by first instituting his suit to enforce his lien. All stand on the same ground, regardless of any of these conditions, and share *pro rata* in the proceeds of the sale of the property affected.[1]

§ 9. Chancery proceeding, quasi in rem — The enforcement of this lien is an action *in rem*, in so far as it cannot affect other property of the owner until the particular property improved is exhausted. Yet, not such an action *in rem* as to bind others than parties and privies to the action. It is a chancery proceeding, subject to chancery rules, save where the statute has otherwise provided, and will stand on the chancery side of the docket. The statute, with all its proceedings, is a law unto itself, *sui generis*, and may best be denominated a chancery proceeding, *quasi in rem.*[2]

§ 10. If a lien is defeated, suit fails.—In the trial of cases arising under this statute, as between owners and lien claimants, there are but two questions; whether or not there is a lien; if so, for what amount. The owner cannot, by offsets, counterclaims, or damages arising out of the very contract under which the liens are claimed, recover any judgment against the claimant, even if he defeats the claim for lien, or proves such to be far in excess thereof. For any claim of his own, exceeding that which the lien claimant asserts and against such lien claimant, whether for damages under that contract, for defective or delayed performance, or overpayment, or of whatever nature, that owner must resort to another action at law. Such claims cannot be adjudicated in a trial under this statute.[3] All he can be allowed to do in the proceeding to enforce the lien is to defeat the claim to a lien; to utilize his own claims as matters of defense, and for that purpose, and to that extent only. Nor, on the other hand, can the lien claimant recover any judgment unless his lien be established. If his lien on the property be defeated by reason of non-compliance with some statutory requirement, or divested by sale of the property under a prior mort-

---

[1] Sec 14, act 1874, as amended, Wing v Carr, 86 Ill 347

[2] Secs 8, 10, act 1874, as amended, Kimball v Cook, 1 Gilm 423, Shaeffer v Weed, 3 id 511, Kelly v Chapman, 13 Ill 530, Ross v Derr, 18 id 245, Morrison v Stewart, 24 id 24, Sutherland v Ryerson, 24 id 518. Raymond v Ewing, 26 id 329, N P Church v Jevne, 32 id 214 Lomax v Dore, 45 id 379, Crosky v N W Mfg Co, 48 id 481, Clark v Boyle 51 id 104, Dunphy v Riddle, 86 id 22, Paddock v Stout, 121 id 571, Franklin Svgs Bank v Taylor, 131 id 376

[3] McCarthy v. Neu, 93 Ill 455, Green v Sprague, 120 id. 416, adv., 18 Bradw 476, O'Brien v Graham, 38 App 546.

gage, there can be no judgment save for the dismissal of the suit. The fact that the claimant is entitled to a judgment at law for his debt does not warrant a judgment for that debt when his claim is prosecuted under this act.[1] If the owner defeats the lien, whether sued jointly with the principal contractor before a justice of the peace, or other court, or alone, to enforce collection of the debt by enforcement of the lien, he defeats the action, regardless of the justice of the claim, or the right of the plaintiff to recover thereon at law.[2] On both sides the action is narrowed to the limit of lien, or no lien. The decree must be upon the lien as a basis, or there must be no affirmative decree at all[3] The difference between the rights conferred upon owner and lien claimant being, that, if the owner defeats the lien by reason of his claims as proved being in excess of that of his adversary, he can recover no judgment for such excess;[3] the claimant establishing his lien, if an original contractor, is awarded a judgment for any deficiency in the amount decreed him that the proceeds of the sale of the property fail to satisfy;[3] if a sub-contractor or sub-claimant, the same, if the owner's payment to the principal contractor be in violation of his rights as the statute prescribes;[4] or if he sue the owner and contractor jointly by common-law action,[5] which judgment is collectible only by general execution, as in other cases.[6]

§ 11 **Lien covers owner's interest in land.** — While this lien applies solely to real estate, it covers completely the debtor's interest therein, whatever that interest may be, legal or equitable, extends to an estate in fee, for life,[7] for years, or any other estate, or any right of redemption or other interest, which such owner may have in the lot or land at the time of making the contract[8]

---

[1] Green v Sprague, 120 Ill 416, Martin v Swift, id 488, O'Brien v Graham, 33 App 546
[2] Quinn v Allen, 85 Ill 39
[3] Green v Sprague, 120 Ill 416, Martin v Swift, id 488, O'Brien v Graham, 33 App 546, sec 25, act 1874, as amended, Bouton v McDonough Co, 84 Ill 384, Baptist Church v Andrews, 87 id 172, sec 25, act 1871, as amended
[4] Sec 29, act 1874, as amended
[5] Sec 37, act 1874, as amended
[6] Secs 37–38, act 1874, as amended, Baptist Church v Andrews, 87 Ill 172
[7] Osgood v Pacey, 23 App 116 The error of the syllabus of this decision has crept into the digest It does *not* decide that there is no lien under contract with a tenant for life, but that the owner's property is not liable where such tenant made the contract, that the owner's offer to allow certain $100 due on rent if collected, to be paid the mechanic, was no ratification, for that rent was not his to offer He had no interest in it, it was the property of the life tenant This suit was not against the tenant for life, but owner, and the decree against him in favor of the mechanic was reversed. Had the mechanic's suit been against the tenant for life it would doubtless have been successful
[8] Secs 1, 2, act 1874, as amended, Turney v Saunders 4 Scam 527, Garrett v Stevenson, 3 Gilm 261, Steigleman v. McBride, 17 Ill 300, Donaldson v.

§ 12. **Except tenancy at sufferance.** — Tenancy at sufferance, alone, fails to support a lien. Any alienation or incumbrance, *per se*, puts an end to such tenancy, and as this lien extends only to the interest of the owner, the termination of that interest terminates the lien [1]

§ 13 **Extends to after-acquired interest.** — It extends to any interest of the owner acquired subsequent to the contract, as the husband's estate in the wife's realty, where he alone made the contract, and her death subsequent thereto vests such estate in him, or he frees the land from lien of a prior incumbrance by its payment and discharge, or perfects his title under executory contract and procures a deed for the property.[2]

§ 14 **Extends to whole tract of land used for common purposes.** — It extends over not merely the ground that the building stands on, but the whole lot as platted, or the entire tract of land used for one common purpose, as a tract of four hundred acres used for stock yards,[3] or several quarter sections used by a coal company, not simply the quarter section upon which the machinery was placed [4] It may thus extend from a city lot fifteen by fifty feet to a section or more of land

Where two persons jointly owned two tracts, one of eighty acres, one of twenty-two and one-half acres, each living on the respective tracts, the operation of the lien was confined to the interest of the party in the twenty-two and one-half acres who lived on that particular tract and contracted for the improvement thereon.[5] The area of the ground thus depends upon its defined boundaries, or use for one common and distinct business by the owner contracting for the improvement

§ 15. **Judicial notice taken that lots in different sections are different tracts.** — But where the property had been subdivided into lots, though used as a farm, and the improvements were on a farm-house and barn, the court took judicial notice that the different lots being in different sections, were different tracts of land, held, that the lot alone on which the building was situated could be

---

Holmes, 23 id 83. Phillips v Stone, 25 id 67, Stephens v. Holmes, 64 id 336
Canisius v Merrill, 65 id 67, Dobschuetz v Holliday, 82 id 371, Reed v Boyd 84 id 66, Belanger v Hersey, 90 id 70, Paulsen v Manske, 126 id 72, 24 App 95, Chisholm v Williams, 128 Ill 115, Chisholm v Randolph, 21 App 312, Portones v Badenoch, 132 Ill 377, Portones v Holmes, 33 App 312
[1] Proctor v Tows, 115 Ill 138
[2] McCarty v Carter, 49 Ill 53 Phœnix M L Co v Batchen, 6 Bradw 621
[3] Nat'l Stock Yards Co v O'Reilly, 85 Ill 546
[4] Kankakee Coal Co v Crane Bros Mfg Co , 128 Ill 627, 28 App 371
[5] Woodburn v Gifford, 66 Ill 285

sold to satisfy the lien, and that a sale of the entire body comprising all the lots was erroneous[1] The point, however, was not raised in this case that the entire premises were used for a common purpose — the improvement being as necessary for that purpose as machinery for coal mining would be for a tract of many quarter sections devoted to coal business. On the other hand, the statute recognizes the difference between the expressions "lot," or "piece" and "tract" of land[2] If the improvement be on property subdivided into lots, then in order that the lien shall extend to all, there must be in the contract sufficient to apply such improvement to the body of land as a whole, or the fact must appear that the lots are, or are to be improved as an entirety; that is, the improvement for their use as a unit and for a common purpose that applies to and covers all, must be properly averred and proved.[3]

§ 16 **There is no lien against State, county or municipality, but there is against public buildings not so owned or controlled.** — The lien does not attach to public property, as a court-house or school-house, nor for labor or material for sewers, sidewalks or other public improvements[4] But where the property is not paid for by the State, and is not the property of the State, county or municipality, but is an eleemosynary corporation and public, as a normal school that any one may attend, but whose charter the State has no control over, the lien attaches[5]

§ 17. **Lien against homestead.** — The homestead is not exempted from its grip, but dower is; the widow can claim her dower, not only in the land, but also in the improvements made thereon, and in both her interest takes precedence of the lienholder.[6] The chivalry and humanity of both the common law, from which the right of dower descends, and statutory enactment, permits dower to be divested only by the wife's own act in proper form, and extends it to whatever improvements her husband makes on his realty, whether he pays for them or not. Even if she be made a party to proceedings to enforce a mechanic's lien, is duly summoned and defaulted, no judgment can be taken that will affect her dower interest[7] It was held where a mechanic's lien attached prior to the execution

---

[1] Van Lone v Whittemore, 19 Bradw 447
[2] Sec 1, act 1874, as amended
[3] Seiler v Schaefer, 40 App 74
[4] Thomas v. Urbana School District 71 Ill 283, Thomas v Industrial University, id 310, Board of Education v Neidenburger, 78 id 58, Bouton v McDonough County, 84 id 384 Quinn v Allen, 85 id 39
[5] Board of Education v Greenebaum, 39 Ill 610
[6] Shaeffer v Weed 3 Gilm 511, Gove v Cather, 23 Ill 634.
[7] Gove v. Cather, 23 Ill 634

of a trust deed, or mortgage in which the wife joined and released her dower, that a sale under a decree to enforce the mechanic's lien extinguished the title under such trust deed or mortgage, and the dower which was released only for the purpose of the trust deed or mortgage was revived against the purchaser under the decree in the mechanic's lien case.[1]

§ 18. **Statute liberally construed on cases within it —** This lien is enforceable only in the cases and upon the conditions prescribed by the statute,[2] is entirely the creation of the statute, and is controlled absolutely by the provisions, requirements and conditions of the law which created it[3] It confers extraordinary privileges, and it is not proper to stigmatize as a burden, or unreasonable or harsh, the requisition of strict compliance with each and every provision of the statute susceptible of working such hurtful preference to others, whose rights are of equal sanctity, the coupling with the conference of these privileges, the exaction of strictly following the methods prescribed for obtaining, securing, holding and enforcing them. While no construction should be adopted that will defeat the object of the statute,[4] and that construction must be strict in requiring compliance with all its provisions,[5] it must be liberally construed in cases falling clearly within its provisions[6]

§ 19. **Statute strictly construed in bringing case within it.—**It is not extended to cases falling within the reason and spirit, but not provided for by the language of the statute The letter of the law limits its action[7] The court cannot extend the privileges of the act beyond its terms as to party or place[8] Prior and subsequent incumbrancers and creditors were relieved from the onus of the lien, in case the claimant did not prosecute his rights within a limited period, long before a *bona fide* and innocent purchaser was put upon the same footing, accorded the same protection by being named in the

[1] Gove v Cather, 23 Ill 634
[2] Haines v Chaudler, 26 App 400
[3] Swift v Martin, 20 Bradw 515, 27 id 117; Martin v. Swift, 120 Ill 488
[4] Stout v. Sower, 22 App 65, McDonald v Rosengarten, 35 id 71, 134 Ill 126
[5] Cook v. Heald, 21 Ill 425, Senior v Brebnor, 22 id 252, McLurken v Logan, 23 id 77, Brady v Anderson, 24 id 111, Roberts v Gates, 64 id 374, Huntington v Barton, id 502, Canisius v Merrill, 65 id 67, Bryan v Whitford, 66 id 33, Crowl v Nagle 86 id 437, Belanger v Hersey, 90 id 70, Butler & McCracken v Gain, 128 id 23, Kankakee Coal Co v Crane Bros Mfg Co, id 627, McDonald v Rosengarten, 134 id 126, Ruggles v Blank, 15 Bradw 436, Boals v In trup, 40 App 62, Seiler v Schaefer, id 74
[6] Phillips v Stone, 25 Ill 67
[7] Wetherell v Ohlendorff, 61 Ill 283, Stephens v Holmes, 64 id. 336, Rothberger v Dupuy, id 452, Carney v. Tully, 74 id. 375.
[8] Brady v. Anderson, 24 Ill 111.

statute.[1] Nor was there any right of redemption from judicial sales in enforcement of these liens, until the statute relating thereto expressly allowed it.[2]

The act of 1845 gave a lien to the original contractor for erecting or repairing a building. The act of 1869 extended the lien to sub-contractors for altering, beautifying and ornamenting it. Under this the court held, that an original contractor had no lien for altering, beautifying, or ornamenting a building already erected, and not needing repairs from decay and accident.[3] Here the original contractor was put to the ridiculous and absurd necessity of subletting such contract, however small and trifling, to secure his lien. Yet, this being the legislature's work, the court's findings under the law were correct. There is no such absurdity in the present statute,[4] but the principle is the same; it cannot be extended to cases falling within the spirit, but not provided for by the language of the statute.

§ 20. **Must be within language of statute, spirit will not prevail.** — He who seeks the benefit of this act must ground his claim, not on the merit of his work, the worth of his material, the justice of his debt, but show by contract, conduct of claim, pleading and proof that he comes clearly and unmistakably within the provisions of the statute, and in strict conformity to each and every one of those provisions, invokes its remedial agency.[5] None of its requisitions, deemed insignificant, or unreasonably exacting can be slighted or disregarded.[6] The necessity of their uniform observance is absolute; not one will the court regard more technical, less binding than another; non-compliance with any directed duty proves fatal to the claimant's case. Where the interests of only the original parties — the owner and principal contractor — are involved, courts have indulged less critical construction, greater liberality in methods of procedure to enforce payment, but where the interests of third parties are touched, they move with a more cautious tread, and enforce a stricter construction.[7]

[1] Amendment, 1879, Dunphy v. Riddle, 86 Ill. 22
[2] Act March 30, 1869, West v. Flemming, 18 Ill. 248, Armsby v. People, 20 id. 155, Link v. Architectural Iron Works, 24 id. 551, Claycomb v. Cecil, 27 id. 497, James v. Hambleton, 42 id. 308, Schmidt v. Williams, 89 id. 117
[3] Bryan v. Whitford, 66 Ill. 33
[4] The present statute uses the word "beautifying" in sec. 29, referring to sub-contractors, and does not use it in sec. 1 referring to original contractors. It is used in conjunction with ornamenting, and is included in that term. To avoid controversy, there ought to be an amendment making this verbiage of both sections the same.
[5] Notes, secs. 18-19
[6] Carney v. Tully, 74 Ill. 375
[7] Kimball v. Cook, 1 Gilm. 423, Nibbe v. Brauhn, 24 Ill. 268

§ 21 **Every necessary step to perfect lien must be shown.**—
In all cases it is held, that every statutory step necessary for the cre
ation, maintenance and enforcement of the lien must not only be
taken, but affirmatively shown by every claimant of one, whether he
be principal or subordinate contractor, laborer, materialman, architect, superintendent, or other person [1]

§ 22 **Creditor defined** — The term "creditor" in this act
does not mean or refer to creditors at large, but to those who by
contract have a lien for labor or material under it.[2] It is confined to these special lien claimants, save in the limitation of four
months for filing claims, which refers to general creditors, not to
these [3]

Incumbrancer — The term "incumbrancer" means and refers to
one who has a lien by trust deed, mortgage, judgment, or otherwise,
existing at the time of the rendition of the lien claimant's judgment, whether the same were created prior, or subsequent to the
making of the contract under which he seeks to enforce his lien [3]

General creditors who prove claims against a decedent's estate are
regarded as judgment creditors [4]

§ 23 **Must be acquired under statute in force when contract
is made** — The right of the lien is determined by the statute in
force when the contract is made,[5] its manner of enforcement by the
statute in force when the suit is brought.[6]

There is no vested right in a remedy   The legislature may
change the mode of enforcing rights, and the new law will govern
as to proceedings instituted after it goes into effect, no matter when
the right sought to be enforced accrued. [7]

The act of 1869 provided that thereafter there should exist a
right of redemption in cases of mechanic's liens.   It was held that
this could not be construed to affect a decree entered before the act
went into effect, for a sale thereafter, which cut off the right of redemption   Such a decree being proper at the time it was entered.

[1] Shaeffer v Weed, 3 Gilm 511, note 5, § 18
[2] Kimball v Cook, 1 Gilm 423, Shaefter v Weed, 3 id 511
[3] Sec 28, act 1874, as amended, Maxwell v Koeritz, 35 App 300
[4] Reitz v Cover, 83 Ill 28
[5] Berkowsky v Sable, 43 App 410, Hughes v Russell, id. 430
[6] Turner v Saunders, 4 Scam 527, Garrett v. Stevenson, 3 Gilm 261, Knight v
Begole, 56 Ill 122 Arbuckle v I M R R, 81 id 429, Templeton v Horne 82
id 491, Reitz v Cover 83 id 28, Schmidt v Williams, 89 id 117, McDonald v
Rosengarten 134 id 126, 35 App 71, Barton v Steinmetz, 37 id 141, Berkowsky
v Sable, 43 id 410, Hughes v Russell, id 430
[7] Kinney v Sherman, 28 Ill 520, Knight v. Begole, 56 id 122, Templeton v
Horne, 82 id 491

would not, upon the act going into operation before the time fixed for the sale of the property, thereby become erroneous [1]

The act of 1839-40 repealed the previous law, but provided that rights acquired and liabilities incurred under the previous law should not be affected by such repeal. It was held that a lien growing out of a contract entered into before the passage of the later act, but not completed until after it took effect, should be prosecuted under the new act [2]

§ 24. **Power of legislature over contracts.** — A statute cannot affect a contract so as to make a new contract for the parties entirely different in its character, as by making it a lien on land when it was none when the contract was made. The legislature may deal with remedies, but not with contracts which parties have voluntarily made. Courts may relieve from their hardships, or enforce them; the legislature can do neither [3]

§ 25. **Whole statute construed together.** — The entire act must be considered and construed as a whole. If any part of the statute be intricate, obscure, or doubtful, or apparently in conflict with another part, the proper way to discover the intention is to consider the other parts of the act, for the words and meaning of one part of a statute frequently lead to the sense of another, and in the construction of one part of the statute every other part ought to be taken into consideration [4]

In further detail these general principles will be enlarged upon hereafter.

---

[1] Knight v Begole, 56 Ill 122.
[2] Turney v Saunders, 4 Scam 527
[3] Kinney v Sherman, 28 Ill 520
[4] Biggs v Clapp, 74 Ill 335, Chicago S D & B Co v Shaw, 44 App 618.

CHAPTER II.

PERSONS ENTITLED TO LIEN

§ 26 **Only persons named are entitled to lien.** — Only those persons named, and in the character named; not those coming within its spirit, are entitled to the benefit of this statute, nor does the work done in the spirit of the act fare any better.[1] It is the letter of the law that controls the persons as well as the class and character of work entitled to its protection.

§ 27. **Original contractors.** — There are two classes, and only two, to whom the privileges of the act are extended. The first class comprises.

1 Any one who contracts with the owner for the entire building or work — the principal contractor

2 Any one who furnishes material to the owner.

3. Any one who labors for the owner.

4. Any architect, or superintendent, who furnishes service as architect, or as superintendent to the owner, when his service is in accordance with the provisions of the statute and pursuant to the purpose of the original contract.

In brief, the first class embraces those who, pursuant to the statute and the contract, deal directly with the owner — all coming under the head of original contractors.[2]

§ 28 **Sub-contractors.** — The second class of persons entitled to a lien are those who, pursuant to the original contract and the statute —

1 Make a contract for a special part of the work with the original contractor

2. Furnish materials to the original contractor.

3. Do mechanical or common labor for the original contractor.

---

[1] Sec. 18, 19.   [2] Sec 1, act 1874, as amended.

Those, in brief, who, pursuant to the purpose of the original contract, and in accordance with the statute, deal directly with the original contractor, all coming under the head of sub-contractors[1]

§ 29 **Sub-sub-contractor no lien.** — The statute reaches no further than this class. No one who furnishes material or renders services to, or labors for a sub-contractor has a lien[2] Where the statute uses the words "mechanic, laborer," it refers to the skilled or unskilled laborer for the owner or original contractor, not for those of the sub-contractor.

If, however, suits are brought to enforce the lien and the court acquires jurisdiction of the fund coming to the sub-contractor, his sub-contractor or laborer, or whosoever has furnished him material, can make himself a party, and have what is due paid him out of such fund[3]

§ 30. **Each must take the steps designated by statute.** — Each class must pursue its distinct, designated steps to first attach the lien, thereafter fix and establish that inchoate, imperfect lien by an equally distinct method The roads to the result — collection of what is due them — are as different and divergent in some respects as though a separate statute governed each.[4] From the point where a petition is to be filed to enforce the lien on the property improved, the materialman, architect, superintendent, original contractor, sub-contractor, skilled and unskilled laborer, or other person, must proceed exactly as the statute provides

§ 31. **Sub-contractor's lien depends on original contractor's contract.** — The sub-claimant's lien depends, primarily, upon the validity, existence and character of the principal contract. If there were no contract, or a contract with one against whom the law allows no lien, the sub-claimant has none, no matter what the merit of justice of his claim may be; and in such case he cannot successfully maintain an action against the owner, either to enforce that asserted lien, or, at law, to collect his debt, against that owner alone, or against him and the principal contractor jointly[5]

Of primary importance to all are the necessary requisites with respect to that original contract.

[1] Sec 29, act 1874, as amended
[2] Rothberger v Dupuy, 64 Ill 452, Ahern v Evans, 66 id 125, Newhall v Kastens, 70 id 156, Smith Bridge Co v L N A & St L R R. Co, 72 id 506, C & St L R R Co v Watson 85 id 531, Berkowsky v Sable, 13 App 410
[3] Newhall v. Kastens, 70 Ill 156
[4] Maxwell v Koeritz, 35 App 300
[5] Quinn v Allen, 85 Ill 39, Bouton v McDonough County, 84 id 384

CHAPTER III

NECESSARY REQUISITES OF AN ORIGINAL CONTRACTOR'S LIEN.

3

§ 32 Requisites of original contractor's contract.— The necessary requisites to establish a lien in favor of an original contractor are

1 A valid contract.

a This contract must be made with the owner of a lot, piece, or tract of land.

b. This contract must be made to build, alter, repair, or ornament a house or other building or appurtenance thereto on that particular lot, piece or tract of land, or upon some street or alley and connected with a building or appurtenance on such lot or tract of land

c This contract must be made strictly in accordance with section 3 of the statute.

d This contract must be performed, or its non performance excused according to law.

Should the original contract lack any of these requisites, the original contractor has no lien, however just and meritorious in itself his claims may be

§ 33 Contractor must perform his contract — The contract and the statute are kept in common and equal view by the courts in deciding the claims of all concerned.

Whatever is done must be done pursuant to the purposes of that contract with the same strict fidelity as in accordance with the provisions of the statute   The lien is created by the statute, but being dependent upon the contract, owes to each a common fealty. Its terms cannot be changed or varied to suit the interests of any one who labors or furnishes materials for the work done under it   The owner under all circumstances, save where his own fraud or omission of personal or statutory duty impairs it, is entitled to the benefit of that contract   Its terms limit the extent, manner and form of his liability and bound the rights of all others' claims.[1]   The thread of its controlling obligations runs through the whole web and woof of subsequent action, until upon naked ground a building is erected to completion for use or residence, or such is altered or repaired for these purposes, or ornamented to enjoy, beautified to delight   The first legal as well as prudential obligation of all who deal with landed improvement is to ascertain what the contract is, whether or not what the parties to it propose to do is within the limits of the contract and the statute ; what position they occupy in doing what they are asked to do; whether they occupy positions as original contractors, or sub-contractors, or are farther removed from the owner, and so, whether or not they are safe in the undertaking, before they incur the risk

It is not the province of the legislature or courts to supply prudence, or remedy the lack of its ordinary exercise, and this law knows and helps only those who, pursuant to its provisions and the purposes of the contract, safely conduct their business operations Their confidence or credulity cannot carry their meritorious claims into the contract's obligations, or the law's protection, if beyond the fixed boundaries of either.

---

[1] Mehrle v Dunne, 75 Ill 239, Whitcomb v Eustace, 6 Bradw 574

§ 34 **No contract, no lien.**— As before stated, there must be an original, valid contract

It is not the furnishing of materials and labor alone that gives the lien, but the contract and furnishing labor and materials under it[1] If there be no contract there is no lien.[2] Where one contracted to furnish materials for a building, and during the progress of the work took in a partner, and the firm, on firm account, continued to furnish the balance of the materials contracted for, it was held, that the firm could not sustain a lien because no new contract was made by it therefor[2]

§ 35 **Minority, effect on lien.**— Under a contract with parties incompetent to contract, as minors, and persons *non compos mentis*, there is no lien. But minority is both sword and shield. The minor can enforce a lien for his labor or materials, while he escapes liability, if he pleads minority, to those who do the same for him It is his option to make the contract valid or void.[3]

Nor will use of the property, receipt of its rents and profits after arrival at age constitute ratification of a contract by one who was a minor when it was made[3]

§ 36 **Contract must be a valid one.**— There is no lien if the contract be for an immoral purpose, contrary to public policy, without consideration, or for work done prior to contract.[4] Nor is an owner's verbal promise to pay binding, if made after the work is done for, or materials delivered to his contractor[5]

Where H , on credit of the contractor, furnished materials to build G 's house, the building was partly completed and abandoned by the contractor, and G executed this agreement· "This is to certify that I hold myself responsible for all lumber and materials furnished by H., for the erection of store on Halsted St , in course of erection, and will pay all of our accounts for said store when the building is completed," it was held G was liable only for the materials furnished after the date of that agreement; that no consideration for the materials furnished before that time was expressed, or existed ; that if there had been a consideration expressed it would not have created a lien for such materials, because furnished before the contract of G was made.[4]

---

[1] Sutherland v Ryerson, 24 Ill 518, Kinney v Sherman, 28 id 520, Wendt v. Martin, 89 id. 139
[2] Roberts v Gates, 64 id 374, Wetherell v Ohlendorff, 61 id 283
[3] McCarty v Carter, 49 Ill 53 Mathes v Dohschuetz, 72 id 438
[4] Wetherell v Ohlendorff, 61 Ill 283
[5] Tanquary v Walker, 47 App 451

§ 37 **Ultra vires. (Beyond corporate authority.)** — So, if the contract be *ultra vires* (beyond corporate authority) the corporation making it cannot enforce a lien   A corporation whose charter only empowered it to manufacture and deal in lumber, or make and sell brick could not hold a lien for labor performed in the construction of a building, nor would a contract made with members of a corporation who had no authority to bind it sustain a lien against the corporate property   A corporation is bound only by its corporate acts done under corporate authority, not by the acts of its individual members [1]

§ 38. **Ultra vires of public corporation.** — With a public corporation the rule is more stringent than with a private, the law holding that whoever deals with persons purporting to represent a public corporation must know the scope of their authority [1] Nor is there a lien if the contract be made with one who professes to, but in fact does not, have authority to bind the owner

§ 39 **Contract may be made out of State.** — It does not matter if the contract be made out of this State, if the materials are to be delivered, and the labor done in this State. [2] It must possess all the elements of contracts generally as to capacity of parties, authority to contract, consideration, and is to be interpreted by the ordinary rules of law   It may be written or verbal, and needs no stipulation for a lien

§ 40 **Payments in property.** — It need not be for payment in money   It is good if the owner is to pay all, or part, in property, [3] and, if such be its terms, no different payment can be enforced by the sub-contractor, materialman, or other person. If the property be not delivered or conveyed, the price at which it was agreed to be taken becomes a money demand and that amount a lien on the improved property [3]

§ 41 **Fraudulent representations of owner.** — Fraud, as in any thing else, will avoid the terms of the contract, and enable the lien claimant, if he is entitled to a lien, to enforce it for the value of his materials or labor, regardless of the contract price. [4]

Thus, where a painter agreed to do certain work for a certain price upon the representations of the person for whom the work was to be done as to the amount and character of the work re-

---

[1] Bouton v McDonough County, 84 Ill 384, City of Chicago v Shober & Carqueville Lithographing Co , 6 Bradw 560
[2] Gaty v Casey, 15 Ill 190, Paddock v. Stout, 121 id 571. Stout v Sower, 22 App 65
[3] Welch v Sherer, 93 Ill 64, Barstow v McLachlan, 99 id 641.
[4] Sec 29, act 1874, as amended, Martine v Nelson, 51 Ill. 422

quired, and did not see it until after his employees had done it, he was awarded a lien for the actual value of the work done in excess of the price stated in the contract   But if after the contract, and before the work was done he had personally inspected the work and found it to be of a more expensive character than represented, it would have been his duty to have notified the party before doing it [1]

Fraud is not presumed; it must be clearly proved to overthrow a contract's stated terms; nor will it, under any circumstances, confer a lien.   It only affects the amount of the lien   The claimant must have a lien under the contract, but fraud as to the terms of the contract may make it cover what his work is worth, regardless of the contract price

§ 42 **Architects.** — The rights, duties and powers of no one connected with building operations are more generally misunderstood than are those of architects and superintendents

They are as much original contractors as masons, carpenters or others who contract with the owner   Their contract, then employment equally distinct, and the same rules treated of hereafter as applicable to original contractors are applicable to them

The statute gives them a lien only for their services *as* architect or *as* superintendent,- and none for settling with contractors, etc [2] For any services they may render not included under the special character of such professional employment they have no lien [3] If the charge for their services be a gross one. and include compensation for services not strictly architectural, not strictly within a superintendent's duties, there would be no lien in their favor for any thing [3] For any services outside of a strictly professional character they must keep a separate account, make a separate charge, and collect as any ordinary debt

§ 43 **Powers and duties of architect.** — The province of the architect is to draw the plans, specifications and details for the building, or improvement thereof, upon a particular lot or tract of land   He may be employed as both architect and superintendent, in which event he would have a right to a lien for a joint charge. As architect simply he has no power to let contracts, order material or labor, or in any way obligate either owner or contractor.   He is not the agent of either, has nothing to do with any of the work outside of his own for the owner.

---

[1] Sec 29, act 1874, as amended, Martine v Nelson, 51 Ill 422.
[2] Sec 1, act 1874, as amended
[3] Adler v World's Pastime Co , 126 Ill 373, 26 App 528

The owner, by written or verbal authority, may give him full power to let contracts, supervise the work, enforce its performance according to the plans and specifications, or, in default of the contractor so doing, have it done.

As a rule, contracts are let upon condition that the work is to be done to the satisfaction of subject to the approval of the architect In such case he becomes the absolute arbiter between owner and contractor, his decision final and binding upon both, where honestly and understandingly made[1]

Whether the work be good or bad, in such case, if he is satisfied, disputes must end[2] His decision can be overruled only when made through fraud or mistake To impeach that decision, the owner or contractor who attacks it must prove clearly and conclusively, either that he wilfully did not exercise an honest judgment, or was so mistaken in the facts that he did not exercise his real judgment, such judgment as he would have exercised upon a correct understanding of the matters passed upon

Where so empowered he acts in a professional-judicial capacity. It becomes his duty to withhold certificates from the contractor whose work or materials he deems not in accordance with the plans, specifications and contract, and if occasion requires to have it done in the time and of the quality and character called for, and his acts under such power are binding upon all the parties concerned.

Where either he or the superintendent orders work done or materials furnished, those who do either must learn from the owner or the contract whether or not he has authority to do so, or look to him personally for payment for what he orders.

§ 44 **Powers and duties of superintendent.**— The province of the superintendent is to give constant supervision as the work progresses, and see that it is done as the plans, specifications and contract call for His duties and powers are wholly supervisory He has authority to stop work or refuse to accept materials not of the standard required, but, unless specially authorized, no authority to contract for either or obligate owner or contractor for their payment

When the owner empowers either to supervise, control and direct the work, let contracts, procure proper materials, or the contractor accepts a contract wherein they are so empowered, their authority is superior to both owner and contractor

[1] Downey v O'Donnell 86 Ill 49 92 id 559 Ewing v Fiedler, 80 App 202 see also, Wolf v Michaelis 27 id 336 Michaelis v Wolf, 33 id 645, Davidson v Provost, 35 id 126 Watrous v Davies, id 542.
[2] McAuley v Carter, 22 Ill 53

§ 45 **No lien where no contract with owner** — This contract must be made with the owner of a lot or tract of land.

There is no lien for materials furnished, or work done on the credit of an original contractor only, or of one not the owner.[1]

If a house be built upon an owner's lot, without his knowledge or consent, it becomes his house, and the builder can neither enforce a lien for it, nor remove it. The law imposes no obligation upon such owner to pay for it, or abstain from its use. It then becomes his, absolutely, clear from all claims of every one — whether the party who built it, or his creditors, and any interference therewith is as much a trespass as if the owner had built and paid for it.[2]

The general rule is that improvements of a permanent character made upon real estate and attached thereto without the consent of the owner of the fee, by one having no title or interest, becomes a part of the realty and vests in the owner of the fee.[3] There is an equitable lien for improvements, but only where made by a party under claim of title which turns out to be defective, or under some legal mistake concerning his rights, or is induced to incur expenditures in that behalf through fraud or deception of the owner, but such equitable liens are not in the contemplation of this statute.[3]

§ 46 **No lien where sale is on personal credit.**—A., being unwilling to credit L., sold lumber to B. for L., and delivered it to L. on L.'s lot. Held, that A had no lien, because he did not contract with, only delivered the lumber to the lot-owner. This case also decides that one who guarantees payment for material has no lien.[4]

C sold lumber to K., who owned lots 1 and 2, and had them inclosed with lot 7, which he did not own, and on which he built. U bought lots 1 and 2, and bought the house on lot 7 and moved it on to lot 2. C. brought suit to enforce his lien, and lost. The court held there was no lien on lot 7, because the contract was not made with the owner of it. There being no lien to start with, none could follow the house. Though under a common inclosure, it was C.'s

[1] Secs 1 and 2, act 1874 as amended. Dawson v Harrington 12 Ill 300, Underhill v Corwin, 15 id 556 Burns v Lane, 23 App 504, Burkhart v Reisig, 24 Ill 530 Wetherell v Ohlendorff, 61 id 283, Woodburn v Gifford 66 id 255 Tracy v Rogers, 69 id 662, Mathis v Dobschuetz, 72 id 138 Strawn v O'Hara, 86 id 53 Wendt v Martin, 89 id 139, Proctor v Tows 115 id 138 Paulsen v Manske 126 id 72, Campbell v Jacobson, 145 id 389, Austin v Wohler, 5 Bradw 300, Little v Vredenburg, 16 id 189, Osgood v Pacey, 23 App 116, McGraw v Storke, 44 App 311
[2] Mathes v Dobschuetz, 72 Ill 438
[3] Williams v Vanderbilt, 145 Ill 238.
[4] Ruggles v Blank, 15 Bradw 436

duty to examine into the title of the property; and his failure to
do so, and loss of lien in consequence, was his own fault.[1]

Where a father in good circumstances built on his daughter's lot.
she knowing of and directing the work, no pretense of his acting
as her agent, it was held that there was no lien, because she, the
owner, did not make the contract.[2]

§ 47 **Removal of material.**—It is also held that severance of the
improvement from the land, unless wrongfully made by the party
against whom the lien exists, or his privies, though the lien continue against the land, converts the improvement into personalty
and prevents the lien following it to a new location.[3] However, if
that new location belongs to the same owner, and the materials be
removed to it under contract with him, there will be a lien thereon
to the extent of the value of the labor and materials put upon it.
If it does not belong to the same owner, but to an innocent and
bona fide purchaser of the materials and improvement, the lien
does not follow.[1]

§ 48. **Owners.**—By owner is meant, not only one who of record
owns the fee-simple title, but who owns an estate for life, for years.
or any other estate or right of redemption, or other interest which
such owner may have in the lot or land at the time of making the
contract to the extent of that right or interest.[4]

The statute gives a lien to any person for any thing furnished by
contract to the owner of any interest which becomes attached to the
premises, and becomes the property of the owner as part of his interest.[5] There is no lien on a lot or building in the temporary use
of one who has it improved when it belongs to another,[6] mere possession is not evidence of authority to bind any interest but that of
the possessor.[7] In order for a mechanic's lien to attach, the party
with whom the contract is made must have some interest or estate
in the premises on which the improvement is made or building
erected. The possessor is the owner only to the extent of the interest he has, and that interest is what the mechanic's lien affects.[8]

[1] Underhill v Corwin 15 Ill 556
[2] Strawn v O'Hara, 86 Ill 53
[3] Steigleman v McBride, 17 Ill 300
[4] Sec 2, act 1874, as amended, McCarty v Carter, 49 Ill 53, Portones v
Holmes, 33 App 312, Portones v Badenoch, 132 Ill 377
[5] Portones v Badenoch, 132 Ill 377
[6] Tracy v Rogers 69 Ill 662
[7] Baxter v Hutchings, 49 Ill 116
[8] Paulsen v Manske, 126 Ill 72, 24 App 95

There is no lien on a tenancy at sufferance,[1] nor is there a lien where a building is erected on land without the owner's knowledge or consent, nor will his use of it, or receipt of its rents thereafter, ratify its unauthorized erection, or make him liable for it.[1]

§ 49 **Agency.**—This contract, as any other, may be made by the owner's agent.[2]

Even if the agent does not mention or disclose the owner, but acts in his own (the agent's) name, and the materials are delivered to, work done for the agent, the contract signed by the agent merely in his own name, the owner is liable, if the agency be proved, and the agent acted within the scope of his authority, unless the circumstances show that an exclusive credit was given to the agent.[4] Where the husband contracted as agent of the wife, she had notice thereof, and gave her approval and consent, she and her property were bound by the contract.[5] Where the father made the contract in his own name for building on his daughter's land, but she was present, directed all that was done, promised to pay what was due, and did pay $1,300 toward the balance due, her land was held subject to the lien; her conduct authority for, and her payment ratification of his agency.[6]

§ 50 **Declarations of agent do not prove agency.** — But where the fact of agency is in issue, the declarations of the agent, not made in the presence of the owner, and not approved by him thereafter, are no proof of his agency, and it is improper for the court to admit evidence of such declarations.[7] And where the prices agreed to be paid by the agent are attacked by the owner on the ground of fraud and collusion between seller and agent, only the market value of the materials, labor or contract work can be recovered, instead of what was agreed to be paid But such agreed price is *prima facie* evidence of their value.

§ 51. **Ratification of agency** — Ratification of an agent's acts done without the owner's knowledge, or authority, will relate back to and confirm such acts from the time done, and bind the owner as fully as if authorized beforehand, but such ratification must be on the full knowledge by the owner of all the facts, and if misled or mistaken as to any such facts, such ratification is held not to have

[1] Proctor v Tows, 115 Ill 138
[2] Burns v Lane 23 App 504 McCarty v Carter 49 Ill 53
[3] Schwartz v Saunders, 46 Ill 18, Greenleaf v Beebe 80 id 520
[4] Paulsen v Manske, 24 App 95, id , 126 Ill 72
[5] Greenleaf v Beebe, 80 Ill 520
[6] Burns v Lane, 23 App 504
[7] Proctor v. Tows, 115 Ill 138, Osgood v Pacey, 23 App 116

been made, is not binding ' Ratification is not to be implied from the use of the property, or from collecting its rents ' Though the agent purchase the property for the owner and occupy it, this does not give authority to improve it ' Nor does authority to build imply authority to build on credit, where the agent is furnished a specific amount with which to build ' Nor will a general agency to care for property sustain a lien for extensive improvements.[2]

The party doing work or furnishing materials, knowing the owner, should inquire as to the agent's authority before he incurs a risk The title being of record, he should ascertain the same and the extent of the authority of the agent before constructing.[3]

The fact that the husband has acted as the wife's agent in some cases does not prove that in all he is her agent,[3] nor does a party's agency in respect to one or more affairs prove the existence of a general agency.

§ 52 **Owner authorizing improvement, lien attaches.** — Where the owner authorizes another to improve his property, though not as his agent, such authority carries with it the statutory incident of the lien.[4]

The owner of a lot entered into an agreement with P., whereby the latter was to erect certain buildings on a certain lot, those on a certain designated part of the lot to cost $5,846, in consideration of which the lot-owner was to convey the remaining portion, being ninety-five feet, to P The owner was to execute mortgages on the whole lot to raise money to enable P to make the proposed improvement It was held that P. had such an interest in the portion of the lot which was to be conveyed to him under this agreement as would authorize a mechanic's lien, that the lot-owner, having authorized P to contract for the buildings, and having received the benefit of the improvements, could not have his property improved and escape the liability to the mechanics and materialmen, and it was subject to their liens

§ 53 **Three classes of owners whose contract will not sustain lien.** — There are three classes of owners whose contracts will not sustain a lien .

---

[1] Proctor v Tows, 115 Ill 138 , see St Louis Nat'l Stock Yards v O'Reilly, 85 id 546
[2] Burns v Lane, 23 App 504, McCarty v Carter, 49 Ill 53, Baxter v. Hutchings, id 116
[3] Franklin Savings Bank v Taylor, 131 Ill 376
[4] Paulsen v Manske, 126 Ill 72, 24 App 95, Henderson v Connelly, 123 Ill 98, 23 App 601
[5] Paulsen v. Manske, 126 Ill 72, 24 App 95

1. Where the property was conveyed to a trustee to hold for the use and benefit of another — the trust was an active one and not to exercise powers in default of the *cestui que trust* performing certain obligations — and the deed of conveyance creating such trust authorized the trustee to improve the property by adding to, altering or removing buildings thereon, and to sell part to improve the remaining portion, but contained the clause, " Provided, always, there shall be no lien, incumbrance or charge created thereby on said premises," though the *cestui que trust* procured, and the trustee authorized the improvement, it was held that no such lien could be created therefor in contravention of this clause in the deed of conveyance [1]   As to whether or not such clause in a trust deed or mortgage given to secure the payment of purchase or loaned money or other indebtedness would bar the creation of a mechanic's lien has not been decided

No question of greater importance can be addressed to those who take security upon realty for purchase or loaned money, or other indebtedness.   There is no doubt but what the enforcement of such liens may result in the scaling of such debts secured by first mortgage or trust deed, where the instrument of security contains no such clause, as will be hereafter shown   The majority, indeed almost all instruments of such security contain no clause prohibiting such liens, and the debts they secure are, in consequence, in peril It is questionable, in view of the statute's provision as to incumbrances,[2] if such instrument can be so drawn as to make the security absolute and protect it from impairment by the owner's improvement of the property it covers

2. A contract made, work done, or materials furnished after foreclosure proceedings are begun will not sustain a lien.   The purchaser under decree and sale takes the property free from claim of such liens, and the mortgagor or maker of a trust deed, in such case, though in possession, is held not to be such an owner as can impose a lien upon the property [3]

3 The purchaser in possession under a recorded contract to convey on payment of the stated purchase-price, cannot create a lien to the prejudice of his vendor   Such vendor must be paid in full before the lien can attach to the property   His vendee cannot im-

---

[1] Franklin Savings Bank v Taylor, 131 Ill 376
[2] Sec 17, act 1874, as amended
[3] Tracy v Rogers 69 Ill 662, Davis v Conn Mut L Ins Co, 84 id 508, Green v. Sprague, 120 id 416, adv , 18 App 476

pair his title or give the mechanic a better title than the vendee
has[1]

The purchaser of such vendor's title, taking an assignment of the
contract as well as an assignment of the notes given by such condi-
tional purchaser, takes with the same rights as the original vendor[2]

§ 54. **Except where contract of sale authorized improvement.** — But where such contract authorizes the purchaser to build,
it carries with such authority the statutory incident of the lien, the
rule is different, and the purchaser is held to be such an owner as
whose contract will sustain a lien against the vendor's and his own
interest.[3]

October 17, 1884, H sold to S. a lot for $2,150, payable $75
cash, $30 per month on the first of each month from from Feb-
ruary 1, 1885, until February 1, 1888, when the whole sum remaining should become due In case of failure to make payments, H was to have the right to forfeit the contract, provided
S. should have four months in which to make good any delinquency
in payment before any forfeiture or re-entry should be made. H
also agreed when S. had expended $325 in the erection of a dwell-
ing-house upon same, to advance S. as the progress of the building,
in his opinion, justified, $875 to aid in the completion thereof.
December 1, 1884, S contracted with C for certain work on said
house, who did such work During progress, H advanced S $350,
April 16, and $350, May 15, 1885 In July or August, work
having stopped about June 1, and S having only paid the first
$75, H took possession and completed the house C filed his
petition to enforce a lien for amount due and unpaid him. The
court decreed in his favor, ordered the property sold, his claim paid
first out of the proceeds and the purchase-money claim of H next
On appeal decree confirmed, the court holding, that H. had the right
to forfeit the contract on June 1, so far as S. was concerned ; but
before the right of forfeiture accrued, the lien of C. attached to the
premises, that no steps had been taken by H., by notice of forfeiture, or otherwise, to terminate the contract ; that the case differed
from one wherein the vendor gave no authority to improve ; that
in giving this authority, H subjected his title to the property to the

---

[1] Wing v Carr, 86 Ill 347 Hickox v Greenwood, 94 id 266, Ruggles v.
Blank 15 Bradw 436
[2] Wood v Rawlings, 76 Ill 206 Ruggles v Blank, 15 Bradw 436
[3] Henderson v. Connelly, 123 Ill 98, 23 App. 601, Paulsen v Manske, 24 id 95,
126 Ill 72.

lien of the mechanic, and the decree properly gave that mechanic priority of payment [1]

§ 55 **Contract made with purchaser under contract of sale will sustain lien subject to vendor's rights.**—The purchaser under a contract to convey has the right to improve the property, subject to the rights of his vendor   But the statute gives to the contractor a lien on that purchaser's interest at the date of the contract for the improvement. As between such vendor and purchaser, non-payment does not, of itself, work a forfeiture of the contract. The vendor can elect to enforce performance of the contract, sue for the promised payment. The contract is not forfeited until the vendor exercises his right and expressly declares it forfeited. And where a lien for improvement attaches prior thereto, the rights of the contractor who held it must be regarded

So in the case of a contract to convey, with forfeiture in case of non payment ; non-payment does not of itself terminate the contract, forfeit the title and leave the mechanic remediless, who before such default put materials or labor into the improvement   He can pay the purchase-money, save the title and enforce his lien, if he see fit, or he can enforce a sale of the property, and the proceeds of the sale, in excess of what is due the vendor, must be paid to him [1]

The vendor in such cases must do some overt act — declare the forfeiture to effect it   Until this is done the contract continues mutually binding on the parties, and the contract of the purchaser thereunder will sustain a lien.[2] Nor can the vendor forfeit the contract after a lien attaches without notice to the mechanic, and giving him the opportunity to assume and carry out the contract of the vendee, and thereby secure his debt for labor or material [3]

On May 28, 1868, A , by contract, sold to B. a lot for $750, the first payment falling due May, 1870, the last, May, 1878, interest payable annually. The contract contained a clause of forfeiture for non-payment of interest, and was not recorded   A also loaned B $300 to help build on the lot. C and others, under contract with B for such improvement, acquired liens; on June 19, 1869, filed a petition against B to enforce them, making A a party, and alleging that B held the premises under contract of purchase from A , who was summoned and made default. At the judicial sale, C pur-

---

[1] Henderson v Connelly, 23 App 601, 123 Ill 98
[2] Moore v Smith, 24 Ill 513, Wing v Carr, 86 id 347, Phœnix Mut Life Ins Co v Batchen, 6 Bradw 621
[3] Henderson v Connelly, 123 Ill 98, 23 App 601.

chased the interest of B. in the property for the amount of his own
and other liens, paid off the latter, and brought suit against A,
having tendered him the amount of the purchase-money due by B.
to compel specific performance of the contract with B, and to con
vey the property to him as purchaser of B's interest. The lower
court refused so to decree, and ordered the property to be sold,
from the proceeds, first, to pay the original purchase-money; next,
the lien of C; next, the loan of A.; and, lastly, the lien claims
paid by C. The Supreme Court reversed the decree, and held that
no sale but specific performance should have been decreed, that A
had no lien for his loan; that not having declared the contract forfeited, as he might have done on B.'s default of paying interest in
May, 1869, nor answered in the mechanic's lien suit when made a
party, he could not, therefore, declare it, and C. was entitled to conveyance on payment of only the original purchase-money, with interest, as named in the bond of conveyance.[1]

§ 56. **Trustee with power to build consenting to improvement
by cestui que trust confers lien.**—Where the title is in a trustee,
with power to build, his ownership is such as will sustain a lien[2]

In this case, it was held where the beneficiary of the trust alone
made the contracts and built with the acquiescence and knowledge
of the trustee, there was a lien. Justices McAllister and Walker
dissented from this opinion, holding that the trustee must be a
party to the contract, if written, by signing it; if verbal, by join
ing in making it

§ 57 **Ownership by estoppel sustains lien.**— Ownership by
estoppel is such as will sustain a lien. That is, where A, who is
the real owner, allows B. to hold himself out as the owner to the
party contracting, that party can enforce his lien on the property as
if B held the title in fee[3]

Where the owner stands by and suffers credit to be given another
on the supposition that he owns the land, and aids in creating such
belief, he cannot defeat the claim of the mechanic by claim of ownership. If the owner suffers another to hold himself out as having
full disposition of the property, he is estopped to deny the liability
created thereon by such party.[3]

---

[1] Fitzhugh v Smith, 62 Ill 486
[2] Taylor v Gilsdorff, 74 Ill 354
[3] Higgins v Ferguson, 14 Ill. 269, Donaldson v Holmes, 23 id 83, Schwartz
v Saunders, 46 id 18, Anderson v Armistead, 69 id 452, Powell v Rogers 105
id 318, adv., 1 Bradw 631, Price v Hudson, 125 Ill. 285; Campbell v Jacobson
145 id 389; 46 App 287. Wilson v Schuck, 5 Bradw 572, Geary v. Hennessy,
9 id 17, Little v. Vredenberg, 16 id 189, Bruck v Bowermaster, 36 App 510

Where a party fails to make known his rights when equity and good conscience requires that he should do so to protect the interests of others, he cannot be heard as against them to assert such rights.

§ 58 **Husband improving wife's land.** — These cases have generally arisen when the land was that of the wife, and the husband contracted for the labor and materials to improve it, and was insolvent when he did.

Where the credit is given to the husband on his own account, the rule that the contract must be with the owner applies, and there can be no lien enforced against her land [1]

The husband as well as a stranger may in good faith make improvements on a wife's land as a gift, or may make them in discharge of *bona fide* indebtedness to her   In such cases she is not bound for payment of what they cost   And if no false or fraudulent representations are made, the contract made on the husband's credit, she is not estopped to set up her title [2] In this case it was held that the mere fact the contract was made in her presence, and the improvement made under her daily inspection, did not make her liable for a contract with her husband who did not profess to own the property or to be her agent. Here, neither she nor her husband made any false representations. The contract was written and with her husband

Again, where a husband purchased materials which were used by him in repairing a house owned by his wife, and in so doing did not purchase for her, or profess to act in her behalf, but bought on his own account and solely on his own credit, giving his note for the price, it was held, no lien was created upon the premises of the wife [3]

Where a married woman's title is of record, she is not estopped from claiming her ownership, unless her acts are tantamount to representations that the title is in her husband   Where she is not apprised of his making claim of ownership, and does not by word or act confirm the same, she can assert her title against the lien claimant [4]

In this case, though the wife borrowed money by mortgage, in which her husband joined, to finish paying for the house, her title was of record, the proof showed no knowledge by her of her hus-

---

[1] Little v Vredenberg, 16 Bradw 189. McGraw v Storke. 44 App 311 Clement v Newton, 78 Ill 427, Wendt v Martin, 89 id 139 Campbell v Jacobson, 145 id 389
[2] Geary v Hennessy, 9 Bradw 17
[3] Wendt v Martin, 89 Ill 139
[4] Campbell v Jacobson, 145 Ill. 389, 46 App 287

band's claim of ownership, but that he promised to build the house for her, told her after work had progressed some time he was unable to complete it, and that she had never held him out or recognized him as agent or owner, and the lien was defeated

§ 59 **If wife misleads contractor lien attaches** — But our courts have gone very far in declaring her non-action as well as conduct works an estoppel; having held that if a married woman sees the work go on, gives her approval and consent, takes no step to prevent it, she is estopped to set up her title adverse to the lien claimant [1]

Where the deed to the wife was made on June 1, recorded July 28, the husband, claiming ownership, made the contract on July 24, it was held, that holding the deed off record enabled him to represent himself as owner, and as she saw the work go on without information of her title to those furnishing material for and doing it, and moved into the house, she was estopped to set up her title [2]

The most advanced position, wherein also the husband was charged and held to have acted as the wife's agent, is that, if, after the contract with the husband by one ignorant of the wife's interest, the wife knowing what was done, does not disclose her interest and stop the work, she is estopped to set up her rights as a defense to a mechanic's lien [3]

Each case seems to have stood upon its own special merits, and to have been decided upon its own circumstances and surroundings.

§ 60. **Estoppel in general.** In all cases estoppel is based upon a fraudulent purpose on the owner's part, and a consequent injurious and fraudulent result to the party complaining. There must be deception and change of conduct in consequence thereof, to estop the party against whom it is pleaded from showing the truth. Where it is by conduct there must be a positive obligation to speak out and not maintain silence, and that silence must have induced the party complaining of it to have acted as he would not have otherwise done [4]

The mere assertion of ownership by one party, unknown to the actual owner, and unconfirmed, unaided by his conduct, does not estop that owner from asserting his title against all who would subject it to their claims. He must aid or abet the assertion to bind him [5]

[1] Schwartz v Saunders, 46 Ill. 18
[2] Anderson v Armistead, 69 Ill 452
[3] Bruck v Bowermaster, 36 App 510, Watson v Carpenter, 27 id. 492.
[4] Powell v Rogers, 105 Ill 318, adv. 1 Bradw 631

Estoppel can only be set up to prevent injustice that it directly and positively occasions, and, if the element of fraud or injury is absent, there is no estoppel. If both parties are equally cognizant of the facts, and the declarations or silence of one produces no change in the conduct of the other, he acting solely on his own judgment, there is no estoppel.[1] And where the misrepresentations could not have misled the mechanic or materialman, or induced him to do labor or furnish material on the faith of it, there is no lien by estoppel, as where, after contract made, the contractor falsely represents himself to be the owner.[2]

§ 61. **Improvement must be with owner's consent.**—Where machinery was put into a mill under a contract with a former owner, but after transfer of title, and without the knowledge or consent of the new owner, and he immediately disclaimed authority for so doing and removed it, no lien was held to exist.[3]

Where work is done or materials are furnished after rescission of the contract by the owner, there is no lien. The action of contractor, materialman, or mechanic must then be, not to enforce a lien, but for breach of contract.[4]

§ 62 **Landlord and tenant.**—Contract with a tenant, other than at sufferance, will sustain a lien as to his interest, but cannot affect the rights or interest of the landlord. Cannot extend to or bind the interest of the owner.[5] The voluntary surrender of the lease to the owner of the fee before the expiration of his term cannot affect the lien upon the estate of the lessee, which attached during the existence of the lease, and the merger of the estate of the lessee with that of the owner of the fee will not destroy the previous lien. But in case of forfeiture, and not voluntary surrender, the case is different. The forfeiture destroys the lien.[6] A decree against the owner who accepts the surrender is good as to the improvements made and the term of the lease. The owner must either accept the lien claimant as tenant for the term, or pay off the lien.[6] A similar rule to that in cases of contract for sale prevails with landlord and tenant. Non-payment of rent does not, *per se*, work a forfeiture of the tenancy. The landlord must show the facts warranting the forfeiture, and declare it before the tenancy is

[1] Powell v. Rogers, 105 Ill. 318 1 Bradw 631
[2] Rothberger v. Dupuy, 64 Ill 452
[3] Cox v Colles, 17 Bradw 503
[4] Horr v Slavik, 35 App. 140
[5] Judson v Stephen, 75 Ill 255
[6] Williams v Vanderbilt, 145 Ill. 238, 40 App. 298; Dobschuetz v Holliday, 82 Ill 371

terminated. If the lien attaches before such forfeiture it is good. The lien claimant can then pay the rent and enforce his lien on the term of the leasehold. Forfeitures are not favored at law, either in contracts to convey or leases, and where rights of third parties intervene are still less regarded. If the vendor is paid his purchase-price, the landlord his rent, they can ask no more.[1]

§ 63. Lessor authorizing improvements, lien on property. — Where the lessor agrees to pay the lessee a given sum toward the erection of a house on the leased premises, the estate of the lessor is bound by the mechanic's lien.[2]

If, by the provisions of the lease, the improvements, when made, become the property of the lessor, it is no bar to the lien, because of the authority to build carrying with it the statutory incident of lien, and he takes them subject to the lien claim. He cannot take the benefit of the improvement and escape liability for it.

The lien will attach to the leasehold for work on machinery which the tenant may remove under the terms of his lease.[3] If the lessee has the right to remove any improvements he makes, this right is acquired by the purchaser under sale in enforcement of the lien.[3]

In event the lease provides for the purchase of improvements by the landlord at the expiration of the term, unless specially so made, it is not a covenant running with the land, and is not binding upon the grantee of the lessor, and the lien will not continue as against such grantee.[4]

§ 64. No lien for improvements by insurance company. — Where a house is rebuilt or repaired by an insurance company in case of fire, no lien can be sustained, because that is an affair of such company, not of the owner. Nor can an administrator subject the estate thereto. An executor could, if empowered to improve by the will.

§ 65. Contractor buying as agent; if he pays, no lien. — If a contractor, as agent of the owner, procures materials in the name and on the credit of the owner, and pays for them, he has no lien, but would have to sue at law to recover therefor.[5]

§ 66. Where one of several owners contracts, his interest bound. — Where one of several who contract is an owner, the lien

[1] Sec 55, ante
[2] Williams v Vanderbilt, 145 Ill 238, 40 App 298
[3] Moore v Smith, 24 Ill 513, Smith v. Moore, 26 id 392, Dobschuetz v Holliday, 82 id 371
[4] Watson v Gardner, 119 Ill 312, adv 18 App 386
[5] C & V. R R v Fackney, 78 Ill 116, Ruggles v Blank, 15 Bradw 436

is good as against his interest;[1] but where one of several owners does not join in the contract, his interest is not bound

§ 67 **Joint and co-tenants no lien as against each other.**—Joint and co-tenants have no right of lien for improvements as against each other.[2]

§ 68. **No lien for party-wall without consent of adjacent owner.**—There is no lien on an adjacent lot for a party-wall, unless the owner of that lot agrees to its erection And where improvements are made on an adjacent lot not owned, but used by the party for whom the work is done, the lien exists only for the labor and material on the lot owned.[3]

§ 69. **Corporation's contracts sustain lien.**—A corporation is an owner whose contracts will support a lien where the same are made by corporate authority, and it is bound by the acts of its authorized agents just as an individual[4]

[1] Van Court v Bushnell, 21 Ill 624, Roach v Chapin, 27 id. 194
[2] Welch v. Sherer, 93 Ill 64
[3] Tracy v Rogers, 69 Ill 662
[4] Board of Education v. Greenebaum, 39 Ill. 610

The contract must be made to build, alter, repair or ornament a house, or other building, or appurtenance thereto on a particular lot or tract of land, or upon some street or alley, and connected with a building or appurtenance on such lot or tract of land.

§ 70. **Contract must be to improve particular lot.**—An architect would have no lien simply for plans and specifications for a building, or to alter, repair or ornament a hypothetical one The owner who procures his services must intend to erect same, or to alter, repair or ornament one already in existence on some definite lot or piece of land The same rule prevails with contractors and materialmen The language of the statute is, that any person who shall, by contract * * * with the owner of any lot or piece of land, furnish labor or material, or services as an architect, or super intendent, in building, altering or ornamenting any house or other building, or appurtenance thereto, on *such* lot, * * * shall have a lien on the whole of *such* tract of land or lot [1]

The logic and language of the statute are to make this statutory mortgage a lien on a certain definite piece of real estate, as much as a duly executed and recorded mortgage on that real estate The formalities for the latter are its description of the property, signing and acknowledging the same by the owner and recording it by the mortgagee, according to law. The formalities for the mechanics lien are the purchase of material, or contract for work for the erection or improvement of a building on certain property, furnishing the material or doing the work on that property, and filing the claim as the statute prescribes. Neither ordinary nor statutory mortgage would be a lien on any other than the real estate described in the one, or intended to be improved under the other. Both are particular liens on specific property The labor or material must be for some particular lot or tract of land whose improvement is in view, is intended at the time of contracting therefor, and is so understood by all the parties to the transaction to sustain the mechanic's lien [2]

§ 71 **No lien for material on open account without reference to particular lot.**—In furnishing lumber on open account, with

---

[1] Sec 1 act 1874, as amended, Hill v Bishop, 25 Ill 307, Burkhart v Reisig 24 id 530, Croskey v Corey, 48 id 442, Lombard v Johnson, 76 id. 559
[2] Croskey v Corey, 48 Ill 442, Wendt v Martin, 89 id 139, Clark v Manning, 90 id 380, Burns v Lane, 23 App 504

out reference to being placed in any particular building, it was held there was no lien; that it would have been no violation of the agreement by the purchaser if used in making furniture, or any other personal property [1]

Where the contract was simply to put up an engine, boiler, etc., for the defendant in Chicago, it was held there was no lien, for, so far as the contract showed, it could be put up on any lot in Chicago [2]

In both cases, it was held that the purchase must be for the definite purpose of use on a definite lot or tract of land, that the contract must have reference to the land sought to be subjected to the lien

The same rule would apply to stone, brick, or any other material sold on open account, without reference to any particular lot on which they were to be used

§ 72. Does not extend to adjacent lot of same owner, even if inclosed.--A lien existing for work done on and material used in a building on one lot, cannot be made to extend to an adjacent lot of the owner, even if in the same inclosure, unless by proper averments both lots are to be considered as one [3] And courts will take judicial notice that lots in different townships are in different tracts, and enforce the lien only on the lot on which the improvement stands [4]

§ 73. In block of buildings different roofs make different liens. — Where more than one lot is covered by the improvement the extent, quantity, or area of property covered by the lien is determined by there being one common roof, or different roofs   The improvement may form in front and rear a solid block, but if there are dividing walls and different roofs the lien will be against that under each roof for what material is used or what work is done under each roof.[5]

If the contract be to build a number of distinct and separate buildings on separate lots, the lien is on each one for the labor done on or material used in it, the same as where in a compact body, but under different roofs.[6]

If a common roof cover all it makes the whole improvement a

[1] Hill v Bishop, 25 Ill 307
[2] Burkhart v Reisig, 24 Ill 530
[3] Seiler v Schaefer, 40 App 74
[4] Van Lone v Whittemore 19 Bradw 447
[5] Steigleman v McBride, 17 Ill 300, Culver v Elwell, 73 id 536, Portones v Badenoch 132 id 377, Portones v Holmes, 33 App 312, Major v Collins, 11 Bradw 658

unity, and one lien will cover the whole improvement The principle and rule is the same as if one lot were improved [1]

The contract itself is good in either event, if it be an entire contract for all and the intention be to so improve the lots, but regard must be had to the manner in which the accounts are kept and liens asserted. If under different roofs, or on different lots, the account for what material is furnished, or for what work is done on each must be carefully kept separate, and the lien asserted in the same manner [2] Notwithstanding the entirety of the contract, the lien cannot be enforced generally on all the buildings that the contract provides for [3]

§ 74. If more than one building on same lot or tract, one lien for all. — If, however, more than one building be on the same tract, though there are different contracts for each, if between the same parties, the whole tract will be covered by the same lien and it can be enforced as a common lien against all.[3] In this case the tract consisted of several hundred acres, the contracts were made and performed at different times. So, in cities where distinct buildings under distinct roofs are erected each upon a half, third, or less portion of a lot — say two, or three, on a fifty-foot lot, the lien would be good on all, without regard to what labor or material went into each Their being on one lot would avoid the necessity of separate accounts and separate liens for each

§ 75. Where materials removed from one lot to another of owner, lien on each for amount on each. — Where, at the owner's instance, part of the material was removed from one lot to another belonging to him, and put into a building on the latter lot, the lien was enforced on each lot, respectively, to the extent of the value of the labor and material put upon it.[4] Though the contract were made only for the improvement of the first lot, in such case, the law would create a new and implied contract to improve the latter with the usual consequences of such contracts.

§ 76. If tract used for common purpose or a number of lots for common purpose, lien covers all. — And if the improvement be upon a tract of land used for a common purpose or business, though it be upon a small portion of the tract, the lien will cover

---

[1] James v Hambleton, 42 Ill 308, Orr v N W. Mut Life Ins Co , 86 id 260, Seiler v Schaefer, 40 App 74
[2] Steigleman v McBride, 17 Ill 300 Culver v Ellwell, 73 id 536 , Portones v Badenoch, 132 id 377, Portones v Holmes, 33 App 312. Major v Collins, 11 Bradw 658
[3] St Louis Nat Stock Yards v O'Reilly, 85 Ill. 546
[4] Steigleman v McBride, 17 Ill 300

the entire tract, as machinery on part of an eighty-acre tract where a section or more was held for development in coal mining, and the machinery was to be used in the general development of the entire property as time passed and work progressed[1]

The same principle would extend the lien over a number of lots, where the land had been so subdivided, in case all the lots were used as common ground for a business. For instance, if a block composed of several distinct lots were used for a foundry or manufacturing plant, and the improvement were only on one or more of those so used, the lien would extend to all on properly averring and proving their use for a common purpose, which purpose the improvement subserved and was made for.

§ 77 **Contract need not be for definite amount of material nor provide for lien, nor describe property.** — The contract need not be for any definite amount of material, for whatever may be used in the particular improvement is sufficient[2] It is not necessary for the contract to provide for a lien   The law provides for that, and it has been held that where it is attempted to make a lien by contract between the parties, such contract must be in writing, that a verbal contract therefor was not sufficient.[3] Nor is it necessary for the contract to describe the property   While the contract for work or material must have reference to some particular lot, or tract of land, it does not follow that the legal description of the lot or land must be in the contract. The description of the real estate seldom if ever, beyond mere location is considered by the parties when the contract is made. By other evidence it may be shown, but shown it must be, that the material was sold for that lot, or that tract of land sought to be charged[4]

§ 78 **Less particularity of description of property necessary where house or building under process of construction.** — A distinction has been made between materials bought for a house in process of construction, or to put in one already built, so far as the degree of particularity necessary in designating the property when the contract for materials was made. Where the contract was to alter or add to a building already erected, as to place machinery in a mill in Charleston, Ill, owned by the second party, it was held

[1] Kankakee Coal Co v Crane Bros Mfg Co, 128 Ill 627, 26 App 371, St Louis National Stock Yards v O'Reilly, 85 Ill 546
[2] Thielman v Carr, 75 Ill 385 Brown v Lowell, 79 id 184
[3] Smith v Kennedy, 89 Ill 485
[4] Burns v Lane, 23 App 504 Strawn v Cogswell, 28 Ill 457, Power v McCord 36 id 214, Lombard v. Johnson 76 id 599, Clark v Manning, 90 id 380, Burns v Lane, 23 App. 504

sufficiently definite, though it was no further described. Where the building was in process of construction, a contract to furnish materials therefor, without specifically describing where it was, was held sufficient   Both decisions holding if it appeared that the material was used in such building, the jury or court might properly infer it was bought for that purpose[1] But this inference would not be justified where no building was being erected and the goods sold on general account.

§ 79 **Appurtenances must be on the same lot or tract.**—The appurtenances must be on the same lot, or tract of land, on the same premises, or upon a street or alley, and connected with such building or appurtenance[2]

Where the contract was for a mill on one lot it was held, the lien did not extend to a crib and wagon sheds on another lot across the street, though used in connection with the mill.[3]

Where the contract was simply to curb, grade and pave the street in front of the house, and did not embrace either building or improvement of a building on the lot, it was held, no lien existed[4]

It was also held, that no lien existed for a vault under sidewalk adjacent to a building, and that both the building and the appurtenance being provided for in the same contract, no distinct price for each, on account of the indivisibility of the demand, there was no lien for either[5]

This decision was rendered while the act of 1845 was in force A comparison of the first section of that act with the first section of the present act shows wherein it is not now applicable The phraseology of the present law is different,[6] and undoubtedly made so in consequence of that, then correct, decision disclosing the injustice done the contractor In large cities extensive, costly and valuable improvements are made under adjacent sidewalks, such as vaults, and other apartments for business purposes and occupancy If the appurtenance, under the present statute, be not only on the lot but upon any street or alley and connected with the building or the appurtenance of the building, the lien on the lot is good, and the

---

[1] Power v McCord, 36 Ill 214, Martin v Eversal, id 223 Chisholm v Randolph, 21 App 312, Austin v Wohler, 5 Bradw 300, Burns v Lane 23 App 504, Lombard v Johnson, 76 Ill 599 Buckley v Boutellier 61 id 293
[2] Sec 1, act 1874, as amended, Parmelee v Hambleton, 19 Ill 615, Adler v World's Pastime Co, 126 Ill 373, 26 App 528, Tracy v Rogers, 69 Ill. 662
[3] Paddock v Stout, 121 Ill 571, Stout v Sower, 22 App 65
[4] Smith v Kennedy 89 Ill 485
[5] Parmelee v Hambleton, 19 Ill 615
[6] Sec 1, act 1874, as amended

lien for the indivisible demand enforceable   While the word " side-walk" is not used, it is part of the street, the part for pedestrians, and would be included in it

Liens were sustained for putting in a furnace,[1] but not for stoves, for painting,[2] but not for a lightning rod;[3] also for boxes for hoisting coal put in in connecting with an engine and hoisting apparatus,[4] and for cars used in connection with a drier in a brick-yard,[5] on the theory that they were part and parcel of one system of machinery, and though not attached to the land or building, yet were an essential part of that which was attached, were necessary appurtenances of the main improvement; but fencing on a farm was held not to be such an appurtenance as came within the purview of this statute[6]

[1] Thielman v Carr, 75 Ill 385
[2] Martine v Nelson 51 Ill 422
[3] Drew v Mason, 81 Ill 498
[4] Dobschuetz v Holliday, 82 Ill 371
[5] Curran v Smith, 37 App 69
[6] Canisius v Merrill 65 Ill 67

This contract must be made in strict accordance with the statute creating these liens.

§ 80 **Contract must be according to statute.** — The earlier acts applied solely to express contracts. The many decisions thereunder hold that the contract (express) must affirmatively show on its face — must state — the time when the labor was to be completed, the materials furnished and the payment made therefor, as well as the time of commencing such labor and delivery of materials, that unless the time for the completion of such labor, or of furnishing the material, as stated in the contract, was within three years from the commencement thereof, and the time of payment within one year from such completion, there was no lien, even if the labor were all done, the material all furnished in one month, or a few months after the commencement thereof [1]

§ 81 **Change by act of 1861, allowing liens under implied contracts.** — Many of the cases adjudicated presented these very hardships. To remedy this, the legislature, in 1861, amended the act as follows ·

" That chapter 65 of the Revised Statutes of 1845, entitled ' Liens,' shall be held to include implied as well as express contracts under which labor or materials are furnished at the request of any owner of land or town lot, for erecting or repairing any building or the appurtenances of any building on such land or town lot, when no price is agreed upon or no time is expressly fixed for the payment of such labor or the furnishing of such labor or materials ; Provided, that the work is done or materials furnished within one year from the commencement of the work, or the commencement of furnishing said materials."[2]

Prior to the passage of this amendment the courts held, excepting where it was intimated in *Cook v. Vreeland*, 21 Ill 431, that time of payment might be implied, time of completion being fixed, that the court could not imply a time for either, that the contract stating and conditioning that completion and payment should be within a

---

[1] Cook v Heald, 21 Ill 425, Cook v Vreeland, id 431, Senior v Brebnor 22 id 252, McLurken v Logan, 23 id 79, Rogers v Ward, id 473, Brady v Anderson, 24 id 111, Moser v Matt, id 199, Burkhart v Reisig, id 530, Phillips v Stone, 25 id 67, Columbus Machine Manfg Co v Dorwin, id 153, Scott v Keeling, id 316, Kinzey v Thomas 28 id 502, Kinney v Sherman, id 520, Rowley v James, 31 id 298, Coburn v Tyler, 41 id 354 (Fish v Stubbings, 65 id 492 Powell v Webber, 79 id 134, so held but were overruled in Clark v. Manning, 90 Ill 380, as contrary to amendment of 1861)

[2] Appendix, amendment of February 19, 1861

reasonable time, as soon as possible, etc., was insufficient and fatally defective

After this amendment, the legislative definition of an implied contract was adopted by the courts — that a contract which did not fix a date for completion or payment, was not an express, but an implied contract; that the law would imply that completion was to be in a reasonable time after commencing work, or delivery of material, that within a year thereafter was a reasonable time, that there was a promise to pay on completion [1]

§ 82. **Present law.**—The present act provides that when the contract is expressed, no lien shall be created, if the time stipulated for the completion of the work or furnishing materials is beyond three years from the commencement thereof, or the time of payment beyond one year from the time stipulated for the completion thereof.[2] If the work is done or materials are furnished under implied contract, no lien shall be had by virtue of this act unless the work shall be done or the materials be furnished within one year from the commencement of the work or delivery of the materials,[3] and includes a third class of contracts, partly expressed, partly implied, concerning which no limitations are laid down [4]

A contract for furnishing materials to be used in a building, fixing the prices of articles to be delivered, but leaving all other matters to be implied, is not an express contract within the meaning of the term in the lien law, but of the latter class. In such cases, if the materials are all furnished within one year from the commencement of delivery thereof, the materialman will be entitled to a lien [4]

While the statute is silent as to contracts partly expressed and partly implied, the courts hold that such parts as are expressed shall

[1] Roach v Chapin, 27 Ill 194, Claycomb v Cecil, id 197 Coburn v Tyler, 11 id 351, Baxter v Hutchings, 49 id 116 Corey v Croskey 57 id 251, Chicago Artesian Well Co v Corey, 60 id 73, Schnell v Clements, 73 id 613 Cunningham v Ferry, 74 id 426, Reed v Boyd, 84 id 66 Orr v N W Mut Life Ins Co , 86 id 260, Belanger v Hersey, 90 id 70, Grundeis v Hartwell id 324 Clark v Manning, id 380 Driver v Ford, id 595, Powell v Rogers, 105 id 318 Paddock v Stout 121 id 571, Portones v Badenoch, 132 id 377 McDonald v Rosengarten, 134 id 126, Peck v Standart, 1 Bradw 228 Rogers v Powell, id 631 Graham v Meehan, 4 id 522, Austin v Wohler, 5 id 300, Younger v Louks, 7 id 280, Jacoby v Scougale, 26 App 46 Haines v Chandler, id 400 Adler v World's Pastime Co , id 528, Kankakee Coal Co v Crane Bros Mfg Co 28 id 371, Harwood v. Brownell, 32 id 347, Lehman v Clark, 33 id 33, Portones v Holmes, id 312, Rittenhouse v Sable, 43 id 558
[2] Sec 3, act 1874, as amended McDonald v Rosengarten, 134 Ill 126
[3] Sec 3, act 1874, as amended, Grundeis v Hartwell, 90 Ill 324
[4] Sec 3, act 1874, as amended Orr v N W Mut Life Ins Co , 86 Ill 260, Grundeis v Hartwell, 90 id 324, Austin v Wohler, 5 Brad 300, Younger v Louks, 7 id 280

be governed by the rules relating to express contracts, such parts as
are implied, by the rules relating to implied contracts.[1]

§ 83 **Terms of contract as made decide lien.** — There are no
peculiar formalities requisite to be observed in making the contract
different from other contracts. As stated, it may be written or verbal, express, implied, or partly expressed and partly implied. But
the time within which it is to be performed and payment is to be
made does decide whether or not there is a lien under it, and, if so,
how it is fixed and enforced.[2]

§ 84 **Lien depends on original contract, not on changes made
in it.** — The right to the lien depends upon the contract as originally
made, not what may be done thereafter in the execution of it.[3] If
it did not then comply with the statute no subsequent changes or
amendments will help it, nor will its execution in time be of aid.
If an express contract, for instance, as originally made provide for
completion more than three years after commencement of the work,
changing the terms thereafter so as to make it within the three
years, or completion within that period, will not restore the lien lost
by its making. So if it provide for final payment more than one
year after completion, a subsequent agreement changing the time to
within one year will have no different result.

And if the lien once attaches it will not be divested, so far as the
owner is concerned, by subsequent change, as indulgence of time of
payment. A subsequent change of time of payment, if the original
contract fixes the same within one year from the completion, will not
divest the lien. Where a note was taken payable one year after completion and renewed, the renewal falling due after the expiration of
the year, it was held, such extension did not defeat the lien, because
the terms of the original contract were within the statutory period.[4]

The question is not whether the parties do, or do not agree, after
the execution of the contract, to an extension or abbreviation of the
time of performance or payment, the question is as to terms of the
contract. And the filing of the claim required within four months
from the date of the last payment must be done with regard to the
date fixed in that original contract.[5]

---

[1] Orr v N W Mut Life Ins. Co., 86 Ill 260
[2] Sec. 2, act 1874, as amended
[3] Simons v Blocks, 16 Bradw 450, Crowl v Nagle, 86 Ill. 437, McCarthy v.
New, 93 id 455, Paddock v Stout, 121 id 571, Chisholm v Williams 128 id
115, Simon v Blocks, 16 Bradw 450, Chisholm v Randolph, 21 App 312, Stout
v. Sower, 22 id 65
[4] Chisholm v Williams, 128 Ill. 115, Id v Randolph, 21 App 312.
[5] Brady v. Anderson, 24 Ill. 111, Moser v. Matt, 24 id. 199.

§ 85. **Express contract, example of.**—An express contract made to commence work January 1, 1894, stating that the work was to be completed, or materials furnished by or before January 1, 1897, final payment, January 1, 1898, would sustain a lien

If it made completion January 2, 1897, there would be no lien, though final payment was made due on completion. If it made completion January 1, 1897, and final payment January 2, 1898, there would be no lien; or, if it made completion to be in a month, final payment due more than a year after that month, there would be no lien   So if the contract to build a house or furnish materials is made to commence on January 1, 1894, no time specified for completion of contract or delivery of materials, or payment, and the performance of any part of the work or delivery of any part of the materials is prolonged to January 2, 1895, the lien for all is lost

Contract dated March 14, 1867, to complete May 1, 1867, payment $560 ; $100 cash, balance, $10 per month, held, entitled to no lien, payments being extended beyond one year [1]

§ 86 **Extension of time on condition; without condition.**—But if payment be extended beyond one year on condition that a mortgage on the property be executed at the expiration of the year, to secure balance due, this becomes a condition precedent to the extension of time, and if the mortgage is not given, the debt then becomes due and a lien can be enforced [2] If, however, the contract provides absolutely that payment shall be by note due two years after completion, the giving of the note is not a condition precedent. The condition puts the case beyond the statute and there is no lien, whether the note is or is not given [3] To save his lien the mechanic should provide in the contract if such note is not given the debt shall at once become due

If notes be given due one year after completion, the three days' grace of commercial usage extended for payment will not vitiate the lien [4]

§ 87. **Not necessary to fix a certain date for completion or payment.**—It is not necessary to fix a certain day and date of a certain month for completion or payment, but a time within the period named by the statute

[1] Beasle v Webster, 64 Ill 458   In this case the purchaser assumed and agreed to pay the contractor's bill, and the court held, that such contract being for the contractor's benefit, though he was not a party to it, he could recover the debt from the purchaser even if his lien was lost

[2] Gardner v Hall, 29 Ill 277

[3] Simon v Blocks, 16 Bradw 450

[4] Paddock v Stout, 121 Ill 571, Stout v Sower, 22 App 65

A contract dated March 22, 1872, to complete on or about July 15, 1872, payment 85 per cent as work progresses, balance on completion, was held sufficiently definite as to time and payment.[1]

A contract stating that payment shall be made in installments of 10 per cent as the work progresses, the work to be completed within three years from the date of contract, and all payments to be made within one year from the time of completion, without fixing a precise day for either, is good   When the contract provided for a day certain for completion, as August 1, but a working test is provided, the date of that test will be held the date of completion, be it sooner or later than the date fixed in the contract[2]

§ 88. **Must do one of two things.** — In the absence of an express contract limiting the time in which to furnish materials or perform the contract within three years after commencement thereof, no lien is created, unless the materials are in fact furnished or the contract is performed inside of one year   It is equally necessary to do one of two things — either to make an express contract limiting the time of performance to within three years after commencement of what is to be done under it, or to complete that performance within one year from its commencement[4]

§ 89 **No time stated for performance or payment.** — A contract to furnish materials as needed, no prices being specified, nor amounts, nor times for completion of delivery, will sustain a lien if performed within one year[5]

A party agreed with the owner of property about to build to let him have hardware from time to time as needed in the construction of the building.   No amount of hardware was specified, and no time fixed for the completion of the building   The contract was made in October, and it was understood, though not agreed, that the building was to be completed by January 1, following   The hardware was furnished according to the contract, beginning in October and ending in November.   Held, that this was a contract partly expressed and partly implied, within the meaning of the statute, and the party furnishing the material was entitled to a lien.   That the intention of the legislature in adopting the Mechanic's Lien Law of 1874 was, where the terms of a contract are partly expressed and partly implied,

[1] Schnell v Clements, 73 Ill 613
[2] Reed v Boyd, 84 Ill 66
[3] Paddock v Stout, 121 Ill 571, Stout v Sower, 22 App 65
[4] Haines v. Chandler, 26 App 400, McDonald v Rosengarten, 134 Ill 126 35 App 71.
[5] Orr v N W Mut Life Ins Co, 86 Ill 260, § 81 note

to limit the express terms by the same limitations, so far as applicable, as is applied to express contracts, and the implied terms, by the same limitations, so far as applicable, as is applied to implied contracts, though the statute does not fix any limitation whatever when the contract is partly expressed and partly implied

Under a contract to build for $2,800, $1,000 as work progresses, balance when finished; held, contract good, if the work was finished within a year [1]

Where the delivery of materials was begun on June 19, 1883, and last delivery was made in November, 1884, there was held to be no lien. [2]

Where delivery was begun May 22, 1887, and last delivery was made May 31, 1888, there was no lien. [3]

§ 90 **Law requires only request by owner and compliance within year.** — The law requires only, in order to create a lien, as far as the agreement of the owner of the land and the mechanic or materialman are concerned, that labor or material should be furnished at the request of the owner of the land, for erecting, repairing or ornamenting any building thereon, when no price is agreed upon, or no time is expressly fixed for the payment of such labor or materials, that the work be done or materials furnished within one year from the commencement of the work, or the commencement of furnishing the materials   A contract arises by implication from these facts, the existence of which creates a lien on the land   To bring a case within the law, it is only necessary for a materialman to show that he was requested by the owner of the land to furnish him with materials for making improvements on the land, and that afterward, in compliance with this request, he furnished the materials, and they were used for the purpose indicated   Then a lien is created for the value of the material, provided they are furnished in one year, and there need not be any other agreement, express or implied, in order to the creation of the lien. [4]

This decision was rendered under the act of 1861, but applies to the present law.

§ 91 **Where contract express, except as to time of completion, lien if completed in year.**—Where the contract is silent as to the time of completion, and express as to all other terms, there is a lien if the work be done within a year from its commencement [5]

[1] Clark v Manning, 90 Ill 380
[2] Haines v Chandler, 26 App 400
[3] Harwood v Brownell, 32 App 347
[4] Chicago Artesian Well Co v Corey, 60 Ill 73
[5] Younger v Louks, 7 Bradw. 280

§ 92. **Where working test fixes date of completion, date of test controls lien.** —It is held that where the date of completion is fixed by a working test, as when machinery is finished and started to satisfactory results, such test, regardless of the day and date named in the contract for completion, is the time of completion Hence, if the test were made more than one year after commencement of work, and the contract is an implied contract, there would be no lien [1]

§ 93. **Importance of distinction between express and implied contract.** —While the liberality of later decisions relieves from much of the rigor of former interpretations of the contract as to whether it is express or implied, the distinction is yet important for, as is later shown, when suit is brought, the claimant must set out in his petition what character of contract he relies upon for recovery, and is bound by what he claims it to be.[2]

If it is an implied contract, he must state it to be such. And in event it is, there is no lien if the labor or delivery of materials be prolonged for over a year after the same are commenced.[3]

§ 94 **Character of labor or material must be such as statute provides for.** —The service must be such as the statute provides for If the contract embrace work or materials for which no lien is allowed by the statute, and there be one price for all, the vicious leaven of no lien for part will leaven the whole and vitiate the lien for the entire contract [4] In such case, if there were a separate price for that portion for which a lien was allowed, and for which it was not allowed, the demands divisible, the lien would be good for that portion provided for by the statute, lost only as to the other.

For this reason, it was held that a plumber had no lien for the hire of his license to another plumber who had none, in order that the latter might purchase material and carry out a contract he had entered into ,[4] that an architect had no lien for clerical services, such as settling with contractors, keeping books, auditing accounts, nor for supervising the improvement of grounds and accessories,[5] and that there was no lien for the mere removal of a house from one lot to another;[6] nor for any other work, material or purpose other than that which the statute expressly names

---

[1] Paddock v Stout, 121 Ill 571
[2] *Post*, § 214.
[3] Parmelee v. Hambleton, 19 Ill 614, Adler v. World's Pastime Co., 126 id 373, 26 App 528
[4] Burnside v O'Hara, 35 App 150
[5] Adler v World's Pastime Co , *supra*.
[6] Stephens v Holmes, 64 Ill 886

The contract must be performed, or its non-performance excused according to law.

§ 95 **Contract must be performed, or non-performance excused.**—Two things must co exist to sustain the lien.

1. The contract made, as heretofore shown, and possessing all of the statutory requirements stated.

2. Performance of that contract, or its non-performance excused according to law.

As a distinction is made in the decisions between what constitutes performance on the part of the contractor, and what on the part of materialmen and others, this performance will be treated of with regard to the respective parties

§ 96 **No lien for work unless done.**—First, as to the contractor for the work

The contractor for work cannot enforce a lien where there is simply a contract, but no work done under it.[1] In the event the owner, after making the contract, refuses to permit him to start the work, his remedy is at law for breach of contract, not under this statute to enforce the lien.[2] If, after he starts the work, the owner either wrongfully refuses to permit him to go on with and complete it, or wrongfully discharges him, he can enforce his lien for the value of what he has done, according to the contract price, and recover under the act therefor,[3] but not for damages based on prospective profits. For such he can maintain a separate action at law, but there is no lien therefor.[4] The lien is only for what is done *in* building, altering, repairing or ornamenting a building or appurtenance thereto, as heretofore shown.

Where work is done without the owner's consent, and after rescission of a contract, this general rule applies, because, then, there is no contract to support the lien.[5]

If defects are complained of and the contractor offers to remedy them, and is denied, he has a lien.[6] And if there is a substantial performance of the contract, the work is accepted and the performance of the balance thereby waived, the lien exists[6]

---

[1] Wendt v Martin, 89 Ill 139, Horr v Slavik, 35 App 140(a)
[2] Horr v Slavik, 35 App 140
[3] McAuley v Carter, 22 Ill 53, Sanger v City of Chicago 65 id 506 Herman v Schroeder, 74 id 158. Kipp v Massin, 15 Bradw 300, Watrous v Davies, 35 App 542, sec. 11, act 1874, as amended
[4] Sanger v. City of Chicago, 65 Ill. 506.
[5] Welch v Sherer, 93 Ill 64
[6] Havighorst v Lindberg, 67 Ill. 463.

§ 97. If contract for entire work, no lien if property burned or destroyed. — But if a contractor undertakes to erect an entire building, and it is destroyed, blown down or burned before completion, there is no lien for what has been done.[1] Where a party undertakes an entire work not impossible, he must do it, or he cannot recover.[1]

He can neither maintain an action for work partly done, nor to enforce a lien therefor, unless reasons exist for not doing it all which are recognized as sufficient by the law.[2]

In such case he cannot quit when he chooses, without cause, and enforce a lien for such portion of the work as he may have performed. He has no power to split up an entire demand, and maintain several suits, and enforce several liens, and thus harass and vex the owner with costs. He must perform his contract unless wrongfully prevented, before he can enforce his lien. Any other construction of the statute would render it liable to be made an engine of oppression, instead of the means of obtaining justice.[3] If he were only to do part, as the carpenter work, he would have a lien, in case of destruction.[3]

§ 98. Non-payment excuses abandonment, and lien for what done. — It has been repeatedly held, that mere non-payment of installments, as agreed, is no excuse for non-performance of the contract, or abandoning it, unless such payments are expressly made a condition precedent to going on with the work.[3] This is undoubtedly the common-law interpretation, but the statute now provides for such cases.[4] When the owner of the land shall have failed to perform his part of the contract by failing to advance to the contractor moneys justly due him under the contract, at the time when the same should have been paid to the contractor, or has failed to perform his contract in any other manner, and by reason thereof, the other party shall, without his own default, have been prevented from performing his part, he shall be entitled to a reasonable compensation for as much thereof as has been performed, in proportion to the price stipulated for the whole, and the court shall adjust his claim and allow him a lien accordingly.[5]

If the contractor be without the means, and dependent upon the

---

[1] Sontag v Brennan, 75 Ill 279 Schwartz v Saunders, 46 id 18, Thomas v Industrial University, 71 id 310

[2] Thomas v Industrial University, 71 Ill 310

[3] Kinney v Sherman, 28 Ill 520, Geary v. Bangs, 33 App. 582 This decision was prior to the amendment of sec. 11, April 22, 1891

[4] Sec 11, act 1874, as amended

[5] Sec 11, act 1874, as amended

agreed payments to furnish the money for carrying on the work, this protects him and secures him the value of what he has done

And wherever it becomes necessary to enforce the lien on the *quantum meruit*, the action must be brought under section 11 of the act [1]

§ 99 **Where contractor is delayed, he has lien for extra expense.** — Where the contract provides that in case of delay caused by the failure of other contractors to complete their work in time extra time should be allowed, such provision will not preclude the contractor making it from recovering damages resulting from the delay.[2] It is incumbent upon one erecting a building to keep the work in such a state of forwardness as to enable the respective contractors to complete their respective contracts in the time limited. In this case the contract provided that, in case the parties failed to agree as to the value of extra or deducted work, or the amount of extra time to be allowed in case of delay, the decision of the architect should be final and binding, the same in case of any disagreement between the parties relating to the performance of any covenant or agreement in the contract   The court held that the claim made by the contractor was not within the clause of the contract relating to questions which the architect should decide; that the rise in wages in consequence of the delay having made the work cost the contractor $473 20 more than it would if he had not been so delayed, he could recover such sum from the owner and enforce his lien therefor

§ 100 **Extra work provided for by contract is part of same.** — Where the contract is to do certain work for a certain price, but provides for extra work, such, however much it may be, is part and parcel of the original contract, and a lien for extra payment therefor beyond the price for the stated work exists as completely as for the work named in the specifications, whether a specific sum, or what is just and reasonable, be agreed to be paid for the extra work [3]

§ 101. **Promise to pay increased price not binding without consideration.** — But where the work is undertaken for a certain sum, there must be a consideration shown to support a claim for extra pay for doing that work. Even a promise to pay additional therefor is not binding on the owner making it, unless there is a con-

[1] Watrous v Davies, 35 App 542
[2] Nelson v. Pickwick Associated Co , 30 App 333
[3] Brown v Lowell, 79 Ill 484

sideration to support his promise.[1] If it is shown that such consideration existed, and that the promise of extra pay was made on account of it, the lien exists.[2]

Where a party employed under a special verbal contract to furnish materials and erect a building, finding himself unable to perform without great loss, owing to a rise in prices, informed his employer that he would not comply with the contract, and the employer directed him to go on and finish the work, and he would pay him what was right for it, it was held, that the new agreement was based upon a sufficient consideration and valid. The mutual promises of the parties were sufficient to support the new agreement.[3]

Where it was claimed there was a mistake of $500 in the price of the work, and the contractor refused to go on with it, and the owner agreed to pay that sum in addition to the contract price, the new and supplemental agreement was held valid, and that such modification changed no other terms of the contract but the price.[b]

§ 102 **Allowing work after time provided for completion waives forfeiture.** — Suffering the contractor to go on with the work after the agreed time for completion waives any forfeiture of the contract, as an entirety, stipulated for non-completion at a certain date, but does not waive or change any of the other terms of the contract, or preclude the owner claiming damages for non-completion in time.[?]

§ 103. **Architect's certificate.** — If the contract provides that the architect's certificates must be procured for all payments, or that vouchers showing the contractor's bills are paid must be presented, these must be produced before the contractor can sustain a lien on demand for and refusal of payment; but if the owner refuses to pay without demanding compliance with these conditions precedent as a basis for payment, the contractor is excused from compliance with the conditions.[4]

Where the contract makes the time for completing the work essential, and provides for a forfeiture of so much per day for every day the work shall remain unfinished, as liquidated damages, the architect's certificate of the completion of the work, and the sum due the contractor, but which fails to state the completion of the

[1] Nelson v. Pickwick Associated Co., 30 App. 333
[2] Bishop v. Busse, 69 Ill. 403(a), Cook v. Murphy 70 id. 96 (b)
[3] Nibbe v. Brauhn. 24 Ill. 268, Eyster v. Parrott, 83 id. 517, St Louis Nat Stock Yards v. O'Reilly, 85 id. 546
[4] Downes v. O'Donnell, 86 Ill. 49, 92 id. 559 Ewing v. Fiedler, 30 App. 202 Wolf v. Michaelis, 27 id. 336, Michaelis v. Wolf, 33 id. 643

work, within the time fixed, will not preclude the other party from insisting upon the damages agreed upon for delay in finishing and delivering up the building, and it is error to exclude evidence showing such delay.[1]

The form of the certificate must be according to the contract. The architect's omission to state "complete according to plans and specifications" does not impair the certificates, unless the contract so required.[2]

If the contract requires completion within a certain time, without providing for damages at so much per day, and the architect does not certify the work was completed in time, the owner can claim damages for delay, if any, in reduction of the contractor's claim, or to defeat the lien.[3]

Fraud or such mistake as clearly shows the architect was misled, deluded, and so far misapprehended the facts that he did not exercise his real judgment in the case, invalidates the certificate and justifies the owner's refusal to pay on production thereof.[4]

It has also been held that the owner, notwithstanding the issuance of the certificate, ought to be allowed to show that the contractor had not followed the plans and specifications whereby the owner was injured, where such showing would disclose such gross negligence on the part of the architect as to raise a presumption of fraud or mistake. In that case the architect admitted he had never looked to see if certain parts of the specifications were complied with.[4]

But the architect's certificates are binding and conclusive on both parties where he is made the arbiter, unless impeached for fraud or mistake, and if such be charged, it must be clearly shown as previously set forth.[5]

The death of one of a firm of architects terminates the authority of the survivor, unless both parties recognize his certificates, in which case they have the same force as of both.[4]

Breach of contract by owner dispenses with necessity of certificates. Where the contractor is wrongfully discharged he does not need the architect's certificate. He is relieved of all the terms of the contract by his wrongful discharge, except the value of his work, which is to be measured, as before stated, in proportion to the price

---

[1] McAuley v Carter, 22 Ill 53
[2] Downey v O Donnell, 86 Ill 49, 92 id 559   Ewing v Fiedler, 30 App 202, Wolf v Michaelis, 27 id 336, Michaelis v Wolf, 33 id 645
[3] Ewing v Fiedler, 30 App 202
[4] Davidson v Provost, 35 App 126
[5] Downey v O Donnell 86 Ill 49, 92 id 559

stipulated for the whole.¹ And destruction of the premises by fire, or otherwise, is an excuse for not obtaining or producing the certificate.²

§ 104 **Damages where work not done according to contract.**
— The measure of damages, where the work is done, but not according to contract, yet is retained and used, is the difference between the value of the article furnished and that contracted for, and loss of use while necessary changes are being made to make it susceptible of use; nor will receiving and using estop the owner from claiming damages if the work or material be defective.³

The damages resulting from failure to complete according to contract, are what it will cost to so complete the work.⁴ Damages are allowed also under certain circumstances for supervision of work and gathering materials by the owner for that purpose.⁵

Damages for delay are regarded as waived by the owner, if not claimed at the time, and when once waived, they cannot be set off in enforcing a lien.⁶

The purchaser can recoup in damages for defective performance of the contract when the lien is sought to be enforced on the property, the same as his vendor could, and avail himself of any defenses to discharge the lien that such vendor might.⁷

§ 105. **Materialman no liens, unless materials used.**—As to materialmen and others, the decisions hold that something more must be done than what universal usage, recognizes as completion of their contract — something that they have nothing whatever to do with; that rests wholly beyond their power; that is, incorporation of the material into and attaching it to the land.

The language of the statute is who performs the services, or furnishes the materials "*in* building, altering, repairing or ornamenting."⁸

§ 106. **As to architects.**—According to this, an architect has no lien, though he completes and delivers the plans and specifications does all that his contract obligates him to do, unless the contemplated improvement is in part or whole put on the realty. He, as others named in the statute, cannot assert his lien on any lot of the owner

---

¹ Watrous v Davies, 35 App 542
² Sontag v Brennan, 75 Ill 279
³ Strawn v Cogswell, 28 Ill 457
⁴ Hellman v Schneider 75 Ill 422
⁵ Metz v Lowell, 83 Ill 565
⁶ St Louis Nat Stock Yards v O'Reilly, 85 Ill 546
⁷ Cox v Colles, 17 Bradw 503
⁸ Sec. 1, act 1874, as amended

He can assert it only on the lot his work was done for, and if nothing were done on that lot through indecision, caprice, or change of mind on the part of the owner, he would have no security

The statute may mean who performs services for the purposes of such improvement shall have a lien on the lot or tract intended to be improved, but it does not say so   The architect must risk the doing of what his work is a guide of and preparation for to enable him to establish his lien

§ 107. **As to materialmen.**—When the materialman has delivered the materials at or on the premises to be improved, he has completed his contract, done all he was to or could do   He has no power to put the material into the building, and to hold him to the duty of himself seeing it is attached, or detailing an agent to do so, is to impose a hardship unreasonable, if not absurd   Yet our courts hold that unless the materials are attached to the realty, the materialman has no lien.

§ 108. **Right of materialman to recover on furnishing material whether used or not, and discussion of cases in regard thereto.**—So many losses have been incurred by reason of inability of materialmen to prove incorporation of their material, properly delivered, into the improvement, and by reason of fraudulent diversion of such delivered material by the purchaser, that it may be well to examine these decisions and see whether or not there has been a full consideration of the language of the statute, whether or not legislation is needed to change the verbiage of the law, or a change of decision is warranted.

In the first case, where it is so held, the question was whether there was a lien for materials sold out of, but used in this State

There was no question of diversion; they were used   The court held that the use of the material furnished upon the premises, putting them into the building, attaching them to the freehold, gave the lien, no matter where the residence of the seller [1]

In the next case, where the question was with regard to priority of lien between mechanic and mortgagee, wherein it was held that the mechanic's lien attached on completion of the work or delivery of material, and use of them, by connecting them to the freehold, not the date of the contract (the contrary of which our courts now hold), this case is approved. But the court say, by delivery of material * * * means are offered others to know something of

---

[1] Gaty v. Casey, 15 Ill. 190

8

such cliams for the time that may follow, within which the right of lien must be asserted [1]

There was no question of diver- n, and delivery of the material seems to be regarded decisive of the lien

In the next case, an innocent purchaser held the property when enforcement of the lien was sought, and the court held, as follows.

The (lower) court substantially construed this law as giving the lien whenever a contract has been made for the furnishing of materials to be put in a building on the lot, and, in pursuance of such contract, materials have been furnished, whether those materials, thus furnished, were actually used in the erection of such building or not   We do not so understand this law   The legislature only intended to give this lien for the materials actually used in, or the labor really bestowed upon, the building situated upon the premises against which the lien is sought to be established   The object of the law was to allow the party to pursue the thing actually furnished.   Two things must concur to create the lien, first, the contract: and second, the furnishing of the material actually used Suppose, in this case, there was a contract made, and, in pursuance thereof, the lumber was furnished, which was found to be unsuitable for the building, and was, consequently, sold to other parties. and never put in the building at all, but the lumber actually used was furnished by another, under another contract.   The statute certainly gives a lien to the one who furnished the lumber which was used in the building, and to the workmen who did the work in the erection of the building, and yet, according to the construction given by the court below, the party who made the first contract, and furnished lumber never used upon the premises, may also have a lien upon the same building and premises.   Not for any thing which he has done to enhance their value, nor by reason of any in cumbrance upon them, but because the owner of the premises had purchased lumber for the purpose of using it on the premises, but which he never did so use

Under the construction given to this law, who has the prior lien? The party who furnished the materials with which the build ing was erected, or the one whose materials were not put in the house? The legislature intended to create no such conflicting claims. The very essence of the lien created by this statute is the furnishing the materials of which the building is constructed.   The act con

---

[1] Williams v. Chapman, 17 Ill. 423.

tinues in the party furnishing the materials of which the building is erected, a *quasi* property in those materials, and others with which it has been commingled in the building, and allows him to follow it, thus transformed, for the purpose of getting his pay   If materials are furnished me for the purpose of being put upon lot 1, and I put them on a building in lot 2, the lien is upon the last lot, where they were actually used, and not on the first   There is no lien upon the premises till the material is put upon them   Under this construction, if a man goes to Chicago, and buys lumber to build a house on a particular lot in Chillicothe, and in transit the lumber is burned up, the vendor shall have his lien upon the lot for the amount so furnished   Such is not the true construction of this law   The legislature never so intended [1]

These cases are next approvingly referred to in a case where dower, only, not diversion, was involved, and referred to to show that they did not sustain the position of the counsel who cited them [2]

The next case was decided on a question of practice, not of diversion, but it holds that it is not the furnishing of materials and labor alone, which creates this lien, but it is the contract of the parties, and the furnishing of labor and materials under it, which have that effect. [3]

In the next case, where diversion of materials was claimed, it was held, there was no error in the decree for a lien if it appeared the materials were purchased to be used in improving the lot on which it was attempted to enforce the lien [4] Subsequently it was held, that the testimony showed the material in this case was purchased for and used in the buildings on the lot, and the lien sustained [5] But in a later decision, in the same case, though the lien was sustained, there is some uncertainty created by the language of the court, with regard to diversion of materials for other purposes than improvement of other property of the owner who purchased them, it being held, that as between the owner and materialman, diversion of part of the materials would not release the lien, and in the same decision that to claim exemption from the lien on this account the proof of the quantity diverted should be clear [6] If such proof were clear, it would seem to follow from the decision that there would be no lien for the material so diverted.

---

[1] Hunter v Blanchard, 18 Ill 318
[2] Gove v Cather, 23 Ill 634
[3] Sutherland v Ryerson, 24 Ill 518
[4] Croskey v Corey, 48 Ill 442
[5] Corey v Croskey, 57 Ill 251
[6] Chicago Artesian Well Co v Corey, 60 Ill 73

In the next case, wherein the question was whether or not the owner made the contract, whether the wife was liable for the contract of the husband, it was held, it is the contract of the parties and the furnishing of labor or material under that contract, that creates a lien under the statute.[1]

Again, where the question was as to labor done and materials furnished after rescission of the contract, the court held, where no part of the work is done on, nor any part of the material attached to the premises there is no lien, and the leading case on this point is cited as authority.[2]

The section of the statute under which these decisions are rendered would be relieved of all ambiguity, and justice to all secured if it read, after furnish materials, "which may be used in the construction," or as follows:

"That any person who shall, by contract, express or implied, or partly expressed and partly implied, with the owner of any lot or tract of land, furnish materials or perform services as an architect for the purpose of, or furnish labor, or perform services as superintendent in building, altering, repairing or ornamenting any house or other building or appurtenance thereto on such lot, or upon any street or alley, and connected with such building or appurtenance, shall have a lien upon the whole of such tract of land or lot, and upon such house and appurtenance, for the amount due to him for such labor, material or service, but as between purchasers, and incumbrancers and other creditors the lien for materials shall be held to secure only the amount due for what are used on the premises improved, the lien for architect's services only in case the work be undertaken."

In view of these decisions, can a court of equity construe and administer the law as if it so read?

As has been seen, a number of decisions go no further than furnishing of the materials as a requisite for the lien. Will the leading case, directly in point on this question, stand review?

The section at that time read, "for," not "in" building, was even stronger than the present section. But is its interpretation of the legislative intention correct? Was not and is not that intention to make the realty a security for what is furnished for the purpose of, as well as done in its improvement? It would be a hardship where lumber was destroyed in transit, and for that reason was not

---

[1] Wendt v Martin, 89 Ill 139   [2] Horr v Slavik, 35 App 140

attached to the premises, to enforce a lien for it ahead of one for him whose lumber did go into it   But in that case both owner and purchaser would be blameless   A court of equity would violate its character and duty to so enforce it   The equity existing in favor of him whose material went into the property is strongest and would prevail on general equity principles   So it might be asked, if more material is ordered than is used, has the materialman a lien for that not used as well as that used?   As between him and the owner why not?   Must he either go to the expense of freighting back his material, probably deteriorated by exposure, or leave it to be destroyed where delivered?

Would not equity put the burden on him whose fault was greatest?   Would it make the materialman bear the burden of an improvident buyer's reckless calculations?   In the very nature of things the work must be done to entitle him who did it to a lien.   In its very nature delivery of material by the seller thereof completes his obligation as fully as doing the work by the other   Could the legislature have intended that he who in good faith delivered his material on or at the premises should do more than the nature of his business required, than universal usage regarded as completion of his contract?

It is held that the words used in the statute must have their usual and natural construction, unless some absurd or injurious consequence would result, not foreseen or intended by the legislature[1] Apply this to the language and intention of the legislature here

Could it intend to exact more of him than lay in his power to do?   Could it define completion on his part to be more than law or business or reason ever before defined it to be?   If delivery of his material, parting with control of it, completes his contract, does not the requisition that it must be attached impose an impossible obligation on his part, and make his completion of his contract a trap and snare?   Does the act, so construed, give him any security at all?   Does it not leave him completely in the purchaser's power?   Does it not enable the purchaser, by his fraudulent, or his ill-advised act, to nullify the intent of the statute?   The expression, "completion of a contract," is a relative one.   The legislature could contemplate no more than that the respective parties should do what was completion on the part of each   It would be as great, but no greater, hardship to hold that the owner must use or sell his building before the contractor who had done his work could enforce his

---

[1] Martin v Swift, 120 Ill 488

lien, as to hold that he must use the material before the material-man who delivered it could enforce his. This law does not contemplate reliance upon honesty of purpose and personal integrity It contemplates reliance upon security in the property proposed to be improved. For this reason it requires the sale to be with reference to a particular lot or tract of land that the seller may decide whether or not he regards that lot or tract of land as adequate security for his risk, and act accordingly And when he delivers it with regard to that security he is entitled to the security.

If there were a contract to deliver material for the improvement of lot 1, and the materials were used on lot 2, suit on that contract to enforce the lien on lot 2 would fail It is too well established that the material must be bought to improve the lot it is used on.[1] In such case the lien could be enforced, but it would have to be done, not under that contract, but another, an implied contract to pay for what was used on lot 2.

These are hypothetical cases the court presents On the other hand, take the case of deliberate diversion by the purchaser; where he sells the delivered material and appropriates the proceeds; where the seller seeks to enforce the lien only against him, is not the equity for such enforcement of equal strength to that raised in behalf of him whose materials were used in consequence of the owner not receiving the first material? Suppose in cities where blocks of buildings of the same character (exact duplicates) are erected, A and B, owners respectively of adjoining lots 1 and 2, decide to so improve them. A. buys materials to improve lot 1, B. buys from another party the same class and quantity of materials to improve lot 2 When the materials are delivered, unknown to the sellers, A. and B exchange materials and so erect their houses. He who furnished material for lot 1 could not assert his lien on lot 2, for he had no contract with the owner of that lot, and did not furnish his materials to improve it, and *vice versa* If this decision be correct, the diversion of materials would bar liens on either property. Would a court of equity permit such jugglery under this statute?

In most of the States the actual use of the materials is not requisite if they were furnished for a particular building or improvement, and a contrary rule is held on similar statutes to that of Illinois.[2] By very distinguished authority it is held · — To require

---

[1] Hill v Bishop, 25 Ill 307, Croskey v Corey, 48 id 442, Wendt v Martin, 89 id. 139.

[2] Jones on Liens (2d ed.), sec. 1329

direct and positive testimony as to each specific article delivered, that it was in fact used in the building, would make the Mechanics' Lien Law more of a burden and a trap than a blessing and a help[1]

In the sparse settlements of early times materialmen could and did know the progress of improvements and were able to keep watch of what purchasers were doing. In the populous cities that now crowd this State, the vast volume of such business makes such an impossibility. It would require an army of men for material dealers to see that their delivered goods were attached to improvements, impose an obligation that would weigh down and wreck their business. The legislature could intend no such hampering of one of its most important industries, nor to delude those engaged in it by a fancied security, easily made to vanish by the unknown and unpreventable act of the owner who deliberately imposed upon their faith in him and in the law

The course of our State's legislation is proof of the recognition of these facts, and a change in the phraseology of the statute in consequence The act of 1825, the first passed with relation to liens, awards a lien to whoever has "furnished materials, which shall have been used in the construction" The act of 1833, the next passed, "which *may* have been used in the construction" The act of 1839-40 drops this condition and reads, "for erecting or repairing" The act of 1845 and the act of February 16, 1861, use the same language. The act of February 14, 1863, applicable only to sub contractors, "in building;" that of same date, extending liens where the work was done over the lot line, "for building" The act of April 5, 1869, and subsequent acts, "in building"[2]

As will be seen, the words, "for" and "in," were used in different acts of the same date, February 14, 1863 The legislature must have intended the same thing by both expressions, but the omission in all legislation of, "which shall (or may) have been used in the construction," subsequent to the acts of 1825 and 1833, must have been done for a purpose That purpose could be but one, to give the lien when the materials were furnished The legislature must have considered the requirement, "used in the construction," as being too strict, as being short of doing justice to those who had gone to the limit of their ability and duty in furnishing materials for the purpose, and have omitted it and used other language for the express purpose of giving them a lien when they had furnished

---

[1] Justice Brewer, Rice v Hodge, 26 Kans 164
[2] See respective acts in Appendix

the materials. The history of our legislation on this matter can bear no other construction as to legislative intention.

The earlier decisions must have been made with the earlier acts in mind, the court's attention not called to the change in the law and the later decisions followed these as authority, as the court says in *Clark* v *Manning*, 90 Ill 380, overruling *Fish* v *Stubbings*, 65 id 492, and *Powell* v *Webber*, 79 id 134, that the act of 1861 seemed not to have been considered in their rendition, and they were, in consequence, erroneous

Take the section as it reads The word "in," Webster defines, is used in a variety of relations, as "in respect to, or consideration of;" "on account of;" "according to, and the like," "in health," etc, meaning a state or condition. The language of the section is not in *the* building, but *in* building. It is not a strained construction to define it, "on account of," "for the purpose of," "during the course of," or, "while in progress."

The other sections of the act sustain this contention. Section 5 makes the bill or petition sufficient, if it contains a brief statement of the contract on which it is founded, if expressed, or if the work is done or materials are *furnished* under an implied contract, if the bill or petition so states. The statute itself does not require the allegation that the materials were used. Section 17 expressly states that no incumbrance upon land created before or after the making of a contract under the provisions of this act, shall operate upon the building erected, or materials furnished, until the lien in favor of the person doing the work or *furnishing* the materials shall have been satisfied Section 35 requires the contractor, on demand, to give a statement showing, not whose material has been used in the building or improvement, but who are *furnishing* material, and what is due or to become due for materials *furnished*. Construing the whole act — the different sections together — the weight of its authority favors conference of the lien when the materials are furnished

These are chancery cases. Courts of equity are courts of flexible powers The peculiar province of equity has ever been to remedy the law wherein it is defective by reason of its universality. On this principle the hardships of clearly expressed and absolutely certain contracts are relieved from, when the same would be enforceable at law. It acts upon moral grounds, and to secure and enforce justice It is a purchaser's right to reject defective material. His refusal to receive or use it would bar both lien and common-law obligation to pay for it.   His sale, on the ground of being defective, and appropriation of the proceeds, with immunity from lien liability, an excuse of too easy invention for safely appropriating the property of another, for a court of equity to countenance   A more liberal construction has been given this statute in favor of those whom it was designed to protect where only between those parties and owners matters were at issue.[1]   Where these parties alone contest, to hold that the lien for materials furnished covers the property they are furnished to improve, is for the court of equity to be backed by the strongest moral, equitable reason, as well as statutory intention

If the diversion were done without the knowledge or collusion of the seller, he should not be suffered to be robbed of his rights by the fraud of the purchaser, and left only to the vengeful proceeding of an action on the case   While this would bring the defrauding owner who bought to just punishment, it might not secure the seller in payment for his materials.

In such case the court can act on the general chancery principle that he who asks must do equity, that a court of equity aids only him who comes with clean hands, and that a party who perpetrated the fraud would be estopped to plead his own tort in order to escape liability. That having bought the material to be used in his own improvement, he would not be heard to deny that it was so used, or to set up as a defense a diversion that he alone occasioned.   The purpose of the law is to secure materialmen as well as those who, as contractors, do or have work done on real property   Not to enforce the lien in such case would be to defeat the purpose of the law through the fraud of the purchaser, and inability of the seller to prevent it

Nor is it difficult, where other's rights intervene, to do justice to all under the broad jurisdiction and ample powers of a chancery court This would be done by holding that if the owner purchase material to improve a lot, and sell part or all, the lien therefor will cover the lot, so far as the owner is concerned   If others intervene whose materials did go into the property, apply the proceeds of the sale, first to payment of their claims, the surplus to him whose material was diverted   In case of incumbrancers and purchasers, ignorant of the purchase of such materials, hold their rights likewise superior   This would bar the fraudulent purchaser taking advantage of

---

[1] Sec 20, *ante*

his own wrong, do justice to all.   In such case does not the latitude
of a court of equity permit it to so administer the law, and if no
intervening creditor, incumbrancer or purchaser appear, enforce the
lien on the property the materials were represented to have been
bought to improve?

There has been no adjudication where the controversy was between only owner and materialman, and the current of authority in
this State is against the argument offered.   As will be shown hereafter, it is held that such petitioner to enforce a lien must aver both
that the material was bought to improve the particular piece of
property, and that it was used in its improvement[1]

The law may be weak in not in so many words establishing the
lien of the materialman on the realty when his material is delivered
on or at it for its improvement, if such were the legislative intention
The legislature, not the court, may be the sole authority to rectify
the error, if error it be   Yet it may be that our courts, on a review
of the authorities and the legislation, would establish a different
interpretation of the statute, and award a lien to the materialman
when he had completed and performed his contract by a delivery
of the material on or at the property he sold it to be used upon, as
against the owner who bought of him, and without prejudice to the
rights of third parties

---

[1] See chapter 12,

CHAPTER IV.

PERFECTING THE ORIGINAL CONTRACTOR'S LIEN.

§ 109 **Contractor must file claim for lien.** — The making and performance of the contract still leaves the lien an inchoate one. One more step is required to perfect and fix it

The creditor or contractor must file with the clerk of the Circuit Court of the county in which the building, erection, or other improvement to be charged with the lien is situated, a just and true statement or account, or demand due him, after allowing all credits, setting forth the time when such material was furnished, or labor performed, and containing a correct description of the property to be charged with the lien, and verified by an affidavit [1]

§ 110. **Must be against the owner when contract is made.** — The claim must be filed against the owner of the property. [2]

This should be the person who owned the property at the time of and made the contract, not the one who owns it at the time the claim is filed, for whoever purchases the property after the contract is made, purchases subject to the lien under that contract, and is bound by it   There would be no objection in event the property had been sold after the contract was made, to filing the claim against both the original owner and subsequent purchaser — the owner at the time the claim is filed.

[1] Sec 4, act 1874, as amended, Beck Lbr Co v Halsey, 41 App 349, see Limitations, § 179
[2] Campbell v Jacobson, 145 Ill 389

If the owner be a corporation its corporate name should be used: The transposition of some of the words in the corporate name is not material, if it make no essential difference in the sense. As where it was alleged that a contract was entered into by one of the parties by the name and style of "The State Board of Education of Illi nois," when by the act creating the corporation, the name given to it was "The Board of Education of the State of Illinois." Although the words were transposed in the contract, the name and style re mained substantially the same [1]

§ 111 **Must correctly describe the property.** — The claim must give a full and correct description of the property improved, and on which the lien is sought to be enforced The lien can be enforced only on the property thus described, though it may really extend over other property If, for instance, a house be built on lot 1, and the adjoining half of lot 2, the claim describe merely lot 1, the lien would be enforced only on lot 1.[2] Hence the importance of a full description The law contemplates that after the contract is made, time and opportunity is afforded to learn from the records the exact legal description of the property improved, and this legal description the affidavit should set forth. It should be such as to give full record notice of the property to create a *lis pendens* lien, and if the proceedings are carried to a sale, should be such that the deed of the officer selling would properly convey the property, as well as to give purchasers opportunity to examine before sale into what was to be offered under such sale. As this statement must be sworn to, the petition not, it is even more essential that the descrip tion set forth in it should be correct, than that in the petition. If in correct, the error is fatal [3]

§ 112. **Must be itemized and particulars necessary.** — The statement of account should be itemized ; if for materials, what they were ; with dates of respective deliveries, amounts, prices and credits; if for labor or services, of what character, carpentry, masonry, etc , the dates same were rendered and price or value, with the respective dates of all payments made thereon, and of the amount due after allowing all such deductions and credits , if for a contract. set it out in full, state the date when made, and contract price, when to be performed, when it was performed, what deductions, if any, what for and the amounts, the dates and amounts of payments, and the

---

[1] Board of Education v Greenebaum, 39 Ill 610
[2] Watson v Gardner, 119 Ill 312 , Gardner v Watson, 18 Bradw 386, Poitones v. Holmes, 33 id. 312, id v Badenoch, 132 Ill 377
[3] Sec. 4, act 1874, as amended

balance due after allowing all such credits   If the statement fails
to set forth the times when the materials were furnished, or work
done, it is fatally defective,[1] equally so if it fails to set forth the
original amount due, and credits as made[2]

Such requirements are not met by stating the amount due in a
lump sum after deducting credits, without stating any items com-
posing the account, or showing what the credits were ; nor by stating that the work, or contract, was completed at a certain time,
without showing the time when it was commenced, or during which
it was performed, or the period during which the materials were
furnished or labor claimed for was rendered.[2]

§ 113. **Where different houses, claims must be against each.**
— If one roof cover all, one claim is sufficient   Where the improvement consists of a number of houses on different lots and under
different roofs, the claims must be filed against each separately,
although the contract be an entirety, and the payments are to be
made and credited upon them as a whole.[3]   The fact that these lots
are contiguous and when completed the buildings form in front and
rear a solid block, does not alter the rule, if dividing walls and
separate roofs make them distinct buildings[4]   If under one roof,
only one claim need be filed against the whole,[5] and if more than
one building be on the same lot or tract of land, but one claim is
necessary to be filed.[6]

If the work be done or the materials are furnished upon distinct
premises, the claim must be against each of the several premises, according to the value of the work and materials incorporated in each,
and not against both for the aggregate amount[7]

§ 114. **Must be properly verified — Cases of defective verification.**—This statement must be not merely sworn to, but properly
verified.   In one case the following affidavit was made to the claim.

A., being duly sworn, says he is the authorized agent for B., that
B. has performed the labor and furnished the materials set forth in
the above statement of claim for a lien, and there is now due B. from
C., for said labor and materials, after allowing all credits and set offs,
the sum of $175, which affiant charges and alleges is a lien upon the

[1] Campbell v. Jacobson, 145 Ill 389
[2] McDonald v Rosengarten, 134 Ill 126, 35 App 71
[3] Bayard v McGraw, 1 Bradw 134, McGraw v Bayard, 96 Ill 146 Portones
v Badenoch, 132 Ill 377, Portones v Holmes 33 App 312
[4] Note 2, *supra*, A R Beck Lumber Co v Halsey, 41 App 349
[5] James v Hambleton, 42 Ill 308 Orr v N W Mut Life Ins Co, 86 id 260
[6] St Louis Nat Stock Yards v O'Reilly, 85 Ill 546
[7] Steigleman v McBride, 17 Ill 300, Culver v Elwell, 73 id 536

above-described premises The court held that this was no verifica
tion , that it might be true, whether performed in time or not, to
enforce the lien   It was merely a statement that the claimant per
formed labor and furnished materials, not *as* set forth, but set forth

So in the following affidavit ; L , as agent, sold the materials men
tioned in the above statement, and said balance of $113 77, above
set forth, is now due said company on account of materials so fur
nished for the building situated upon said premises. heretofore described, was held to be no verification, and a statement with proper
verification being a statutory condition precedent to the enforcement
of a lien, the failure to provide such affidavit prohibited the enforcement of the lien.[2]

§ 115 **Of proper verification.**—The verification should be, if
the claim be upon a contract, that it was made, at the time, for the
purpose and for the consideration, as set forth in the statement,
that the work under said contract was commenced, performed and
completed at the times as therein set forth ; that payments thereon
were made at the dates and in the amounts as therein set forth , that
all credits to which the said (owner) is entitled are as therein set
forth, and that, after allowing all such credits, there is due the
claimant from said (owner) the amount as therein set forth, which
is yet due and unpaid

If for materials, that the same were purchased to be used in im
proving the property as described, and were so used ; that they were
delivered at the times, and as set forth in the statement, and at the
prices as therein given , that the amounts and dates of payments,
and all credits to which said (owner) is entitled are as therein set
forth ; and after allowing all such credits, there remains yet due and
unpaid the claimant, from said (owner), the amount as therein set
forth. If for services as architect, or superintendent, or labor by
mechanic or laborer, that such services or labor were rendered and
performed at the times set forth in the statement ; that the prices
agreed upon, or value of such services, were as therein set forth ;
that all payments made were in the amounts and at the times as
therein set forth ; and that after allowing all credits to which said
(owner) is entitled, there remains a balance due, owing and unpaid
the claimant, from said (owner), the amount as therein set forth[3]
The affidavit may be made by owner, agent, or employee.

---

[1] McDonald v Rosengarten, 134 Ill 126, 35 App 71.
[2] A R Beck Lumber Co v Halsey, 41 App 349
[3] See form of verification, Appendix, page 201.

§ 116 **Object of claim.**—The purpose of requiring the claim to set forth the time when such materials were furnished or labor performed, is to enable those interested to know from the claim itself that it is such as can be enforced; and verification by affidavit is required as a guarantee of the claim in this as in other respects, and all this is, by section 28 of the act, indispensable to the enforcement of the lien against creditors, incumbrancers, or purchasers [1]

If their examination of the claim as filed discloses that it is not properly made, they may disregard it and deal with the property as if no claim existed

Thus far, the law has been given as applicable to the parties — original contractor, materialman, architect, superintendent, laborer, or other person — who dealt directly with the owner.

As the sub-contractors, or others, who seek to enforce their liens on the property must proceed by petition the same as these, it will be well to ascertain their rights before treating of the petition and subsequent procedure

[1] McDonald v Rosengarten, 134 Ill 126, 35 App 71.

CHAPTER V.

SUB-CONTRACTORS

§ 117. **Earlier laws, no lien to sub-contractors.**— The earlier acts allowed no lien to the sub-contractor. They proceeded in accordance with the universal practice in all other business affairs, that a person should be held only on the contract he made, and by the party with whom he made it, and for reasons heretofore given, were enacted to secure that original contractor. Not until 1863 was any recognition given to sub-contractors[1] Then the statute for their benefit applied only to a few counties Not until 1869 were the provisions for their benefit made a part of the general law and applicable to the whole State. There has been a steady advance in statutory effort to protect the unknown subordinates whose material or labor should add to the value of real estate by building improvements thereon. Somewhat of philanthropy animates this progress The legislature seems to have regarded the laborer less capable of caring for himself, more worthy its protection than any others Its latest effort makes his claim an absolute lien to a certain extent for a certain time,[2] thereafter a preferred one to that of materialmen, or other sub contractors of a higher grade.[3]

This progress is based upon recognition of the progress in build-

[1] See act 1863, Appendix
[2] Sec 33, act 1874, as amended
[3] Sec. 34, act 1874, as amended.

ing operations, the present methods of business. No one party does or can do the entire work The extent of the field enforces special ties Stone and brick work, carpentry, plumbing, plastering, steam fitting, roofing, structural iron, electric apparatus, decoration. are each special branches of trade, distinct vocations, some of which require licenses to prosecute, and are as worthy protection as the sole contractor who in primitive day did the entire work.

§ 118. **Liability of owner where notified.**— Though the owner and sub-contractor make no contract with, are absolutely unknown to each other, the statute, on conditions, brings them into contract relations by statutory force Where the owner is notified according to law that the sub-contractor has been employed, the existing law not only makes him liable to that sub-contractor, but primarily so from the date of that notice ' In such case he is obliged to pay, not the contractor whom he has directly dealt with, but the sub-contractor, to credit such payment on his own promised payment, and pay the balance only to the original contractor ' This notice may be given to the owner either by the statement of the original con tractor, as provided in section 35, or by the sub-contractor, as provided in section 30 of the act of 1874.

There is no legal reason why the sub-contractor should not serve this notice on the owner as soon as he makes his contract. If he wishes to secure his rights beyond question he should do so. Appre- hension of giving offense to his immediate employer, the original con- tractor, doubtless deters such action, but it is the only safe method of fixing and securing his lien that the law places in his power

§ 119 **Amendment of 1891 as to form of statement.**— The amendment of 1891 makes material changes in the law relating to sub-contractors, the duties and liabilities of owners and original contractors As the decisions to date have been rendered under the law as it stood prior to this amendment, as no adjudication has been made upon the present law, it will be well to compare the sections wherein these changes are made.

Section 29, as it now reads, was passed June 16, 1887. At the same time section 35 was enacted as appears in the amendment of that date Under this section it was held, with regard to the form of statement, that the following statement of the original con- tractor, to wit:

---

[1] Secs 29-33, 34, 35, act 1874, as amended, see form of notice
[2] Sec 34, act 1874, as amended. Appendix, page 187
[3] See act June 16, 1887, Appendix.

"The following persons were in my employ on said job, viz: Schultz, Bernard Wieska, Robert Wieska, Otto Pauly, Krampke and Charlie, which all amounts to $125, and which is paid in full" was insufficient. That it did not state the number, names, the rate of wages of any workmen, how much was to be paid to either of them, nor the terms of the contracts with any of them, and was, therefore, not sufficient in form or substance [1]

The present section modifies the requisites of this statement, demands less particular details, requires the original contractor to state simply the number of persons in his employ, and of the subcontractors or other persons furnishing labor or material; giving their names, and how much, if any thing, is due or to become due each of them for work done or material furnished [1] The rate of wages, or terms of contract, need not be stated, but what amount is due or to become due each must be stated. The statement of a lump sum due all would be as vicious under the present as under the former law. The owner must require and be informed of what is due or to become due each, that he may reserve and pay to each what is coming to him.

§ 120. **Necessity of statement under law of 1887.**—It was also held, under the law of June 16, 1887, that the owner must require such statement, not merely before he made each payment to the original contractor, that he must not only retain what was so shown to be due to such sub-contracting parties, but pay it over to them, and not to the original contractor. That this section affected the rights of the parties in their duties and relations to each other under the law, and was not a matter affecting the remedy.[2] That it was not a privilege, but obligation of the owner to demand this statement and so make his payments That the section's provisions were mandatory; and any payment made by the owner, without requiring such statement, was at his peril, was not rightfully made, was in violation of the rights and interests of the sub contractors and persons named in section 29, and would not be taken into account in estimating the amount due the original contractor by the owner in an action by the sub-claimant to enforce his lien That if such sub-claimant served his notice according to the law, within the forty days allowed him, it would secure his lien, notwithstanding

---

[1] Weiska v. Imroth, 43 App 347.
[2] Sec 35, act 1874, as amended
[3] Hughes v Russell, 43 App 430

the owner's having paid the original contractor prior thereto, if he had paid him without such statement[1]

That while the owner could not be compelled to pay more than his original contract price, if he had paid properly, that is, after receiving the original contractor's statement and reserving what it showed to be due the sub-contractors for them, if he paid improperly, that is, without so doing, he would be compelled to pay more than the contract price, for such payments would not be reckoned as against the claim of the sub-contractors. The decisions are broad, but follow the letter of the law[2]

§ 121. **Cases under law of 1887.**—Where the house was to be completed on November 1, the last item of material was delivered on November 7, and the materialman served notice on November 17, and the owner had paid the principal contractor prior thereto, without requiring his statement, the lien of the materialman was sustained[3]

Again, the contractor was to build for $4.750, by contract of May 15, 1889. On July 6, 1889, the owner took his statement, showing due to sub-contractors, mechanics and workmen, $300 01; on August 3, 1889, another statement, showing due, or to become due, $1,190 02, making in all the sum of $1,490.03, but no further statements were taken or required; and, after the last statement, the contractor was paid in full, and the materialmen delivered the materials they contracted to deliver, commencing August 23, 1889, and amounting to $675, and extra material and labor amounting to $76 20, completing the last work October 15, 1889, and served notice on the owner October 23, 1889. It was held, the owner, although he had paid all due the contractor prior to such notice, was liable for making such final payments without demanding further statements, and the materialmen adjudged a lien for the amount of their whole bill, $751 20[4]

Where the contract was for $2,896, and the owner paid $2,808 82 without demanding any statement of the contractor, and the materialmen served notice within forty days from maturity of their bills, amounting to $172 10, it was held, the owner was liable and the lien enforced for payment of that amount.[5]

[1] Butler & McCracken v Gain, 128 Ill 23, adv, 29 App 425, Conklin v Plaut, 34 id 264, Chicago Sash, Door & Blind Co v Shaw, 44 id 618, Hintze v Weiss, 45 id 220
[2] Sec 35, amendment June 16, 1887
[3] Conklin v Plant, 34 App 264
[4] Chicago Sash, Door & Blind Co v Shaw, 44 App 618.
[5] Hintze v Weiss, 45 App 220

The effect of this requirement of the statute, and its apparent conflict with duties imposed and rights conferred upon the sub-claimant, and liabilities that he is subjected to by requirements in other sections, was elaborately discussed in the case referred to, wherein the owner neglected to require the contractor's statement before final payment The conclusions reached were as follows: [1]

" The sections of chapter 82, Revised Statutes, as amended and in force July 1, 1887, necessary to be considered in the determination of this question, provide as follows. Section 29 provides that every sub-contractor shall have a lien for the value of labor and material furnished, but the aggregate of all liens shall not exceed the original contract price, and the owner shall not, in any case, be compelled to pay a greater sum than such contract price, unless payments be made to the original contractor or to his order in violation of the rights and interest of the persons intended to be benefited by section 35 of the act, and except in case of a fraudulently low price   Section 30 provides for the giving of notice by the sub contractor, and that such notice shall not be necessary where the sworn statement of the contractor, provided for in section 35. shall serve to give the owner true notice of the amount due, and to whom due   Section 33 provides that no claim of a sub-contractor shall be a lien under section 29, except so far as the owner may be indebted to the contractor at the time of giving such notice as aforesaid of such claim, or may become indebted to him afterward as such contractor   Section 35, referred to as above, provides that the original contractor shall, whenever any payment of money shall become due from the owner or whenever he desires to draw any money from the owner on such contract, make out and give to the owner a statement, under oath, of the name of every sub-contractor, giving the terms of contract and how much, if any thing, is due or to become due to them, and the owner shall retain out any money then due or to become due to the contractor, an amount sufficient to pay all demands that are due or to become due such sub contractors as shown by such contractor's statement, and pay the same to them according to their respective rights, and all payments so made shall, as between such owner and contractor, be considered the same as if paid to such original contractor   It further provides that until such statement is made, the contractor shall have no right of action or lien against the owner on account of such contract, and any payment made by the owner before such

---

[1] Chicago Sash, Door & Blind Co v Shaw, 44 App 618

statement is made, or without retaining sufficient money, if that amount be due, or is to become due, to pay the sub-contractors as shown by the statement, shall be considered illegal and made in violation of the rights of the persons intended to be benefited by the act, and the rights of such sub-contractor to a lien shall not be affected thereby

It is contended on the part of the defendant in error that it was wholly unnecessary for her to take the sworn statements she did take, and that she was not bound to demand any statement upon making a payment to the contractor or his order, but that she might require such statement, or not, at her pleasure. And it is said that the case of *Butler and McCracken v. Gain*, 128 Ill. 23, sustained this contention We do not so understand that decision. The expressions used must be held to refer to the facts of that case, and to be applicable to like conditions only It cannot be contended that the legislature designed that the statement should only be required as to claims of which the sub-contractor had been already given notice If notice has been served by the sub-contractor, the statement is useless both to him and the owner, for he is already secured and the owner already has the requisite information. In that view of the statute it would be a pertinent query in what way the legislature designed that the sub-contractor should be "benefited" by the statute if he must first make himself secure before the benefit is bestowed upon him. In the case above referred to, Butler and McCracken claimed a lien but had never given notice, and the owner had received no notice by any statement The claim of a lien was founded only upon the fact of furnishing material, and the owner's neglecting to take the sworn statement; and it was held, that the right to a lien cannot be based merely on an omission, but that section 35 was only intended to protect persons who complied with the provisions of the statute so as to be otherwise entitled to enforce the right to a lien The only point in that case was that Butler and McCracken not having taken the necessary steps to perfect their lien, were not in a position to complain of the neglect to demand a sworn statement from the contractor. That case was considered by this court, and referred to in *Conklin v. Plant*, 34 App. 264, and was not then regarded as sustaining the claim now made by defendant in error.

The provisions for the benefit and protection of sub-contractors by requiring a sworn statement and declaring payments made before such statement illegal, were introduced into the statute in 1887 by amendment. The persons intended to be benefited by section 35 are named in the section, and include sub-contractors, who are to be protected in their rights by requiring the owner to take a sworn statement intended to disclose such rights. And the section provides: "Any payment made by the owner before such statement is made, * * * shall be considered illegal and made in violation of the rights of the persons intended to be benefited by this act, and the rights of such sub-contractors, mechanics, workmen or persons furnishing material, to a lien, shall not be affected thereby." At the time of this amendment, section 33, above referred to, was not changed, and it is claimed that by reason of that section plaintiff in error could not have any lien. If this section is found to be irreconcilably inconsistent with the amendment, the latter must prevail, but the various sections should be construed together so as to give some effect to each if possible. Prior to the amendment, the original contractor could lawfully collect or order paid to others money due on his contract as rapidly as it became due, and enforce his rights by action regardless of any claim of a sub-contractor who had not already given notice of his rights, and the owner had a right to disregard the claims of every sub-contractor who had not served notice of a lien.

It was the evident intention of the legislature to impose upon the owner, by the amendment, a duty for the benefit of such persons, by requiring a sworn statement to be taken by the owner, and providing that payments made without such statements should be regarded the same as not having been made, and as though the sums so paid were still due, so far as the right to a lien is concerned. It seems that it could not have been intended that the amount due the contractor, referred to by section 33, should be lessened or extinguished by taking account of such payment as the statute declared to be illegal, not affecting the right to a lien.

The rational construction of section 33 would seem to be that, taking account of legal payments only, that is, such as are not made in violation of the statute, the owner shall not be liable for more than the balance due. This affords to him who obeys the law full and ample protection in harmony with the like provisions, as amended in section 29, where it is provided that the owner shall not be liable for any more than the contract price, unless payments are made in violation of the act, in which event it is plainly the legislative intent that he may become liable for more than the contract price. If the owner obeys the plain provisions of the statute and takes the statement, but such statement does not serve to give him notice, and no notice has been served by the sub-contractor, then he may make payment of the amount due, and will not be liable for any more than the contract price. This construction leaves every section of the statute to have some force. To construe the statute otherwise would be to defeat the object of the amendment and leave the law as it was before making the passage of the amendment a vain and useless act

Defendant in error could not lawfully pay to the contractor or his order, without a sworn statement, to the injury of plaintiff in error and against the express prohibition of the statute. This is the very thing that the legislature intended to protect the sub contractor against, and defendant in error having paid to the contractor or to his order, without such statement, sums far in excess of the amounts due plaintiff in error, such payments were by the statute made illegal, and the right of the plaintiff in error to a lien was not affected thereby "[1]

§ 122. **Section 35 amended in 1891.** — Section 29 remains un changed, and yet refers to section 35 as at first, but the language of the latter section, as amended in 1891, is very different from the one repealed

The former made the original contractor's statement a condition precedent to his demand for payment. He could not demand payment or enforce his lien until the statement was furnished The present section relieves him from this burden, has no provision prohibiting his demand for payment, or enforcement of his lien without such statement. It simply imposes a penalty of $50 on the original contractor for failure to furnish such statement within five days after the owner's demand therefor according to law.

The former, in express words, made the owner's payments without such statement illegal and in violation of the rights of the persons named. The present section has no language thus characterizing payments so made.

The former provided the same penalty of $50, recoverable by the owner for the contractor's failure to furnish the demanded statement, and in addition gave him the protection of immunity from action until that statement was furnished, whether demanded or not The present section furnishes no such protective right The author is of opinion, however, if the owner demanded such state-

---

[1] See also Boals v Intrup, 40 App. 62, Beck Lumber Co v Halsey, 41 id 349, Floyd v Rathledge, id. 371

ment before action brought, the contracter could not maintain a lien proceeding until he had furnished it

The former section's phraseology was, the owner *shall* pay the amount that he was notified was due to the sub-contractor to him. The present section omits this provision altogether, while section 34, instead of making it mandatory, reads, he *may* so pay it The present section reads, the contractor *shall* furnish the statement when the owner demands it in writing No obligation is upon the owner to demand it, save by implication and inference in section 29 In itself it is permissive, a privilege which the owner may exercise but it is a duty which he should exercise, considering other portions of the law

The legislative act that swept out the *onus* of the obligation put upon the original contractor to present this statement with his demand for payment, and made it an absolute condition precedent to such demand, with the same stroke swept out the protection awarded the owner in immunity from suit until it was done, the protection awarded the persons named in section 29, by making his payment illegal and in violation of their rights, and in providing that he *shall* pay to them what he is so notified is due them

Section 35 is not only a weaker section as it now reads, but weaker for the repealed section's existence that it is substituted for.

The owner may say to the sub-contractor that the law empowered him to serve notice of his sub-contract on the day he made it, before he did a stroke of work, or delivered a dollar's worth of material; that if he slept upon his rights, he imperiled them by his own conduct, that he (the owner) obeyed his moral and legal obligation to pay his own contractor as he agreed to do; that there was no law forbidding his so doing, and that he was ready to respond to the sub-contractor's claim so far as he owed the original contractor at the time of the notice, but no farther. That this law was one under which the courts of his State instructed him the letter, not the spirit of the law must be obeyed, and this only would he do as was least inconvenience to him

On the other hand, the sub-contractor could insist that the provisions of section 29 now make the owner's payments in violation of the rights of persons intended to be benefited by section 35, illegal and in contravention of their rights, that he is the person whom that section has in view; that both sections must be construed together to properly interpret the act; that not to regard the privilege or power conferred upon the owner to demand the original

11

contractor's statement prior to any statement as more than permissive, as directory, would be to make the law, as to him, a vain and useless act, and that if he gave his notice to the owner according to law within the forty days allowed him, it secured his impending lien on what the owner owed the original contractor during that period, if he had paid it without requiring such statement

Only a decision of our Supreme Court can settle the uncertainty occasioned by this legislation. The only safe course for owner and sub-contractor to pursue, until such decision is rendered, is for the owner to demand the statement before he pays, the sub contractor to serve his notice as if no such provision existed

§ 123 **Sub-contractor's lien attaches at date of original con tract.** — The original contractor's lien cannot antedate his contract: The sub-contractor's lien, when perfected, regardless of when he makes his contract, is, by the statute, carried back to, and attaches at the same date as that of the principal contractor The statute regards it as part and parcel of the original contract, no matter when it is made, and makes it a lien upon the property from that time, and as the work progresses, as much as the lien for the original con tractor's labor or materials[2] But unlike the original contractor, whose lien is an absolute one, upon the whole of the owner's interests in the property, the sub-contractors have a lien on that property only to the extent of the original contract price for the improvement. The aggregate of all liens of this class cannot exceed the price stipulated in the original contract. In no case shall the owner be compelled to pay a greater sum for or on account of such house, buildings, or other improvements, than the price or sum stipulated in the original contract or agreement, unless payments be made to the original contractor or to his order, in violation of the rights and interests of the persons entitled to be benefited by the provisions in section 35 of the act,[3] or after notice of the sub claimant's claim properly served[3]

§ 124 **Original contractor must furnish statement on written demand.** — Those provisions in the existing statute are as fol lows :

The original contractor shall, as often as requested, in writing, by the owner, lessee, or his agent, make out and give to such owner, lessee, or his agent, a statement of the number of persons in his em-

---

[1] Nibbe v Brauhn, 24 Ill 268 Wetherell v Ohlendorff, 61 id 283
[2] Sec 29, act 1874, as amended
[3] Sec 33, act 1874, as amended

ploy, and of the sub-contractors, or other persons, furnishing labor or materials, giving their names, and how much, if any thing, is due or to become due to each of them for work done or materials furnished, which statement shall be made under oath, if required of him by such owner, lessee or agent   The owner cannot demand such statement from the sub-contractor, or from any one but the original contractor.   The original contractor has a similar right to demand a similar statement, except as to what is to become due, from his sub-contractor[1]   This is for the original contractor's benefit and does not affect the lien, or procedure, one way or the other

The owner can recover before a justice of the peace, a penalty of $50 of the contractor, if he fails to give such statement within five days after demand so made, the original contractor has like recourse upon the sub-contractor

This must not be a verbal, but a formal, written request

This statement must contain :

1 The number of persons in the contractor's employment

2 The names of sub contractors, materialmen, or other persons he has dealt or is dealing with, who have furnished labor, or materials, or are to do so

3 The amounts due, or to become due each.[2]

§ 125 **Effect of this statement.**— What effect does this sworn statement have ?   On its delivery, can the original contractor demand at once payment of what is due him, over and above what he so shows is due his subordinates ; can the owner then safely pay that amount, or must he delay until the forty days have expired within which the sub-contractor is allowed to serve his notice?

In the broadest decision, before cited, rendered under the former more stringent statute, it was held, that if the owner takes the statement, but such statement does not serve to give him notice and no notice has been served by the sub-contractor, then he may make payment of the amount due, and will not be liable for more than the contract price.[3]

When the owner has demanded, the original contractor furnished the statement, both have done all that the law requires   The contractor is then entitled to his money, the owner should pay it promptly, reserving the ten per cent provided for by section 33 of the present law   To postpone the payment for forty days on the

[1] Sec 35, act 1874, as amended, see forms, Appendix, pages 197, 199
[2] See forms, Appendix, pages 198, 200
[3] Chicago Sash, Door & Blind Co v Shaw, 44 App. 618

theory that some sub-contractor might be omitted and might serve his notice, would doubtless work irreparable injury to the original contractor. The law allows no such unreasonable, apprehensive action on the part of the owner. He must take that statement as it is made and act upon it. If such statement, through negligence, oversight, or fraud of the original contractor, be false and fail to notify the owner of all whom the contractor owes or will owe, or the proper amount due or to become due those named, if it omit the name of a sub-claimant or state a less amount than is actually due him, and yet purports to be a full statement of all to whom he is indebted and of the amounts that he is indebted to them, the owner can be held only for the notice it gives him, and will be held harmless for any payment that he makes to the original contractor on faith of such statement prior to any notice by such sub-claimant, whose name has been omitted or the proper amount of whose debt has not been given.

This ruling in the owner's favor is supported by further equitable authority. Where injury is done between two parties, equity holds that he should bear the burden who is most culpable. If the statement furnished by the original contractor to the owner be at fault and by reason thereof the owner pays him to the extent that such owner has no funds remaining wherewith to pay the sub-contractor's claim, under this established practice the court would hold that the sub-contractor, being at liberty to serve his notice at any time after the date of his sub-contract, was more culpable than the owner (if the latter were culpable at all), who did all in his power by procuring the original contractor's statement, and paid on faith of the same, without delay, but before the sub-contractor served his notice, though within the forty days that the law allowed him to serve it

§ 126 **Former section for benefit of sub-contractor.**— It was held that the provisions of section 35 were especially for the benefit and protection of the sub-claimant, and were proper for his protection, since he is not a party to the original contract, nor presumed to be informed of the time when payments are about to be made, or advised when the contractor may become entitled to them. The original contractor may collect or receive from the owner moneys at times not known or anticipated by the sub-contractor, and without the protection of the provisions concerning such statement The sub-contractor might be unpaid through negligence or fraud on the part of the parties to the original contract[1] This decision was rendered while the act of June 16, 1887, was in force

With equal reason and no less force of argument, it may be shown that the present provisions of the same section are for the benefit and protection of the owner, since he is not a party to the sub contracts, nor presumed to be informed of what they amount to, nor when they are to be paid for. Such knowledge on the part of the owner may be of the utmost importance, for he should know how the sub-contractors are to be paid, whether in a portion of the consideration moving from him, if it be other than money, to the end that he may discover whether the sub-contractors will be able to carry out their contracts according to their respective terms, if the original contractor, taking what is contracted to be given him, whether in property or money, can provide for them as he agrees with them. Now before he makes any payment he can thus learn to whom what for, and in what amounts his contractor is or will become indebted, and of his safety in the contract he has made He cannot, if he demands this statement as provided, be sued or forced to make any payment until this is done. The law does not require, but in this provision gives him the opportunity for his own security, to find out if the contractor's liabilities are different from what is thus stated for work and materials furnished for the improvement on his property pursuant to the contract. If original and sub-contractor fraudulently arrange that the latter withholds his notice until the former can collect all that is coming to him, and then that the latter serve notice and collect again what is due him, this section gives the owner power to force disclosure on the part of the original and thus head off the iniquity Again, if the original contractor make such a reckless or ignorant bid as will not enable him to carry out his contract, or if he takes a desperate chance to make one collection for temporary necessity or expediency and then abandon the work, thus leaving his employer and sub contractor in the lurch, exercise of this section's powers will enlighten the owner, before he expends a dollar, and enable him to discharge such contractor, nor will he be compelled to pay him more than what is left of the original contract price, after first paying for the completion of the work according to the original contract It enables him, prior to every stipulated contract payment, to ascertain the progress of the work, in a measure supervise his payments, so that at no time can he be seriously injured, if he observes the legal formulæ

[1] Hintze v Weiss, 45 App 220

§ 127. **Notice to owner makes statutory contract between owner and sub-contractor.**— By whichever method the owner is so notified, upon receipt of that notice, the law makes a sort of statutory contract between the owner and the sub-contractor, though up to that time they have sustained no contract relations, are personally unknown to each other [1] As in all contracts, there are conditions upon both sides as consideration for their respective performance of that statutory contract   The obligations it imposes are mutual They are each, in effect, guarantors of the original contractor to the other

§ 128 **Owner's obligations.**— The owner is, in effect, the guarantor of the principal contractor to them to the extent of the payment he agrees to make for the whole work. He is obliged, when notified, to see that they are paid so far as that payment will accomplish the purpose   The statute permits him to hold it for their satisfaction, to pay the principal contractor no part of it until he has required and been assured by that contractor's sworn statement that they have been paid; if not, to pay them as above stated.[1] It gives them the right to look to the owner for protection up to the limit of the contract price, to give it as assurance for payment to their unsecured creditors — the materialmen, mechanics and laborers who supply and render service for them. He should continue regardful of their rights and at no time make any of the stated payments called for in the contract as work progresses, or on completion, without at each time first requiring such statement as to whom and what amount such contractor owes at that time, or will become indebted to thereafter   He is not compelled to disclose his original contract to them,[2] can be compelled to produce it only on trial,[3] but he will not be permitted to mislead or deceive them in regard to it. If the owner when called upon refuses to show a laborer or sub-contractor the original contract, and says he will see them paid, and work is done, or material furnished on such assurance, he is estopped to set up payment in land, or that the original contractor has been fully paid, and a lien can be enforced for payment in money.[2]

§ 129 **Sub-contractor's obligations.** — The statute is not one sided. These obligations are not imposed upon the owner without the imposition of reciprocal duties and obligations upon these protected persons to the owner. Their extraordinary rights and priv-

---

[1] Secs 29, 34, 35, act of 1874, as amended
[2] Welch v Sherer, 93 Ill 64
[3] Doyle v Munster, 27 App 130

leges are conferred upon certa.n conditions. They cannot claim liens simply upon performance of what they agreed to do. Those liens are based upon the principal contract with the owner His contract rights are strictly regarded Their work must be in pursuance of its terms, and so carried out as to become part and parcel of it, so as to make their respective claims links in the chain of rights [1] Under the law as it formerly stood, it was held that the contractor failing to fulfill his contract was not entitled to a lien, that the sub contractors and materialmen took their contracts subject to the fulfillment by the contractor of his, and were equally bound by it, and if he were not entitled to a lien, they were not; that when he executed to the owner a release of all claims for mechanic's liens, on compromise and settlement, such a release carried with it a release of all under him, and, in consequence, his sub-contractors and materialmen could not enforce their liens [2] But for the amendments to the statute, subsequent to this decision, this position would now be tenable.

The owner and original contractor may change the terms of the original contract, but they cannot thereby change the rights of the sub contractor. These are based upon the original contract regardless of such changes [3]

Those who deal with the principal contractor, either in undertaking a special part as sub-contractors therefor, or in furnishing materials to or laboring for him (being equally sub-contractors) are, in effect, the guarantors of that contractor to the owner, except where the contractor abandons the original contract, and with like exception the statute imposes upon all the obligation to carry out the entire work according to the terms, not only of their respective contracts, but also of the original contract All together must, in any event, take the payment therein specified in satisfaction of their united claims at the times, in the manner and on the terms stipulated [4] Their rights depend upon the performance of the original contract The statute makes them joint obligors thereof. While it gives them the right to demand that the owner shall do all that both it and the contract exacts of him with reference to payments, it does not infringe upon, but preserves his right to demand that all his contract calls for be done in the time, in the manner, as and for what it stipulates. They cannot in law or morals demand

[1] Sec 29, act 1874, as amended
[2] Whitcomb v Eustace, 6 Bradw 574, Mehrle v Dunne, 75 Ill 239
[3] Brown v Lowell, 79 Ill 484
[4] Secs 29-34, act 1874, as amended, Mehrle v Dunne, 75 Ill 239

the owner's performance of payment without the performance in some way of what he promised payment for   They must regard his contract rights with the same sanctity that he regards their statutory rights.   If his contract provides for payment in land, goods, or money, they must look to whatever it be for satisfaction.   If he make that payment by delivery of either, as promised and the statute directs, he is absolved from all other liability.[1]   If the principal contractor underestimate the cost of the work, the materialmen and other subordinates, who deal with him, must bear the burden, for the contract price is all that all of them can get for a *pro rata* distribution[1]   If he overestimate his ability to carry it out, or has taken the contract with fraudulent intent to get one or more payments by playing upon the owner's credulity, and then abandon it, they can hold the owner and the property improved only for what is left, after deducting payments properly made and damages resulting from such abandonment, which include delay and cost of completion[1]

Where the sub-contractor failed to show upon what terms the original contractor undertook to build, whether for cash or real estate, when he was to be paid, or that he had ever completed his contract, or was entitled to any thing, either when the notice was served or at any time thereafter, nor was there any evidence as to the value of the work done by the original contractor, it was held he could not recover.[2]   He must show the terms of the original contract, and what was done under it, either that it has been performed, or abandoned.   The statute provides how he must proceed in either event, as will be hereafter shown   Hence, at the start, the importance of the sub-contractor ascertaining what that contract is, if the owner does not wish to disclose it, securing his guarantee, or saving risk of loss by keeping out of the business

§ 130 **Extent of sub-contractor's lien may exceed that of contractor.**—The sub contractors' liens cover the property to the extent of the contract price, even when the principal contractor has no lien   In case of an express contract, placing completion beyond three years from commencement of work, or placing the final payment beyond one year from the date of completion, or of an implied contract, completion being prolonged beyond one year from commencement of the work, while the principal contractor in either

---

[1] Mehrle v Dunne 75 Ill 239 Culver v Elwell, 73 id 536 Barstow v McLachlan 99 id 641 McGraw v Bayard, 96 id 146, adv., 1 Bradw 134, Welch v Sherer, 93 Ill 64
[2] Marski v Simmerling, 46 App 531

case would have no lien, the sub-contractors would The statute
gives them a lien on the property to the extent of the contract price,
regardless of when and how it is to be paid, or what the consequences to the principal contractor, occasioned by fixing payments
or accomplishing completion, so far as express or implied contracts
are concerned So, where the original contractor lost his lien by
reason of abandoning the contract, the sub-contractor would still
have the right to enforce his, but the extent of the security would
be limited, as hereafter shown.[1] In case of conspiracy between
owner and original contractor, thereby making the price as named
in the contract less than it actually was, the lien of the sub-contractor
would cover the property to the extent of what it should be, and
thereby be more extensive than the lien of the original contractor,
which could only be enforced for that reduced price[2]

The liens of each class depend upon independent provisions of the
statute. Those provisions, up to section 29, except in section 2, apply
solely to original contractors, thereafter to sub-contractors[3] While the
lien of the latter is dependent upon some sort of a contract having been
made by the original contractor, it is independent of that contractor's
lien It depends simply upon the sub-contractor doing his agreed
part pursuant to the terms of the original contract and his own contract, and fixing and perfecting it according to the special statutory
provisions applicable solely to him The manner and amount of
his recovery are controlled by performance or abandonment of the
original contract by the original contractor

§ 131. **Mechanical or other labor.**—Among these preferred and
privileged persons, the laborer (mechanical, skilled, or common),
under the original contractor, enjoys the highest privilege and is
accorded amplest protection

His claim is a lien for twenty days from the date of the last day's
work performed by him to an amount equal to ten per cent of the
proportionate value of the contract completed up to the date of that
last day's work, provided the notice mentioned in section 30 is
served within twenty days from the day when such last day's work
was performed by such person serving such notice[4]

This lien is absolute to the extent of the ten per cent propor-

---

[1] Sec 15, act 1874, as amended
[2] Sec 29, act 1874, as amended
[3] Maxwell v Koeritz, 35 App 300
[4] Sec 38, act 1874, as amended, Metz v Lowell, 83 Ill 565, see form of notice,
Appendix, page 203.

12

tional value of what has been done under the contract, no matter whether the owner has paid the contractor in full or not

The owner is allowed by the law to retain for twenty days such ten per cent out of what money is due or to become due to the contractor.[1] If his own business prudence has not prompted him to reserve a per cent of what is due the contractor as work progresses, this section makes it obligatory upon him to do so   If he does not, he pays the contractor at his own peril

This ten per cent is not in addition to such per cent as the owner may, in his contract, provide for holding back   If the contract provides for payment, eighty-five per cent as the work progresses, fifteen per cent balance when finished, the ten per cent is included in that fifteen per cent   He must pay the original contractor eighty-five per cent, and not withhold ten per cent therefrom.[1]

If the contractor abandons the contract, and it costs the owner more than what he has left out of what he was to pay the contractor, still the laborer's lien covers the ten per centum value of what has been done.   There is no escape from that liability if the laborer serves his notice properly.   The owner's only safety is in his reserving ten per cent of whatever may be due the contractor for twenty days after the last day's labor of any laborer.

The only case wherein the laborer is forced to accept a *pro rata* payment is where this ten per cent and whatever else the owner may owe the original contractor is insufficient to pay all the laborers In that event, and only in that event, he must pro rate with his co laborers, then only, and with them only.[2]

In case the amount due from the owner to the original contractor is insufficient to pay all in full, the laborers must first be paid in full, then the balance pro rated among the other lienholders in proportion to the amount of their respective claims[2]

§ 132   **Owner has ten days to pay sub-contractor.** — If the money due to the person giving notice shall not be paid within ten days after service thereof, or within ten days after the money shall become due and payable, and any money shall then be due from such owner to the original contractor, then such person may thereupon file his petition and enforce his lien, in the same manner as original contractors may[3]

---

[1] Sec 33, act 1874, as amended, Metz v Lowell, 83 Ill. 565, see form of notice, Appendix page 203
[2] Sec 34, act 1874, as amended.
[3] Sec 37, act 1874, as amended.

§ 133 **Suit at law against owner and contractor.** — Instead of thus enforcing his lien he may sue the owner and contractor jointly for the amount due him, in any court having jurisdiction of the amount claimed to be due, and a personal judgment may be rendered thereon as in other cases [1]

His right, however, to a personal judgment is dependent upon the existence of his lien   And to a common-law action against the owner and original contractor, the owner is entitled to make any defense that would defeat the lien.[2]   If that is defeated the defense to the action is complete   If the contractor's statement give no notice to the owner of the sub-claimant's debt, and if notice has not been served by him on the owner in proper form and manner or within the statutory time; if the suit is not brought within three months after the cause of action accrued, if for any reason the sub-claimant has no lien, he cannot maintain the action at law

§ 134 **Wrongful payments.** — Payments made by owner to original contractor, after such owner is notified of the sub-contractor's claims by the statement of the original contractor, provided for by section 35 of the present act,[3] are wrongful payments   Payments made by the owner after notice served by the sub-contractor or materialman, as required, are wrongful payments[4]   Payments made within twenty days after the last day's labor of the laborer, in excess of ninety per cent of the value of what has been done, as to such laborer are wrongful payments.[5]

Any payments made by the owner without demanding the statement of the contractor as required in section 35, were held to be wrongful payments under the law of 1887   The construction of the present statute, as before shown, is doubtful, and it is now the owner's only safety to demand the statement prior to any of such payments [6]

If the money is due the sub-contractor or laborer as the work progresses, but not due from the owner to the original contractor until all the work is completed. or six or twelve months thereafter, such sub-claimants have three months after such payment is due the original contractor within which to bring their suits,[7] and if they

[1] Sec 37, act 1874, as amended
[2] Bouton v McDonough County, 84 Ill 384, Quinn v Allen 85 id 39, Berkowsky v Sable, 43 App 410
[3] Sec 46, act 1874, as amended
[4] Haighorst v Lindberg, 67 Ill 463, Morehouse v Moulding, 74 id 322, Brown v Lowell, 79 id 484
[5] Sec 33, act 1874, as amended
[6] Secs 29, 35, act 1874, as amended
[7] Sec 47, act 1874, as amended, Meeks v. Sims, 84 Ill 422

have properly served notice on the owner, or he has been notified of their claims by the contractor's statement, his payment to the original contractor during that time is a wrongful payment, as either notice binds from the time it is served, or given

Payments made by the owner to the original contractor within forty days after the completion of any sub-contract, or the delivery of any material by the materialman to the contractor, or after payment is due them, might perhaps even yet be held to be wrongful payments, unless made after obtaining the original contractor's statement, and on faith of that statement

§ 135 **Sub-contractor's lien limited to amount due original.** — The amount due or to become due the original contractor at the time of the service of the notice, is all the sub-claimants can recover from[1] The money in, or to be in, the hands of the owner, after all deductions are made and due to the contractor, is the fund and only fund out of which the sub-claimants can be paid[1] These deductions are rightful payments the owner makes to the contractor, damages for delay in completion, which should be fixed at a certain rate per day, and damages for defective construction in manner or material[2]

§ 136 **Abandonment by original contractor.** — Should the original contractor, for any cause, fail to complete and abandon his contract, any person entitled to a lien as aforesaid, may file his petition in any court of record, against the owner and contractor, setting forth the nature of his claim, the amount due, as near as may be, and the names of the parties employed on such house or other improvement subject to liens ; and notice of such suit shall be served on the persons therein named, and such as shall appear shall have their claims adjudicated, and decree shall be entered against the owner and original contractor for so much as the work and materials shall be shown to be reasonably worth, according to the original contract price, first deducting so much as shall have been rightfully paid on said original contract by the owner, and damages, if any, that may be found to be occasioned the owner by reason of the non-fulfillment of the original contract, the balance to be divided between such claimants in proportion to their respective interests, to be ascertained by the court The premises may be sold as in other cases under this act.[3]

[1] Douglas v McCord, 12 Bradw 278 Culver v Elwell, 73 Ill 536
[2] Culver v Elwell, 73 Ill 536, Metz v Lowell 83 id 565, Schultz v Hay, 62 id 157, Biggs v Clapp, 74 id 335, Mehrle v Dunne, 75 id 239, sec 33, act 1874, as amended
[3] Sec 45, act of 1874, as amended.

This section applies solely to the claimants in case of abandonment and non-completion. The questions in such cases are, what is the owner liable for, what have the lienors a right to?

Actions under this section are independent of those under other provisions of the law. The lien claimant can sue at once, after giving notice according to law.

It was held that where the owner had fully paid the abandoning contractor before notice by the sub-contractor, the latter could not recover; but his remedy, if any, was under section 7 of the act of 1869, this section under the present law. It is only under this section that sub-claimants can and must proceed where the contract is abandoned by the original contractor.[1]

The owner is liable in such action, and in such case his liability is for as much as the work and materials are reasonably worth, according to the original contract price. The amount of damages would necessarily be, not only the loss occasioned by delay, but also in addition thereto what it cost the owner to have the original contract carried out. This aggregate amount should be deducted from the original contract price, the balance applied to the liens. If he is compelled to exhaust the original contract price, taking into consideration what he has rightfully paid to the original contractor, he is not required to pay any thing to the sub-claimants.[2] If it fairly and reasonably cost him as much as, but no more than what was left of the contract price, no recovery could be had or lien sustained against him by a sub-claimant. Under the statute, and by the plainest principles of justice, the owner is entitled to the benefit of the contract with his original contractor. Where the notice had been duly served, and there was no money due the original contractor when it was served, it was held, if the owner expended it properly in employing others to complete the work, he was not liable.[1]

§ 137. **Lien for work done after abandonment prior to lien for work done before.** — There is this difference in case of abandonment and in case of continuance of the work by the original contractor. Where the original contractor continues the work, and the owner sees that what is remaining of the contract price will be insufficient to pay for its completion, he cannot prefer the sub-claimants who furnish material and perform labor or services subsequent thereto,

<hr/>

[1] Mehrle v Dunne, 75 Ill 239
[2] Culver v Elwell 73 Ill 536. Morehouse v Moulding, 74 id 322, Biggs v. Clapp, id 335, Schultz v Hay, 62 id 157, Doyle v Munster, 27 App 130

to those who have already existing claims.[1] But in case of abandon ment he can prefer such claims coming due for work done there after. In case of abandonment he has the right to use what remains of the contract price to complete the work, and if he reasonably and justly expends it to so complete it, he will not be liable to those who performed labor or furnished materials prior to the abandonment.

§ 138. **Fraudulently low price in original contract.**— To the rule that the owner shall not be held to pay a larger sum than the original contract price there is one exception. If it shall appear to the court that the owner and contractor, for the purpose of defraud ing sub-contractors, fraudulently fixed an unreasonably low price on their original contract, then the court will ascertain how much of a difference exists between a fair price for the labor and materials furnished in the improvement and the sum named in the original contract, and will, in effect, add such difference to the contract price, as to the sub-contractors, and make the property subject to a lien to that amount, but in no such case will the original contractor's time or profits be secured by lien, beyond the sum named in the original contract or agreement.[3]

The above supposed fraud must be clearly established. It is the duty of the sub-contractors and materialmen to learn what the con tract is before they incur risks in furnishing labor or material. There are but few such who are incapable of forming an approxi mately correct estimate of the cost of an improvement and thereby judging whether or not the contract is fraudulent. Contracts induced by ignorance of the contractor in estimating, his over anxiety to get work, and so start himself in business, even a certain rashness and recklessness in competition do not amount to frauds. The owner often finds out that the lowest is not the best bidder. He is prone to accept such bidder. Such party may underbid his competitor, who proposes to do a good job, and such underbidding may be induced by fraudulent intent on his part to slight the work, to the deceived owner's detriment. The owner may be ignorant as to the value of the contemplated work, and in such case would not be held to be in any way a participant in the fraud. He is as apt to be a victim of as a co-worker in the iniquity. The materialman whose negligent furnishing of materials, without looking into the contract and ascertaining whether or not those whom he deals with

[1] Morehouse v Moulding 74 Ill 322
[2] Biggs v Clapp, 74 Ill 335, Mehtle v. Dunne, 75 id. 239
[3] Sec 29, act 1874, as amended

are original or sub-contractors, has put him in the position of a sub-sub-contractor, and who, as a last resort, attempts to ride over the contract by charging fraud on the part of the owner and those engaged in the work, will find such charge, if he does not fully prove it, recoil upon him and force the court to consider his conduct as unconscionable and dishonest as the iniquity he denounces. Such charge is sometimes made, whereby property is tied up and the record of its title cumbered until the day of trial, when the case is abandoned without even an offer of evidence to sustain it. The statute is short in not providing some penalty for such blackmail litigation, beyond mere costs and self-smirch of character.

Fraud is never presumed, it must be proved. When proved, the court lays a heavy hand on the perpetrators, sweeps the fraudulent contract aside, and awards just reparation to the injured.

§ 139 **Fraud does not aid in establishing lien.**— In no case can fraud, even if it exists, establish or aid in establishing the lien. It can be taken advantage of only by him whose lien has been fixed by his own performance of statutory requirements to enforce payment of what is his due. Carelessness or oversight on the part of the honest dealer may leave him the helpless victim of chicanery.

Where the bill alleged that the house was to be completed on December 1, 1890, that plaintiffs delivered material from April 24 to August 11, 1890 (probably should be July 11), served notice on the owner July 24, 1890, and brought suit January 17, 1891, alleging that the owners fraudulently claimed that S, to whom they furnished the material, was a sub-contractor, whereas he was in fact an original contractor, and that this was done to cheat and defraud them and persons in like circumstances; that the owner yet held back $3,800, not paid the original contractor, a demurrer was sustained to the bill, on the ground that the suit was not brought within the statutory time as provided in section 47 of the statute. The court held that the fund unpaid, even if fraudulently unpaid, and even if S was fraudulently declared to be a sub-contractor so as to place his material creditors in the attitude of sub-sub contractors, could not be subjected to payment of the just claim of those who had no lien, as they had lost it by their own laches in bringing suit too late, or by failing to aver in their petition facts as to when the building was completed, or payment due the contractor, that would have showed the suit to have been brought in time [1]

Rittenhouse v Sable, 43 App 538

CHAPTER VI.

PERFECTING LIEN OF SUB-CONTRACTOR.

§ 140 **Notice not to be filed with clerk.** — It has been shown that the lien of the original contractor is perfected and fixed by filing the claim, as prescribed in section 4, with the clerk of the Circuit Court. This is not only unnecessary on the part of the sub-claimants, but does not accomplish any thing in their behalf, if done. The filing of claim or notice merely with the clerk of the Circuit Court, except where the owner cannot be served with notice in the county, does not affect their lien or bind the owner at all, even if he has personal knowledge, or notice of such filing.

§ 141. **Must be served personally.** — The sub-contractor must serve a written notice on the owner or his agent

This notice must be dated and signed and delivered to the owner or agent in person.[1] Delivery by mail is not sufficient. Even if the owner receives it by mail, it does not bind him, and he may disregard it with impunity.[2]

Preserve a copy and note date of delivery thereof.[3]

---

[1] Wetenkamp v Billgh 27 App 585
[2] Carney v Tully 74 Ill 375
[3] See form, Appendix, page 202.

If there is a contract in writing between the original contractor and sub-contractor, a copy of such sub-contract, if the same can be obtained, shall be served with such notice and attached thereto   If it can be obtained and is not attached, the notice is insufficient [1]

Where the sub-claimant in his notice to the owner gives an erroneous name of the principal contractor, as a firm, Smith & Co, when he should have given the name of an individual, John Smith, if the owner be not misled or harmed by the error, it will not vitiate the notice [2]

§ 142 **Limitation of forty days** — This notice must be served within forty days from the completion of such sub-contract, or within forty days after payment should have been made to the person performing such labor or furnishing such material [1] This provision of the statute is in the alternative, and the sub-contractor has his option to give the notice within forty days after a payment falls due, or within forty days after completing his contract. If given on the payment falling due, or within the time limited therefor, it will complete his lien from that time, and the owner cannot avail of any payment made to the principal contractor after such notice, to defeat the lien of the sub-contractor   But if he delays until forty days after he has completed his contract, he only acquires a lien on whatever the owner may then owe the first contractor. He cannot thus reach any sum paid after his payment falls due and before he gives the notice [3] He cannot recover any greater sum than was due and owing, or to become due the contractor at the time of his notice [4]

It has been held that payments made after notice on orders accepted before notice are good, and that such acceptances are good if only verbal, [5] but this might be different under the present law if such orders were accepted before requiring the contractor's statement.

§ 143 **Action at law against owner.** — Where the owner has funds due the original contractor, at the time of the notice by the sub claimant, he is liable to action at law by such claimant, whether the debt be for wages or material [6] Such would also be the case after notice of sub-contractor's claims by the contractor's statement

[1] Sec 31, act 1874, as amended
[2] Roach v Chapin, 27 Ill 194
[3] Brown v. Lowell, 79 Ill 484   (The time when this decision was rendered was twenty days, the present law makes it forty)
[4] Metz v Lowell, 83 Ill 565
[5] St Louis Nat Stock Yards v O'Reilly, 85 Ill 546
[6] Culver v. Fleming, 61 Ill 498.

13

§ 144. **Garnishment of owner and rights of sub-contractor.—** Where the owner had been garnished on a judgment against the original contractor before the sub-contractor served his notice, it was held, that such garnishment took precedence of the sub-contractor's claim to the extent of the amount garnished, that it was an appropriation *pro tanto* of what the owner owed the original contractor, and to that extent defeated the lien of the sub contractor [1]

But this position is not tenable under the present statute. The lien of the sub-contractor attaches to the property to the extent of the contract price from the date, not of his, but the original contract,' and is as much prior to such garnishment lien as the original contractor's lien to a judgment against the owner subsequent to the date of his contract It continues as the work progresses until the statutory limit allowed him in which to give notice, forty days after completion of his work, or payment due, or notice to the owner by the principal contractor's statement.

The owner cannot safely pay the original contractor during these periods until after he has demanded and received his statement as to what sub claimants he was indebted to, and the amounts of such indebtedness, and, upon receipt of information by such statement or by the sub contractor's notice, it becomes his duty to pay this amount, not to the original but sub-contractor, thus making it, on condition, *ab initio* the sub-contractor's money. Nor can he safely make payment to the contractor until after the time had passed for the sub-contractor's notice where no such statement was obtained, because of the possible danger of that sub-contractor's impending lien By reason of the foregoing the owner cannot answer as to his indebtedness to the original contractor in response to any garnishment proceedings until these sub-claimants shall have had their day. The sub-contractor's notice is retroactive and relates back to the date of the original contract, and as of that date fixes the priority of his lien on what the owner owes the original contractor as against the claim of any judgment-creditor of the original contractor who may garnishee the owner.'

Notice served on the husband of the owner, though he were the agent, has been held not good.' This was prior to the enactment permitting notice to be served on the agent, and illustrates the ne

[1] Nesbit v Dickover, 22 App 140
' Sec 29, act 1874, as amended
' See Manowsky v Conroy, 33 App 141
' Legnard v Armstrong, 18 Bradw 549

cessity of strict compliance with the statute, not simply the spirit of the law, but the very letter.

§ 145. **Service on owners non-resident or not found in county** — If the owner cannot be found in the county in which the improvement is made, or shall not reside therein, the person furnishing such labor and materials must file the sub-contractor's notice in the office of the clerk of the Circuit Court [1] Only in such case has filing this notice with the clerk any thing to do with the claimant's right.

Also, in such case, a copy of the notice must be published in some newspaper printed in the county, for four successive weeks, after filing the notice with the clerk as aforesaid It, however, there be no paper published in the county, then the claimant of the lien must post notices in four of the most public places in the vicinity of the improvement.[1]

The claimant can have the notice published in any newspaper he pleases that is published in the county where the improvement is located

§ 146 **Effect of sub-contractor's notice — extent of lien.** — This notice gives the sub-contractor, materialman, mechanic, laborer, or other person a lien on the property the same as to the original contractor, but only to the extent that the owner is indebted to the original contractor at the time of the service of the notice, or may become indebted to him thereafter as such contractor [2] It would not be a lien on any thing the owner might owe the contractor outside of the indebtedness on that particular job or improvement

§ 147 **Owner must pay to sub-contractor first.** — When the owner or his agent is notified as aforesaid, it becomes his legal duty to retain from any money due or to become due the original contractor, an amount sufficient to pay all demands that are, or will become due such sub-contractor, materialman, workman, mechanic, or other person so notifying him, and to pay over the same to the person entitled thereto, the same as when so notified by the original contractor's statement.[3]

The owner, however, should not act upon the notice without consulting the original contractor. He should ascertain that the persons so notifying him are entitled to what they claim before he pays them. He is entitled to hold out of what is due or to become due the

---

[1] Sec 32, act of 1874, as amended
[2] Sec 33, act of 1874 as amended, Culver v Fleming, 61 Ill 498. Newhall v Kastens, 70 id 156 Culver v Elwell, 73 id 536 Brown v Lowell, 79 id 484
[3] Sec 34, act 1874, as amended

original contractor, the amount, or aggregate amounts claimed, and the contractor cannot maintain a suit against him therefor

§ 148. **General settlement, proceeding for.** — In the event of a dispute between the original contractor and those under him so notifying the owner of their claims, the owner may file a bill of interpleader, making them all parties and set up the facts, and the court will settle their respective rights and liabilities and protect him in the disbursement of the money he has so reserved.[1]

If the owner does not owe the original contractor any thing, a bill of interpleader will not lie. He must then simply defend the suits brought against him, and defeat the lien[2] The owner may file such bill, whether sued or not, where two or more claim the fund owing by him.[3]

All persons who shall be duly notified of such proceedings, and who shall fail to prove their claims, whether the same be in judgment against the owner or not, shall forever lose the benefit of and be precluded from their liens and all claims against the owner[4] And upon the filing of such bill or petition, the court may, on the motion of any person interested, stay any further proceedings upon any judgment against the owner on account of such lien.[5]

On final decree a perpetual injunction to stay such proceedings would be in order.

Only the owner or lienholder can invoke the aid this section affords

Where the husband made a contract to build on his wife's land, and conflicting claims of sub-claimants amounting to more than what remained due to the original contractor were made, and he filed a bill to distribute the amount due between the contractor and other claimants; held, that only the owner or some person having such lien could file a bill under this section, and that these persons not having made the contract with the owner, had no liens, and, therefore, could not file the bill That the husband not being the owner, and the contracts to build being personal with him, he could not file the bill.[6]

§ 149 **When notice not necessary.** — Where the sworn statement of the original contractor, provided for in section 35, shall

---

[1] Sec 39, act 1874, as amended
[2] Hellman v. Schneider, 75 Ill 422.
[3] Newhall v Kastens, 70 Ill 156.
[4] Sec 40, act 1874, as amended
[5] Sec 41, act 1874, as amended.
[6] McGraw v Stoike, 44 App 311

serve to give the owner true notice of the amount due and to whom due the notice required under section 30 is not necessary [1]

If it fails to give that true notice to the owner it does not excuse the failure of the sub-claimant to give the statutory notice required of him, but that notice is then necessary to bind the owner

Under the amendment of June 16, 1887, the decisions heretofore cited went far toward making notice of a sub-claimant on the owner unnecessary, and the statutory requirements for such notice useless. A like, or very different construction may be put upon the present statute. However that may be, there are no idle or nugatory provisions in this statute. Courts do not stretch its construction to favor the interests of any class, however worthy their claims, or deserving themselves This law looks upon owner and employee, dealer and operator with no partial, sympathetic view for one, but impartial view for all Its conferred rights, imposed duties, are equally obligatory upon all within its purview. If the owner had not demanded nor received the statement, and the sub-contractor had not served his notice, the omission of statutory duty on the part of the sub-claimant would certainly close his mouth to complain of a like omission on the part of the owner.[2]

Such being the law, statute rights may be secured by affirmative acts on the part of the respective parties in interest No one, therefore, should rely on the acts or omissions of another, but should himself take such steps as will in any event secure his rights Each should do that which unquestionably secures his lien Failure in any part may be fatal to the claimant's interests.

[1] Sec 30, act 1874, as amended.
[2] Butler & McCracken v Gain, 128 Ill. 23, O'Brien v Graham, 33 App 516

CHAPTER VII.

ARBITRATION ASSIGNMENT.

§ 150. **Arbitration does not release lien.**— Parties concerned in claims arising under this act may submit their rights to arbitration, as in other affairs, nor does such action constitute a waiver or release of the lien.

Bringing suit to enforce the lien after submission to arbitration revokes such submission [1]

Statements made by the owner in arbitration proceedings are competent evidence to prove agency.[1]

§ 151. **Assignability not decided.**— As to whether or not a lien is assignable has not been decided, but it is held that the assignee of such claim can prosecute an action to enforce the lien for same in the name of his assignor, that it should be so prosecuted, and that there is no error in such case in entering a decree in the name of the assignor for the use of the assignee; [2] that the assignee *pendente lite* can make himself a party to the proceedings by supplemental bill, but not by petition; that his position will be the same as his assignor, and that he can utilize the pleadings of his assignor as his own [3] That bringing suit for the use and benefit of another is not tantamount to an assignment so as to present the question as to whether a lien is assignable or not [4] That a receiver being appointed under a creditor's bill against a mechanic entitled to a lien and an

---

[1] Paulsen v Manske 126 Ill 72
[2] Phœnix Mut Life Ins Co v Batchen, 6 Bradw 621, C. & V R. R v Fackney, 78 Ill 116
[3] Lunt v Stephens, 75 Ill 507
[4] Barstow v McLachlan, 99 Ill 641

order on such mechanic to make assignment of property to such receiver, where none is made and the receiver makes no claim to the lien debt, is no waiver or release of the lien, or bar to its prosecution by the lien creditor [1] Where a builder assigns his contract to another, and the owner has knowledge of it, the other becomes the equitable assignee, entitled to the proceeds, and can enforce the lien for his use and benefit, in the name of the assignor In such case the original contractor cannot dismiss the bill and defeat the equitable assignee of his rights set up in the cross-bill.[2]

Where one holds a claim secured by a lien claim assigned as collateral security thereto, he not only can, but it is his duty to enforce the lien securing his debt. His obligations are the same as are imposed upon the holder of any other collateral security.[3] He cannot sell such collateral and buy it in himself [4]

§ 152. **General assignment by owner does not defeat lien.** — A general assignment of a mechanic for the benefit of his creditors does not preclude his prosecution of his lien [5]

Where the owner makes such assignment, proof of such lien claims against his estate constitutes no waiver of the lien; whatever is collected thereby simply goes as a credit on the lien [6] Such assignment does not divest the Circuit Court of its jurisdiction, or give the County Court jurisdiction to enforce the lien [7] The assignee is only entitled to the equity of redemption of the property after it is sold under the mechanic's lien decree [8]

An assignment of a particular piece of property by an owner to pay a particular debt is not such general assignment [9]

§ 153. **General assignment by original contractor.** — The Appellate Court has recently held that a general assignment for the benefit of creditors by an original contractor divests the lien of the sub-contractor, and bars his securing and enforcing it as the statute prescribes.[8] The author submits that such decision is a mistake. The distinguished jurist who voiced the opinion did so under protest, and condemned the precedents that the court felt forced to follow in giving the act a strict construction. The opinion is based on the wording of section 33 of the act, that the sub-contractor has a lien

[1] Barstow v McLachlan, 99 Ill 641
[2] Major v. Collins, 11 Bradw 658
[3] Friedman v Roderick, 20 Bradw 622
[4] Chicago Artesian Well Co v Corey, 60 Ill 73
[5] Paddock v Stout, 121 Ill 571, Stout v Sower, 22 App '65
[6] Paddock v Stout, 121 Ill 171
[7] Haines v Chandler, 26 App 400
[8] Ryerson v Smith, Dec , 1893

only on what is due the contractor at the time of service of his notice on the owner, that such contractor, having made a general assignment, was dead at law, nothing was due him, but all owing to him was due to his assignee

By high authority it is held that the right of a sub-contractor to payment out of moneys due the contractor is not cut off by an assignment for the benefit of creditors made by the contractor.[1] That the assignee has a right to contest the validity of the lien upon every ground available to the owner of the premises [1] But the sub contractor is entitled to proceed the same as if the assignment had not been made.[2]

That recording the claim for lien by an original contractor does not newly incumber the property, but simply fixes and secures upon it a lien already existing [3]

The giving of notice by the sub-contractor to the owner is of the same character, is the statutory method provided him to fix and secure his already existing lien.

By this act the lien of the sub-contractor attaches to the employing owner's property at the time of the making of the original contract,[4] and continues an impending lien, until the original contractor's statement shows it has been paid, or, if no such statement is given, until the forty days have elapsed within which he is entitled to notify the owner thereof

The assignee is undoubtedly entitled to what is owing to his assignor   What is owing to that assignor is the question.

If it be the owner's duty to the sub contractors, before paying the original contractor, to demand of him a statement of his indebtedness to them, to pay them what he learns thereby is due them, and to pay him only the balance, the same duty obliges the owner to pursue the same course with the original contractor's assignee, and pay him in the same manner.   He could not rightfully answer as to his indebtedness to the assignor until he had demanded such statement of the representative of such assignor.[4]   If it be the duty of such assignor to furnish his assignee with information of his property, his assets and liabilities, that duty enforces a full statement, not only of what the owner owes him on the contract, but of what he owes to his sub-contractors under the same contract, so that the

[1] Phillipps on Mechanic's Liens, sec 62h
[2] Phillipps on Mechanic's Liens, sec 295.
[3] Jones on Liens, (2d ed), sec 1550
[4] Sec 29, act 1874, as amended

assignee should be enabled to make the same statement to the owner that the assignor could, and can rightfully demand only what his assignor could — the balance, after leaving with the owner sufficient to pay them

The rights of original and sub-contractors — their liens — depend upon independent provisions of the statute.[1] It plainly says the lien provided for in sections 1 and 29 shall extend to the same property, recognizing each as a distinct and different lien, but covering the same security[2]

If no statement of the original contractor is demanded by the owner, the sub-contractor's right to give his notice exists   That statement simply excuses his not giving it   The statute makes it a personal right of the sub-contractor to give this notice to the owner. It must be given, not to the original contractor, but the owner, and regardless of the physical or legal mortality of the contractor   The sub-contractor has the right to give it, no matter what the original contractor may do, or what his fate   It binds what is coming to the original contractor to the extent of the sub-contractor's claim, regardless of the death of that contractor, or assignment tantamount thereto. If by such assignment the original contractor becomes dead in law, and what is due him vests in his assignee, such consequence cannot divest this primary right of the sub contractor, or vest in the assignee any more than was coming to his assignor   If the original contractor's statement, or the sub-contractor's notice, made in proper form and due time, bars the owner paying any thing to the original contractor beyond the surplus, after paying the claims he is so notified of, either equally bars payment of more to him who stands in his stead, his representative, whether lien, executor, administrator or assignee   The assignee acquires only the " equity of redemption " in the assignor's property covered by a mortgage, whether that mortgage be the ordinary or statutory   The notice, according to law, perfects his inchoate lien that impends thereunder from the very beginning, not of his particular work, but of the contract for the entire work. Notice on the owner by the sub-contractor, within the forty days, must logically and legally have the same effect in fixing and securing his lien as it would have had in case the assignment, with which he had nothing to do, had not been made. The service of that notice within the time provided by the statute makes his claim an original debt of the owner to him, makes

---

[1] Maxwell v Koeritz, 35 App 300   [2] Sec. 2, act 1874, as amended

the owner indebted to the original contractor only for what is left after payment of the bills he is so notified are unpaid,[1] and, perforce of the statute, that amount all that the assignee can claim

Death, or assignment, can no more prevent perfection of a statutory than enforcement of a recorded lien.   To hold otherwise is not only contrary to the letter and spirit of the law, but is to open wide a door to defraud every sub contractor by collusion of the owner and original contractor in the latter's general assignment for the benefit of his creditors, before the sub-contractor had served his notice on the owner, yet within the time the law expressly gave him to serve it

---

[1] Sec. 34, act 1874, as amended

CHAPTER VIII.

INCUMBRANCES

§ 154. **Incumbrances and liens as apportioned.** — Incumbrances on the property covered by mechanics' liens are recognized, adjusted and enforced by this law in its own peculiar way. All other liens by trust deed, mortgage, judgment or otherwise, stand in the order of their record, and are preferred in accordance with their priority as to time. The general rule that whatever is added to an incumbered estate inures to the benefit of and is covered by the incumbrance does not apply when such liens contest with mechanics' liens for enforcement by sale of the property affected. Even the vendor's lien for purchase-money, preserved by timely and fitly-executed document properly recorded, carries with it no special sanctity to demand satisfaction prior to these liens on what is added to the value of the property pursuant to the contracts under which they claim existence. Where property is sold under decree in these proceedings, the proceeds of the sale represent and stand in the place of the land and the building, and all parties who have liens thereon by trust deed, mortgage, judgment, under this statute, or otherwise, have the same proportionate share in the proceeds that they had in the property before it was sold. The sale must wipe out and extinguish all these burdens upon and deliver the title to the property free and clear therefrom to the purchaser. These claimants must look to the fund produced by the sale, after payment of costs, for satisfaction of their claims as this statute directs.[1]

§ 155 **Section 17.** — The statute provides that no incumbrance upon land, created before or after the making of a contract under the provisions thereof, shall operate upon the building erected or materials furnished, until the lien in favor of the person doing the work or furnishing the materials shall have been satisfied; and upon questions arising between previous incumbrances and creditors, the previous incumbrance shall be preferred to the extent of the value of the land at the time of making the contract, and the court shall ascertain, by jury or otherwise, as the case may require, what proportion of the proceeds of any sale shall be paid to the several parties in interest.[2]

§ 156. **Rule of apportionment.** — In interpreting this it is held that neither prior nor subsequent incumbrances can operate upon the buildings erected or materials furnished, to the prejudice of the persons performing the labor and furnishing the materials. A prior incumbrancer is preferred to the extent of the value of the land at

---

[1] Bradley v Simpson, 93 Ill 93, Topping v Brown, 63 id 349
[2] Sec 17, act 1874, as amended, Williams v. Chapman, 17 Ill 423

the time of making the contract for the erection of the building, and he also has a subsequent lien on the building subject to the first lien of the mechanic   The mechanic in the same manner has a prior lien on the improvements he puts on the land to the extent of the additional value those improvements give the premises, and a subsequent lien on the land '·²

Each must look to satisfaction of his debt, first out of the fund on which he has a first lien , if that proves insufficient, to what remains of the other fund after satisfying the prior lien thereon.

§ 157. **Case of apportionment.** — In a proceeding to enforce a mechanic's lien, to which a prior mortgagee was a party defendant, where the court found the proportion of the value of the premises at the time of the decree, which was added thereto by reason of the improvements, out of which the mechanic's lien arose, and then directed that, out of the proceeds of the sale of the premises, the proportion so ascertained, which would arise from the land without the improvements, should be first applied on the mortgage, and the proportion arising from the enhanced value on account of the improvements should be paid on the mechanic's lien ; and any surplus of the latter fund to be applied to satisfy any balance due on the mortgage, it was held, as between the mortgagee and mechanics, the decree was correct ³

§ 158. **Value of land, what meant.** — The value of the land at the time of the contract does not mean the naked ground only, but the land with whatever improvements were upon it at that time. If at the time buildings were upon it, and such were repaired, and for these repairs a lien is enforced, such lien takes priority over the mortgage only to the extent of the additional value given to the property by the improvements.   If a house and lot worth $15,000 are mortgaged, and subsequent thereto the mortgagor improve the same so as to make the premises worth $18,000, the mechanics and materialmen, by whose labor and property these improvements were made, would have a lien to the extent of three-eighteenths of the proceeds of the sale ⁴

§ 159. **Value of improvements, what meant.** — The value of the improvements is not what they cost, but the increased market

---

¹ Sec 17, act 1874, as amended, Williams v Chapman 17 Ill 423

² Raymond v Ewing, 26 Ill 329, Smith v Moore, id 392, North Presbyterian Church v Jevne, 32 id 214, Croskey v N W. Mfg Co , 48 id 481, Dingledine v Hershman, 53 id 280 Howett v Selby, 54 id 151 Tracy v Rogers, 69 id 662 Bradley v Simpson, 93 id 93, Condict v Flower, 106 id 105 Ogle v Murray, 3 Bradw 343, Miller v Ticknor, 7 id 393, Langford v Mackey, 12 id 223

³ Howett v Selby, 54 Ill 151, Dingledine v Hershman, 53 id 280.

⁴ Croskey v N W Mfg Co., 48 Ill 481

value added to the property without reference to the cost of materials and labor actually furnished [1] For instance, if the land is worth $5,000, the improvements, $15,000, total value of land and improvements, $20,000, the prior mortgage has a lien of one fourth, the mechanic's of three-fourths of this total valuation of the property If sold under a decree to enforce the mechanic's lien, for $12,000, the prior mortgage would get one-fourth, or $3,000, the mechanic's, the balance. So that if the proceeds of the sale are not sufficient to pay both, the mortgagee must take such share as the value of the property before the improvements bears to the total value after it

§ 160. **Cases of apportionment.**— Where the land before the improvement was valued at $3,200, enhanced by the improvement $6,290, making a total value after the improvement of $9,492, and the net proceeds of the sale were $3,338 91, though there was due on the prior mortgage, interest and all, $5,657, the prior mortgage was entitled to 3200-9492ds of $3,338 91, or $1,125.63 [2]

Where the land before improvement was valued at $12,000, after, the premises at $30,000, the prior mortgages, without interest, were $9,046, with interest over $10,000, and the gross proceeds of the sale, $8,250, leaving after the costs, $7,889 65 for distribution, the prior mortgages were entitled to 12–30ths, the mechanic's to 18–30ths of that net sum [3] In this case, the oversight of counsel in suffering a wrong decree in the mechanic's favor cost them all share of this, but the rule is distinctly recognized in the case   A proper distribution would have given prior mortgages only $3,159.86.

Where the property was already improved and worth $18,000, after repairs and additions, $25,000, it was held, the mechanics were entitled to 7–25ths, the prior mortgagee to 18–25ths of the proceeds of the sale [4]

§ 161 **Incumbrancer probably cannot prevent scaling.**—Thus it is that under this law a prior mortgage for purchase-money or other indebtedness can be scaled down to the loss of the owner thereof It is questionable if this can be prevented by the party who takes a trust deed or mortgage having a proviso therein that no lien shall be created by the owner in improving, building or rebuilding on the same, to the prejudice of the holder of such trust deed or mortgage, inasmuch as the statute makes express provision limiting the

[1] Gaty v Casey, 15 Ill 190, Croskey v. N W. Mfg. Co , 48 id. 481, Clark v. Moore, 64 id 273
[2] Bradley v. Simpson, 93 Ill 93
[3] Dingledine v Hershman, 53 Ill 280.
[4] Howett v Selby, 54 Ill 151.

extent of such incumbrances Where such proviso was held to be
operative and to bar the creation of mechanic's liens the property
was not in trust to secure a debt, but for the use and benefit of
another [1]

But it is possible that a court of equity would enjoin the owner
of such incumbered property undertaking an improvement thereon,
from making such improvement, in case the incumbrancer should
show that he was not able to pay for the same, and that such improvement would impair his security thereon

§ 162 **Fraudulent incumbrances.**— Any incumbrance, whether
by mortgage, judgment or otherwise, charged and shown to be
fraudulent in respect to creditors, may be set aside by the court, and
the premises made subject to the claimant or petitioner, freed and
discharged from fraudulent incumbrance [3]

§ 163 **Lienholders may contest each others' claims** — Lienholders are privileged to contest the claims of each other, [3] and,
where not made parties, may contest such even after a decree has
been rendered [4]

§ 164 **Lien attaches when contract is made** — As to whether
a mortgage be prior or not to a mechanic's lien depends upon when
that lien attaches, and when the mortgage is put to record. The
same as to date of judgment The earlier cases held that the mechanic's lien did not attach until the work was performed or materials furnished, the contract completed [5]

These decisions have never been expressly, but by implication
have been overruled in the later cases, which hold that the lien attaches when the contract is made, and any incumbrance recorded
subsequent to that date is subsequent to the lien, both on the land
and the improvements, no matter when made [6]

Where the contract was made June 30, 1883, work was completed
October 15, 1883, trust deed made July 2, 1883, recorded July 7,
1883, the mechanic's lien was held prior to the trust deed on land
as well as improvements [7]

[1] Franklin Savings Bank v Taylor, 131 Ill 376
[2] Sec 19, act 1874, as amended, Bennitt v Star Mining Co, 119 Ill 9, 18
App 17
[3] Sec 18, act 1874, as amended
[4] Dunphy v Riddle, 86 Ill 22
[5] McLagan v Brown 11 Ill 519, Gaty v Casey, 15 id 190, Williams v Chap
man, 17 id 423 Hunter v Blanchard, 18 id 318
[6] Clark v Moore, 64 Ill 273, Thielman v Carr, 75 id 385, Hickox v Greenwood, 94 id 266, Paddock v Stout, 121 id 571, Franklin Savings Bank v Taylor,
131 id 376, Stout v Sower, 22 App 65, Freeman v Arnold, 39 id 216
[7] Stout v Sower, 22 App 65, Paddock v Stout, 121 Ill 571

Where the mortgage was made July 17, 1872, recorded September 7, 1872, the owner made contracts, one with Carr, for hardware, on August 17, 1872, one with Fitzsimmons, for lumber, on September 6, 1872, the liens for both of said contracts were held prior on land and improvements to the trust deed [1]

§ 165. **When date of mortgage is important**.—The date of the mortgage cuts no figure in the matter of priority, where it is shown that the mortgage was made before the contract, and it is not shown whether it was recorded before or after the contract was made. Where there are equal and competing equities, the oldest prevails. A mortgage dated April 14, and recorded April 24, was held prior to a contract made on April 24,[2] it not having been shown that the contract was made prior to the record of mortgage.

§ 166 **Lien prior to mortgage void for informality**.—If a mortgage, for informality in its execution, be void, yet such as a court of equity could establish and give validity to, the mechanic's lien, if it attaches prior to such establishment, though subsequent to its record, is prior thereto[3]

A married woman living separate from her husband and transacting business in her own name, executed a mortgage on a lot that was her separate property. The mortgage was executed October 27, 1866, and recorded November 13, 1866, her husband not joining in its execution On July 17, 1869, this lot was sold under a mechanic's lien decree for labor and material furnished in improving that lot after the recording of the mortgage On suit to foreclose that mortgage it was held that the mortgage made by her alone was void, that its execution might be a satisfactory ground upon which the court could establish a lien in equity against her separate property, but no such lien would exist until it was established by a decree of the court. That when so established it could have no retroactive operation. Such a lien, when it takes effect, must act upon the property in the condition in which the decree finds it The mechanic's lien is of a different character. It derives its force from the statute, is *eo instanti*, a lien upon the property, which continues from that moment until the debt is satisfied, unless it is waived, released, or suffered to expire for want of proceedings by the statute made necessary to keep it alive That the mechanic's lien thus became prior

---

[1] Thielman v Carr, 75 Ill 385
[2] Elgin Lumber Co v Langman, 23 App 250
[3] Lewis v Graves, 84 Ill 206

to the mortgage, and the sale under the decree enforcing the lien wiped out the mortgage altogether [1]

§ 167 **Mortgage on equitable estate** —If an equitable owner makes a trust deed or mortgage at the request of the legal owner, such trust deed or mortgage is good The fact that a prior deed of trust was upon an equitable estate will not postpone it to the mechanic's lien [2]

§ 168 **Purchasers** —A sale during the progress of a building, upon which a lien has attached, cannot affect the rights of a mechanic.[3] A party purchasing premises on which buildings are in process of erection is bound to make inquiry as to the rights of parties furnishing material or performing work thereon, and is charged with constructive, if not actual, notice of the lien.[3] A purchase of property after the lien is fixed gives him no rights as against the lien [4]

A purchaser of a building from the owner, pending a proceeding to enforce a mechanic's lien created for its erection, will take the title subject to the lien which may be established in that proceeding; and if such purchaser sell the house to another, and induce him to remove it to another lot, he will hold the proceeds of the sale as a trust fund liable to discharge the lien [5]

Where the person who contracted the debt which created the lien sells to another, who reserves from the purchase-money an amount sufficient to pay the debt, the latter cannot complain of a decree making the debt a lien on his interest in the land [6]

A sale under a deed of trust, prior to the lien, conveys no title to the improvements to the purchaser, or if any title is conveyed, it is subject to the prior lien of the mechanics to have their debt first paid out of the proceeds derived from the sale of such improvements [7] The purchaser who accepts a conveyance of property subject to liens is not liable, personally, therefor [8]

§ 169 **Executory contracts** —Where a vendor, by bond or contract, agrees to convey property on payment of the purchase-money, he differs from the vendor who conveys and takes a mortgage or

---

[1] Lewis v Graves, 84 Ill 206
[2] Lunt v Stephens 75 Ill 507
[3] Clark v Moore, 64 Ill 273, Chicago Artesian Well Co v Corey, 60 id 73 Work v Hall, 79 id 196, Bennitt v Star Mining Co , 119 id 9, 18 App 17
[4] Chicago Artesian Well Co. v. Corey, 60 Ill 73, Austin v Wohler, 5 Bradw 300
[5] Ellett v Tyler, 41 Ill 449
[6] Kidder v Aholtz, 36 Ill 478
[7] Gaty v. Casey, 15 Ill 190
[8] Condict v Flower, 106 Ill 105, Work v. Hall, 79 id 196

15

trust deed to secure the same, he must be paid in full, and is not held to be a prior incumbrancer. The purchaser of the notes held by such vendor enjoys the same protection accorded the vendor.[1]

Where such vendor, at the time of making the bond or contract to convey, makes a loan to his vendee, and the contract for conveyance obligates the payment of both purchase-money and loan, as an aggregate sum, as a condition precedent to conveyance, the purchase-money lien is absolute, but that of the loan prior as to the land, second as to the improvement Where such vendor, after the purchaser has contracted for the erection of a building upon the premises, loans the purchaser money and gives a new bond or contract for a deed to be made upon the payment of the original price, and the sum thus loaned, the vendor, as to the mechanic who erects the building, will in equity occupy the position of a subsequent incumbrancer as to the sum loaned, and be postponed to the rights of the mechanic, but not as to the purchase-money due under the original contract of sale[2] The fact that the new contract is made after the contract to build does not alter his position as to the purchase-money, but does alter it as to the loan.[3] If, however, instead of executing a new contract to convey on payment of the purchase-money, he execute a deed conveying the property, and take back a trust deed or mortgage to secure the payment of the purchase-money, he changes his position, and, while his lien is prior to that of the mechanic on the land, it is subsequent as to the improvements, is still a prior incumbrance, but only as any other prior incumbrance, first on the land, second on the improvements[3] Where he simply executes a new contract to convey on payment of the purchase-money, he does not part with his title, and that title cannot be affected. He must be paid in full; his lien is absolute In conveying he does part with his title, and though the trust deed be for the same purchase-money, the conveyance has stripped it of the absolute right to payment.

Where the vendor repurchases the property, and as part consideration agrees to pay the notes executed by the vendee for improvements, the land and entire property, not merely the improvements, become subject to the lien[4]

Where A. borrows of B, and instead of a mortgage gives B a deed of the property, taking his bond for reconveyance on payment

[1] Wood v Rawlings, 76 Ill 206
[2] Hickox v Greenwood, 94 Ill 266
[3] Wing v Carr, 86 Ill 347
[4] Adams v Russell, 85 Ill 284

of the loan, it is different from an actual vendor's bond; such is only a mortgage and prior, as any other mortgage, on the land, second on the improvements.[1]

§ 170. **First lienholder accepting subsequent mortgage releases first lien.** — Contracts for materials have priority over a subsequent incumbrance by trust deed placed upon the premises, and where the holder of a trust deed for purchase-money, made prior to the contracts for materials, which would be the first lien, releases such incumbrance in consideration of the assignment to him of a subsequent incumbrance, or third lien, placed upon the premises, he, by such act, necessarily yields precedence to the lien for materials, which in the order of priority stood ahead of the last trust deed. The first lien had no power to impart to the third any of its precedence so as to give the latter priority to the extent of the incumbrance thus retired behind it. In this case, A., the vendor, held the property subject to an incumbrance of $16,000 to B. for purchase-money. A. sold the property to C., took back an incumbrance from C. for $33,000 purchase-money, which incumbrance was by agreement made second to one of $45,000 to D. for money borrowed to improve the property. Prior to the record of the latter trust deed to D., mechanics' liens attached for the improvement of the property so that in order of priority the lien stood: First, to B. for $16,000; second, the mechanic's; third, to C. for $45,000, and thereafter to A. for $33,000 purchase-money. The court held the latter a third incumbrance, though the mechanics' liens attached prior to its record, and by contract it was made second to that of $45,000. A. assigned to B. a portion of the trust deeds securing his $33,000, in consideration of B. releasing his first lien under his trust deed for $16,000, and the court, as stated, held that B.'s lien became a third incumbrance in consequence, that a first lien has no power to impart to a third any of its precedence so as to give the latter priority over a second lien. If the first is released, the second becomes first in priority.[2]

§ 171. **Extending time beyond statutory period.** — A party who has furnished materials cannot contract with his debtor for an extension of time for payment beyond the statutory period, so as to extend his lien upon the premises to the prejudice of a mortgagee, or other incumbrancer, mechanic or purchaser. If he give time to his debtor beyond the statutory period for filing claim, serving no-

---

[1] Langford v. Mackey, 12 Bradw. 223
[2] Phoenix Mutual Life Ins. Co. v. Batchen, 6 Bradw. 621

tice or exacting payment according to the terms of the original contract as between him and such others, whether their liens be prior or subsequent, his lien is lost[1]

§ 172 **Improvements paid for by owner and mortgagee.** — The enhanced value given to property by such improvements, as the owner pays for, inures to the benefit of the mortgagee, not the mechanic, and all improvements paid for by the money of the mortgagee, prior or subsequent to the mechanic's lien, inure to his benefit The subsequent mortgage may have been given to secure the very money paid on the improvement[2]

§ 173 **Lienholders pro rate.** — Lienholders must be paid *pro rata* If one be overpaid, receive more than his *pro rata* share, the other lien creditors have the right to sue for the excess[3]

§ 174 **Sale subject to prior mortgage.** — While the owner cannot complain if a sale be ordered subject to the lien of a prior trust deed,[4] the mechanic or materialman can, because the same is thereby made an absolute preference to his claim, whereas, as to him, it is only a lien to the extent of the value of the land, whether due or not due

§ 175 **Claims not yet due.** — Where the property is incumbered by a prior mortgage, the decree may direct a sale of the premises in fee, notwithstanding the mortgage may not then be due.[5] And when an entire sale has been made of the whole property, and some of the debts secured are not then due, in ascertaining the proper amounts to be paid upon such debts, there must be a rebate of interest from the date of the judgment to the maturity of the respective debts[6] This applies, however, only to mechanic's lien claims not due, not to mortgage debts[7]

It has been held that where the prior mortgage is not due, the decree cannot order the owner to pay it before due[8] Courts cannot make new contracts for parties, can only enforce those made But the law gives such mortgage a preference only as to the value of the land,[9] and where it becomes necessary to sell the property in the enforcement of a mechanic's lien, such mortgage must be paid its

---

[1] Brown v Moore, 26 Ill 422, Kelly v Kellogg, 79 id 477
[2] Clark v Moore, 64 Ill. 273
[3] Buchter v Dew, 39 Ill 40, Mehrle v. Dunne, 75 id 239, Ogle v Murray, 3 Bradw 343
[4] Portones v Badenoch, 132 Ill 377
[5] Croskey v N W Manuf Co., 48 Ill 481
[6] Sec 16, act 1874, as amended
[7] North Presbyterian Church v Jevne, 32 Ill 214
[8] Strawn v O'Hara, 96 Ill 53
[9] Sec 17, act 1874, as amended

proportionate share of the proceeds of the sale, the same as if it were due

§ 176 **May sell first and take testimony as to value afterward.** — There is some confusion in the cases as to what date these valuations should be made   It is held that it is not error for the court to direct a sale of the property, and then direct the master to take evidence, and report to the court of the comparative value of the land and the improvements at the time of the sale, such value being determined in reference to the day of the sale, that evidence after the sale would be more satisfactory [1]   But the statute plainly says, the previous incumbrance shall be preferred to the extent of the value of the land *at the time* of making the contract   This may be a very different value from that at the time of making the decree or the sale thereunder, especially in towns and cities where rapid growth and change in location of public, manufacturing, or transportation enterprises rapidly change values   The value of property, improved or unimproved, at the date of the contract, is not difficult of ascertainment   The decretal sale may be far from determining it   That sale may decide the value of the improved premises when it is made, must decide the fund for distribution.   But other and better proof can be had as to the value of the property when the contract was made   That is a fact in existence before even suit is brought, as determinable before as after the sale, and the proof should be as to the value of the land at the date of the contract

---

[1] Croskey v N W Manuf Co , 48 Ill 481

CHAPTER IX.

LIMITATIONS

§ 177. **General statute does not apply** — The general statute of limitations does not apply to mechanic's liens   The Lien Act is a law unto itself, the limitations provided therein only applicable to cases thereunder [1]

The statute fixes definite periods within which the work must be performed, or material delivered after the commencement of the

---
[1] Kinney v Hudnut, 2 Scam 472, Clark v. Manning. 4 Bradw. 649, 90 Ill 380.

work or delivery of the materials,[1] and within which, after completion of work or delivery of materials, payment therefor must be made, dependent upon whether the contract be express or implied,[1] within which a claim for lien must be filed by original contractors and parties dealing directly with the owner, and within which suit must be brought thereafter,[2] within which notice to the owner must be given by the sub-claimant,[3] and within which he must bring suit,[4] and within which, on demand of the owner on any parties claiming liens, they must bring suit[5] If such claimants or holders of liens do not comply with these regulations, their liens will be lost   To file the claim, serve the notice, or begin the suit before the regular statutory time is as fatal as to do so after that time[6]

§ 178. **None as to when work is to be begun.**— There is no limitation fixed within what time the work shall commence after the contract is made[1]   There exists no statutory reason why a contract could not be made for work to begin one, two or three years after its date, and from the date of commencing work the limitation as to completion and payment would run   In large cities, where buildings, once considered magnificent structures, have become inadequate to the demand and out of proportion to the value of the ground, consequent upon increased growth, where it is expedient and profitable to erect more commodious and taller edifices, where leases of part or of all of such would not expire for a year or more, and possession could not be had to tear down the old, and erect the new building until they did expire; where contracts for such new and large buildings required extensive preparation, contracts are not only probable, but in such conditions are made to commence work a year or more after the making thereof   From the date of that contract the lien attaches, and becomes prior to subsequent incumbrances placed on the property by the owner, or judgments recovered against him ;[7] from the date of commencing work under it the limitations as to when it must be completed and paid for[8]

---

[1] Sec 3, act 1874, as amended.
[2] Sec 28, act 1874, as amended
[3] Sec 31, act 1874, as amended
[4] Sec 37, act 1874, as amended, Huntington v Barton, 64 Ill 502
[5] Sec 52, act 1874, as amended
[6] Kinney v. Hudnut, 2 Scam 472
[7] Sec 17, act 1874, as amended, Clark v Moore, 64 Ill 273, Theilman v Carr, 75 id 385, Hickox v Greenwood 94 id 266 Paddock v Stout, 121 id 571, Franklin Savings Bank v Taylor, 131 id 376, Stout v Sower, 22 App 65 Freeman v. Arnold, 39 id 216
[8] Sec 3, act 1874, as amended

§ 179. Limitation for filing claim for lien — As between original contractor and owner there is no time within which the original contractor must file his claim for a lien.[1] Hence his delay in doing so does not impair his lien as between them

As between contractor and other creditors, incumbrancers, or purchasers, whether their claim or rights be prior or subsequent to the mechanic's lien, the claim for that lien must be filed, as required, within four months after the last payment falls due according to the terms of the contract as originally made.[2] Any amendment of the claim must be filed within the four months named.[3] This provision is for the benefit of these parties only, and they, only, can plead the delay of four months in filing the claim as a bar to the lien as against them[4]

If the contract be completed, either for work on the building or delivery of materials, on January 1, 1894, the last payment is to be on January 1, 1895, the claim is good if filed on April 30, 1895 So that for sixteen months after completion the rule *caveat emptor* must be heeded During all that time, though there be no record evidence of the lien, the party who loans money on security of the improved property, credits the owner of it on faith of his responsibility through ownership of it, or buys it, does so at his peril. The law imposes no obligation on the original contractor to reveal his secret, unrecorded claim, or break his silence in regard thereto during that time.

A loan might be made, trust deed or mortgage therefor duly recorded, or purchase be consummated, full payment made, warranty deed recorded, possession taken, at any time during 1894, or even up to April 29, 1895 If the claim for lien were filed April 30, 1895, it would take precedence of the mortgage, trust, or warranty deed

Well may our courts enforce a strict construction of the statute whose provisions make easily possible a fraud on, perversion of justice against the innocent, who must make their rights a matter of public record to secure them Important is it, too, that owners improving should preserve their original contracts showing when payments were to be made, especially the final payment; and not only

---

[1] Sec 4, act 1874, as amended, Turney v. Saunders, 4 Scam 527, Garrett v Stevenson, 3 Gilm. 261, Van Pelt v Dunford, 58 Ill 145, Jennings v Hinkle, 81 id 183
[2] Sec 28 act 1874, as amended. Huntington v Barton, 64 Ill 502, Lunt v Stephens, 75 id 507
[3] McDonald v Rosengarten 134 Ill 126, 35 App 71
[4] Van Pelt v Dunford, 58 Ill 145

take receipts in full, but waiver or release of liens from all who furnish materials, or render labor on, or services for such improvements, stating that such parties did all the work named, or furnished all the material of the class specified therefor, that in event of incumbering or selling such property during this period, they may present as clear evidences as possible that no such hidden liens incumber it The special contractor who did the masonry, carpentry, plumbing, painting, heating, etc, could give the statement that he did all the work; the materialman's statement could be only so far as he knew; for others, unknown to him, might have furnished the same class of goods for the improvements Some other evidence, as of the architect, superintendent, foreman, or mechanic, who saw or directed the use of such material, or put it into the building, should be secured at the time that all of such material used came from such materialman

Objections made by attorneys, in examining titles for loans, or purchasers, that such proofs of payment are wanting, are not captious. They should be provided for. Titles cannot be passed upon mere faith, nor too great care exercised in keeping them clean and perfect.

§ 180 **Limitations as to sub-contractor's notice.**—The sub-contractor can serve his notice on the owner at any time, but must serve it within forty days after his claim is due, or contract completed, or his lien will be lost,[1] unless excused by the owner's demand and receipt of the principal contractor's statement, as required, and such statement giving the owner true notice of his claim

§ 181 **Limitations as to laborer's notice**—The laborer must serve his notice within twenty days after his last day's work in order to claim a lien on ten per cent of the value of the improvement made;[2] if served after twenty and within forty days, he has a lien as any other sub-claimant,[3] except that it is preferred over materialmen and others not laborers,[4] if after forty days, no lien at all

§ 182 **As affected by terms of original contract.**—The limitation as to the original contractor runs from the time of final payment as fixed in the original contract, not from the time thereafter fixed or extended by the parties. The law regards the terms of the original contract, not what the parties may subsequently do in the

[1] Sec 31 act 1874, as amended
[2] Sec 30, act 1874, as amended
[3] Sec 33, act 1874, as amended
[4] Sec. 34, act 1874, as amended

16

execution of it.[1] The question is not whether the parties do or do not agree, after the execution of the contract, to an extension of the time for payment. The question is as to the terms of the contract. The lien depends upon the provision which the contract makes as to the time of payment, and the limitation runs from that time.[1] Thus, where the original contract stipulated for payment on, or six months after completion, and the parties could extend that time further without releasing the lien as to them; if such be done, and no claim filed within four months from the time first fixed, the lien is released as to all others.

Where payment is to be made on completion, whether of work or delivery of materials, the time of completion is the date from which limitations will run, whether completion be accomplished on the day fixed, or before or after that day.[2] So, where, after delivery of possession to and acceptance by the owner, defects are discovered and are remedied by the sub-contractor, the time of completion as to him will date from the time such defects are remedied, and limitation runs from that time as to service of notice on the owner.[3]

If a working test — as where machinery is to be finished and started to satisfactory working order — is the date of payment, regardless of the date fixed in the contract, payment is not due, limitation does not begin to run until that satisfactory test is made; that test marks the time of completion and start of limitation.[4] Where such completion was to be on August 1, but was not accomplished until September 15, the latter date was held the time from which the limitation ran.[5]

Where the original contract is for a specific sum, but with an agreement for alterations and change in plans, and an agreement by the owner to pay what is equitable therefor, any work growing out of such alterations is not extra work, but part of the original, entire contract, the lien of the contractor attaches thereto the same as for work done under the specifications, and from the completion of the

[1] Cook v Heald, 21 Ill 425, Cook v Vreeland, id 431, Beasley v Webster, 64 id 458, Huntington v. Barton, id 502, Lunt v Stephens, 75 id 507, Crowl v Nagle, 86 id 437, Belanger v Hersey, 90 id 70, McCarthy v Neu, 93 id 455, Paddock v Stout, 121 id 571, Chisholm v Williams 128 id 115, Simon v Block, 16 Bradw 450, Chisholm v Randolph, 21 App 312, Stout v Sower, 22 id 65

[2] Paddock v. Stout, 121 Ill 571, Stout v Sower, 22 App 65.
[3] St Louis Nat Stock Yards v O'Reilly, 85 Ill 546
[4] Paddock v Stout, 121 Ill 571, Stout v Sower, 22 App 65
[5] Chisholm v Randolph, 21 App 312, Chisholm v. Williams 128 Ill. 115.

contract, including such alterations, is the date from which limitations will run [1]

Where payment is agreed to be extended in case a mortgage to secure same is given, the giving of the mortgage is a condition precedent, and if not given, the debt at once becomes due, and the limitation then commences [2] But where it is simply agreed that the time shall be extended and the debtor shall execute notes and give security therefor, the execution of the notes is not a condition precedent, and their non-execution will not make the debt due, or change the terms In such case, where the time for which the notes were to be given is beyond a year from completion, there will be no lien, and the limitation of the statute as to claim or notice does not concern it [3]

§ 183. **Entire contract, lien runs from completion.**— As to when the limitation will begin to run as to the original and sub-claimants, depends upon the character of the contract under which the labor was performed or materials furnished

If it is an entire contract, as to do all of the work on the whole building, or all of a certain class of work, or to furnish all of a certain class of materials, as brick, lumber, or hardware, the party who does the work or furnishes the materials has no claim in law or fact until the entire contract has been performed He cannot split up his claim and file separate claims, or give separate notices He must wait until the last act is done, the contract fully completed. But when, under a contract to do all the labor and furnish all the materials of a certain kind for the erection of such buildings and appurtenances as the owner might require for certain purposes, the contractor did all the work he was required to do, or nearly so, on the buildings required to be erected, and settled for the same, showing a certain amount due him, and, after the Chicago fire of 1871, and a temporary suspension of the owner, growing out of the fire, furnished labor and materials in the following year on other buildings connected with the first, but which could have been omitted, and then filed his petition to enforce his lien for the several sums due him, including that due in the first year, it was held, in favor of intervening creditors, who were sought to be postponed on the whole of the contractor's claims, that the last work could not be held to be a continuation of the first, but rather as a new and inde-

[1] Brown v Lowell, 79 Ill 484
[2] Gardner v Hall, 29 Ill 277
[3] Beasley v Webster, 64 Ill 458

pendent contract That no number of buildings being specified, and
it not being known just what buildings the company would require,
the contractor had no right to insist upon the erection of any certain number of buildings, but only such as the company elected to
have erected and that the limitation run as to the work done the previous year from the time it was done in favor of intervening creditors.[1]

§ 184 **Those proving claims in probate court are judgment-
creditors.**—A materialman cannot enforce his lien against the estate of the owner who dies, and with whom he contracted directly,
after the statutory limit has run, so as to cut off other creditors who
have proved their claims, where the personal estate is insufficient for
their payment Creditors who have proved their claims against a
decedent's estate are regarded as judgment-creditors In such case
he stands as any other general creditor.[2]

§ 185. **Limitation runs from maturity of debt.**—Where the
bill of material is purchased on six months' time, the time of the six
months runs from date of delivery of the entire bill — the last item,
and the limitation from six months thereafter If the vendee wrongfully delays delivery the seller may make a tender of the materials,
and the time will run from the date of such tender. Where such
materials are bulky, as lumber and shingles, setting them apart and
notice to the purchaser is a sufficient tender.[3]

§ 186 **Extension of time by sub-contractor may release
owner**—The apprehension of offending a customer, the desire to
give customary accommodation to a patron, the gentlemanly aversion
to what may appear harsh and exacting in business, often induces
materialmen to delay or omit to follow the strict requirements of
the statute, but courts cannot make this law indulge a corresponding
lemency They must construe it without regard to well-intentioned
civility or generous motives. Such indulgence wrecks their rights
to a lien , the attention of a conscientious customer called to this fact
prevent his asking it Extension of time between contractor and
materialman, without the knowledge of the owner, does not prevent
the limitation running from the day when it was first due.[4]

Where payment, according to the contract, is due at a certain
date, extension of time by the sub-claimant will release the owner if
notice be not served with regard to the original date of payment.[4]

[1] Lunt v Stephens, 75 Ill 507
[2] Reitz v Coyer, 83 Ill 28
[3] Langford v Mackey, 12 Bradw 223
[4] Brown v Moore, 26 Ill 422, Kelly v Kellogg, 79 id. 477, Paddock v. Stout,
121 id 571, Chisholm v Williams, 128 id 115

Where no time of payment for materials is fixed by the contract, or agreed upon, or no established custom of trade to the contrary, the price therefor becomes due and payable as soon as the delivery is completed, and the law will imply that payment should then be made In such case the time must be counted from the day the last item of material is delivered for filing claim by an original contractor, or for serving notice, or bringing suit by a sub-claimant [1]

§ 187 **Customs as to date of payment.**— But where there is a uniform custom to demand payment at the close of each month, or on the first of the month for all goods delivered the previous month, and such custom is known to the other, there arises by implication an understanding between the parties that credit is given until the close of each month, and limitation will run from the first of the month as to the previous month's bills, and notice must be served on the owner within forty days from the first day of the month as to such bills [2]

.r the creditor indulge the contractor until the first of the next month — as for instance, on the December bill, due January 1, to February, and incorporate same with the bill of January and serve notice after February 9, but within forty days of February 1, the bar of limitations will run as to the December bill, in the owner's favor [1] It is not in the power of the original contractor and materialman to extend the time of payment, and thus extend the statutory liability of the owner, without his knowledge or consent. In this case all bills were payable on the first of the month for goods delivered the previous month The statement for materials delivered in December was duly sent on January 1. The contractor and materialman agreed to postpone payment thereof until February 1, by which time all wanted would be delivered and would be paid for They were not paid for, the materialman served notice on the owner within forty days after February 1, namely, on February 17, but not within forty days after January 1, and it was held on account thereof the materialman had no lien against the owner for the December bill.[3]

§ 188. **Limitation as to suit by original contractor.** — The original contractor cannot bring suit to foreclose his lien until his

[1] Kelly v Kellogg, 79 Ill 477, Phœnix Mut Life Ins Co v Batchen, 6 Bradw 621
[2] Notes 1, 4 *supra*, 4 *ante*, Claycomb v Cecil, 27 Ill 497
[3] Kelly v Kellogg, 79 Ill 477.

claim for a lien is filed, as provided,[1] nor before the day of payment stated in the contract, or thereafter agreed upon The debt must be due when the suit is brought.[2] If notes are taken, suit cannot be maintained until notes are due,[3] but separate liens can be enforced on the separate notes as they fall due Giving notes for a pre-existing debt extends the time and suspends the remedy until respective maturity of such notes.[3] Nor can he enforce it at all, unless he shall commence his suit within two years after filing of such statement.[4]

Once filed, the suit must be brought within two years, or the lien is discharged, the owner as well as all others relieved from its burden.

§ 189. **Limitation as to suit by sub-contractor.** — The sub-claimant, in case the money is due him from the original contractor at the time his notice is served, must delay ten days before bringing his action

In case it is not then due, ten days after it becomes due.

In case the money is not due the original contractor at either of these times, but later, then he must delay action until the same is due the original contractor [5]

The owner has the right to freedom from suit until these periods have passed, and if harassed by suits earlier, the court will dismiss the same at the claimant's cost.

But he must bring his suit, regardless of the time his notice is served, within three months after his cause of action accrues, provided the money is then due from the owner to the original contractor, if not, within three months after it becomes due the original contractor. Failure to bring suit within that time is a bar to recovery [5]

If any delay be occasioned by reason of the payment not being due the original contractor, the time of such delay shall not be counted. A suit by a sub-contractor is in time, if filed within three months after the money becomes due the original contractor from the owner, although it is more than three months after it is due from the original contractor to such sub-contractor. Where notice was served September 14, 1874, the money was not due the original con-

---

[1] Sec 4, act 1874, as amended. McDonald v Rosengarten, 134 Ill. 126, 35 App 71, Boals v Intrup, 40 id 82, Shinn v. Matheny, 48 id. 135
[2] Kinney v Hudnut, 2 Scam 472
[3] Cox v Keiser, 15 Bradw 432
[4] Sec 28, act 1874, as amended
[5] Sec 37, act 1874, as amended Huntington v Barton, 64 Ill 502, Rittenhouse v. Sable, 43 App 558.

tractor from the owner until a settlement was had between them, which was had in April, 1875, and suit was brought June 12, 1875, it was held brought in time — within three months after it was due from the owner to the original contractor [1]

§ 190. **New parties by amendment** — Where new parties are brought in by amendment, the suit is regarded as brought against such parties at the time such amendment is made, not at the time of filing the original petition [2]

The statute formerly provided that no mechanic should be allowed to enforce his lien " as against or to the prejudice of any other creditor, or of any incumbrance, unless suit be instituted to enforce such lien within six months after the last payment for labor or material shall have become due and payable," and where a suit was brought against the contracting party to enforce a mechanic's lien within six months after the last payment became due, but an incumbrancer and a purchaser under the incumbrance were not made parties within such time, but were brought into the case by amendment after the expiration of the statutory period, it was held no lien could be enforced as against such new parties to affect their rights The remedy given is purely statutory, and unless enforced in the manner and within the time prescribed in the statute, it cannot prevail against other creditors, and if one not made a party at the time of filing the petition shall afterward be made defendant, as to such defendant the suit will be regarded as commenced at the time he was made a party, and not before It is not sufficient to make only the trustee a party; the owner of the indebtedness himself, as his interest alone is to be affected by the decree, is an indispensable party. The time of a creditor being made a party, either in the original proceeding, or any amendment, must be regarded as the time of the commencement of a suit as to him, and if he is not a party his rights will not be affected, although the suit was instituted in time as to others [3] Under the present act, as suit must be brought within two years after filing the claim, unless such persons are made parties by the petition or amendment within that two years, the lien is discharged as to them The same consequence befalls the sub-contractor who fails to make them parties within the three months that he must bring suit.

---

[1] Meeks v Sims, 84 Ill 422
[2] Dunphy v Riddle, 86 Ill 22, Crowl v Nagle, id 437 Clark v Manning 90 id 380, 95 id 580, 4 Bradw 649, McGraw v Bayard, 96 Ill 146, adv , 1 Bradw 134, Bennit v Star Mining Co , 119 Ill 9, 18 Bradw 17, Watson v Gardner, 119 Ill 312, 18 App 386

§ 191. **Suit to be commenced within thirty days on demand.**— Upon the written demand of the owner or his agent, or any person interested in the real estate, served on the person or his agent claim- ing the lien, requiring suit to be commenced to enforce the lien, such suit shall be commenced within thirty days thereafter or the lien shall be forfeited [1]

§ 192. **Importance of limitations.**— Limitation runs from the day the claimant can enforce payment, and once run, is a perpetual bar, and under this law is a bar as much in favor of subsequent as prior creditors.[2]

In view of the statutory requirements with regard to filing the claim by an original claimant with the circuit clerk ; the service of notice on the owner and bringing suit by the sub-claimant, the time when the work is completed, when the debt became due, when the materials are delivered, whether the materials are to be paid for when all are delivered, or each month's deliveries on the first of the succeeding month, are matters of vital interest to those concerned Not only the very existence, but perfecting and keeping the lien alive depends upon them

The limitation of the time for filing the claim with the circuit clerk is not for the benefit of the owner, but for his creditors ; for purchasers of the property ; for those who may loan money on it, whether their loans be prior or subsequent to the making of the contract, or completion of the improvement.[3]

As the sub-claimant deals, not with the owner, but original con- tractor, the limitations with regard to him are for the benefit of both owner and other creditors.

The limitation for bringing suit after the claim is filed is for the benefit of all — owner and creditors.

---

[1] Sec 52, act 1874, as amended, see form of demand, Appendix, page 202
[2] Kinney v Hudnut, 2 Scam 472. Brown v Moore, 26 Ill 422, Rietz v Coyer, 83 id 28, Watson v Gardner, 119 id 312
[3] Van Pelt v Dunford, 58 Ill, 145

CHAPTER X.

§ 193 **Redemption.** — Upon all sales in mechanic's lien cases, the right of redemption exists in favor of the same persons, and may be made in the same manner as is or may be provided for redemption of real estate from sales under judgments and executions at common law.[1]

A judgment creditor can only redeem after, not within twelve months from the date of sale[2]

§ 194. **Neglect to satisfy lien paid: penalty.** — Whenever a lien has been claimed by filing the same with the clerk of the Circuit Court, and is afterward paid, the person filing same shall acknowledge satisfaction thereof in the proper book in such office in writing, and on neglect to do so for ten days after the claim has been paid, he shall forfeit to the owner the sum of $25[3]

While this release is to be made by the claimant in person, when the payment is made to and release executed by his attorney, the claimant will not be liable for not releasing, when the acts of his attorney are unknown to him.[4] This clause of the act applies only to an original claimant; there is no penalty for a sub-claimant not releasing.[4]

§ 195. **Circuit clerk's fee; abstract.** — The clerk of the Circuit Court where such a lien shall be filed, shall indorse on every such claim for a lien filed, the date of filing, and make abstract thereof in a book kept for that purpose and properly indexed, containing the name of the person filing the lien, the amount of the lien, the date of filing, the name of the person against whom the lien is filed, and a description of the property charged with the

---

[1] Sec 24, act 1874, as amended
[2] Armsby v People, 20 Ill 155

[3] Sec 54, act 1874 as amended
[4] Lavery v Brooke, 37 App 51

22

lien, and for which the person filing shall pay one dollar to the clerk.[1]

In all cases where the owner cannot be found in the county in which said improvement is made, or shall not reside therein, the person furnishing labor or materials shall file said notice in the office of the clerk of the Circuit Court, who shall enter in a book to be kept for that purpose, alphabetically, the names of the owners, and opposite thereto the names of the persons claiming liens, for which the clerk shall receive a fee of fifty cents[2]

The abstract of the clerk does not take the place of the claim. The only purpose of that is to furnish a convenient and ample reference to the claim, and the error of the clerk, if any, will not invalidate it.[3]

---

[1] Sec 53, act 1874, as amended   This applies to the claims of original contractors only, not to sub-contractors' claims
[2] Sec 32 act 1874 as amended   This applies to the claims of sub-contractors only, not to original contractors' claims
[3] McDonald v. Rosengarten, 134 Ill. 126, 35 App 71

CHAPTER XI.

WAIVER AND RELEASE

§ 196. **Taking note prima facie does not.** — The lien may be waived or released by express agreement of the parties, or by the act of the party entitled to it (see forms, Appendix, page 204).

It is waived if the owner's note be taken as payment. *Prima facie*, the taking of a note is not payment, and does not release the lien;[1] nor will it be a release even if assigned and suit be brought thereon, and judgment obtained by such assignee Before the lien can be enforced, however, the note or judgment thereon must be canceled by the party seeking to enforce the lien.[2] Suing at law does not release the lien.

§ 197 **Release by estoppel.** — Where mechanics made a settlement with an owner, and accepted notes which they assigned to third parties, and also a warranty deed of certain real estate in excess of the lien, and for the excess gave in return their notes to the owner, during all of which time the mechanics knew the owner was negotiating for a loan on the building and made no objection, it was held the mechanics were estopped by their conduct from insisting that the lien of the loaner was subordinate to their lien[3]

But where a sub-contractor was present at a settlement between the owner and contractor, as to the sum due for the erection of a

---

[1] Van Court v Bushnell, 21 Ill 624; Brady v Anderson 24 id 111, Crowl v Nagle, 86 id 437 Meeks v Sims, 84 id 422, Paddock v Stout, 121 id 571, Cox v Colles 17 Bradw 503
[2] Clement v Newton, 78 Ill 427 Bayard v McGraw, 1 Bradw 134 McGraw v Bayard 96 Ill 146 Kankakee Coal Co v Crane Bros Mfg Co , 128 id 627
[3] McGraw v. Bayard, 96 Ill. 146, adv., 1 Bradw 134

house, and for extra work, at which time the owner accepted an order of the contractor for the balance due in favor of a third person, but the former did not say or do any thing that could have led the owner to believe he was paid or had released him, it was held that he was not estopped from enforcing his lien against the owner, from the mere fact of his being present at the settlement [1]

§ 198. **Acceptance of draft or order.** — The acceptance by the owner of a building of an order drawn on him by the contractor in favor of a sub-contractor, unless received by such sub-contractor as absolute payment, is not a discharge of his lien on the building.[2]

§ 199. **Taking other security releases lien.** — The taking of other security, either on property or that of individuals not parties to the transaction, will have the effect to discharge the premises from the lien.[3] The guaranty of a note by a third party waives the lien[4] So if the note of a firm be taken in satisfaction of a claim for work and materials furnished to one of the partners, though the settlement was made in the usual mode of doing business between the parties, a mechanic's lien cannot afterward be sustained for the same against a *bona fide* purchaser;[5] but if the firm had ordered the materials placed on the premises, and they were used in the improvement of the same, and the firm afterward gave their note for the amount, it would not discharge the lien[6]

The receiving of an assignment of an insurance policy, without evidence that the lien claimant received it with the intention of its being in full satisfaction of or security for his claim, will not operate as a release or waiver of his lien, nor will taking a more efficient security on the same property release it[7]

§ 200 **Part payment in real estate no release as to rest** — Receiving a conveyance of real estate as part payment of a claim for erecting a building thereon, is not a waiver of the lien, for the residue, any more than the acceptance of money as part payment would be[8]

§ 201. **Accepting dividend in general assignment does not release** — Proving the claim against an owner who had made a

[1] Havighorst v Lindberg, 67 Ill 463
[2] Meeks v Sims, 84 Ill 422
[3] Brady v. Anderson, 24 Ill 111 Kinzey v. Thomas, 28 id. 502, Gardner v Hall, 29 id 277
[4] Kankakee Coal Co v Crane Bros Mfg Co , 138 Ill. 207.
[5] Benneson v Thayer 23 Ill 317
[6] Croskey v Corey, 48 Ill 442
[7] Clark v Moore 64 Ill 273
[8] Bayard v McGraw, 1 Bradw 134, adv , 96 Ill 146.

general assignment, and accepting a dividend from his estate thereon is not a release or waiver of the lien. Such dividend will simply go as a credit on the lien [1]

§ 202 **Appointing receiver and assignment to him ordered, but not made, no release.** — The mere appointment of a receiver under a creditor's bill against one entitled to a lien, with an order to make an assignment to him, where none is shown to have been made, and the receiver has made no claim to the debt, will not operate to release the lien [2]

§ 203 **Limitations release lien** — Failure, on the part of the original contractor, to file his claim within four months after final payment is due waives and releases the lien as to prior or subsequent incumbrancers and purchasers ; to bring suit within two years after filing such claim as to owners as well as to these ;[3] on the part of the sub-claimant to bring suit within three months after his cause of action accrues, or if nothing is due the original contractor at that time, within three months after it becomes due him,[4] failure to bring suit on the part of any claimant, within thirty days after written demand by the owner or his agent, discharges the lien.[5]

§ 204. **Release for particular purpose does not release as to others.** — Where a release is executed to a mortgagee by the contractor to enable the owner to draw money on a loan, it is a release only for the benefit of the mortgagee, for no other party, and for that sole purpose [6] So where the release was executed by a sub-contractor to enable the original contractor to draw a particular installment, as the payment due when the plastering is done or floors laid, it was held that the sub-contractor could not complain of the owner paying such installment, whether the work were done or not, that it was a release so far as that installment was concerned [7]

If the release does not state the purpose or terms of its execution, proof thereof can be made and thereby such purpose established and the intended effect and no more will be enforced by the court. Where the release names no one and no consideration is given, the court will look to extrinsic facts to determine both the consideration and in whose favor the release was executed [6]

[1] Paddock v Stout, 121 Ill 571. Stout v Sower, 22 App 65
[2] Burstow v McLachlan, 99 Ill 641
[3] Sec. 28, act 1874, as amended
[4] Sec. 47, act 1874, as amended, Huntington v Barton, 64 Ill 502, Meeks v. Sims, 84 id 422
[5] Sec. 52, act 1874, as amended
[6] Paulsen v Manske. 126 Ill 72, see Dunphy v Riddle 86 id 22.
[7] Biggs v. Clapp, 74 Ill 335

CHAPTER XII.

PLEADING AND PRACTICE.

GENERAL CHARACTER OF SUIT

§ 205 Nature of action.—The institution of an action to enforce a mechanic's lien is practically enforcing a general assignment *in rem*, that is, it operates to subject the property affected to the payment of all claims that are liens upon it, whether on the part of record creditors, as incumbrancers and holders of judgments, or lien claimants. The rights of these, of purchasers, of all concerned in that property, to the extent of the owner's interest therein, must be finally and fully settled in that action

Of the same nature are the proceedings for general settlement by the owner or lienholder where the amount coming to the contractor is insufficient to pay all claims Hence the absolute necessity of making all such persons parties

Any omitted party remains unbound by the decree, his rights as unaffected by it as if it had never been rendered, and is at liberty to contest that decree, the claim upon which it was rendered, the lien itself, the sale made in pursuance of it, just as if it had never been rendered, and the action was begun *de novo* against all

The original contractor need not make sub-claimants parties His claim covers theirs; so far as he is concerned, they are improper and unnecessary parties. He must make all incumbrancers, prior or subsequent, and purchasers parties

He must make not only trustees, but *cestui que trusts* parties If the trustee is made a party, but not the *cestui que trust*, the latter is

18

not bound or affected by the decree. But if the *cestui que trust* only is made a party and suffers a decree to be rendered on a trial on the merits of the case, without objecting to the omission of his trustee as a party, his estate and interest, and that of all who claim under him, will be bound and settled by the decree.

The sub-claimant must make all persons parties whom the original claimant should; and, in addition, that original claimant and all other sub-claimants of liens upon the property. His omission to make them parties imperils whatever decree he may obtain to the same risks, as a similar omission on the part of the original contractor.

Both classes would be compelled to refund out of whatever they collected such *pro rata* share thereof as the omitted party or parties should prove they were entitled to; and could be sued therefor if such parties elected to proceed in that way for their share.

Should the property be sold to a party to the proceedings, the court under whose decree it was sold would be compelled, at the instance of such omitted party, to set aside the sale, as long as such party held the title acquired by such purchase

If such omitted party were a purchaser from the owner, under sale by enforcement of trust deed, mortgage, or judgment, his title would not be affected by sale under such decree, but would be superior to the title of the purchaser under that decree; nor could such decretal purchaser interfere with his possession, or oust him by ejectment or other proceedings

The statute confers ample power upon the court to make all such persons parties, and if the claimant fails to utilize these provisions so as to make the proceedings fully and finally settle his rights, it is his own fault

Only the Circuit Court, or court of concurrent chancery powers, has jurisdiction to enforce a mechanic's lien. Where the suit is not to enforce the lien on the specific property, but is a mere action at law for damages, the suit may be brought in any court having jurisdiction of the amount sued for.

§ 206. **Bill or petition, when to be sworn to.**—The bill or petition, either of original, sub-contractor, or sub-claimant, need not be sworn to, except for general settlement under section 39. If under oath, an amendment need not be sworn to [1]

§ 207 **Petition of the original contractor. Requisites —** The petition of the original contractor must contain, if it is founded

---

[1] Sec 5, act 1874, as amended, Downey v O'Donnell, 92 Ill 559

on an express contract, a brief statement of that contract. If it is founded on a contract partly expressed and partly implied, or an implied contract, it shall state what character of contract it is. It must allege that this contract was made with the owner, performance, and when the work or delivery of materials was begun, and when it was completed; the filing of the claim as required, and set forth; the amount due and unpaid, and when it was due; give a description of the premises subject to the lien, and state what interest the owner has in them, and such other facts as may be necessary to a full understanding of the rights of the parties,[1] which will be hereafter treated of

§ 208 **Original contractor has two forms of action** — The original contractor is allowed two modes of procedure under the statute

1 To enforce his lien for full performance of his contract[2]

2 To enforce it on the *quantum meruit* for part performance where the owner has failed to perform his part of the contract[2]

§ 209 **Sub-contractor has five forms of action.** — The subclaimant has five statutory methods of action to collect his debt ·

1. He can file his petition and foreclose his lien by the same method as the original contractor[3]

2. He can sue the owner at law for the amount that the original contractor's statement shows he is entitled to, or where the owner, at the time of his own notice, has funds due the original contractor.[5]

3 After notice to the owner by himself as directed, he can bring suit at law against the original contractor and owner jointly for the amount due him, in any court having jurisdiction of the amount claimed to be due, and a personal judgment may be rendered thereon, as in other cases.[4] This can only be enforced by general execution, not by a sale of the improved property, and the same is the case where only the owner is sued at law[6]

If this suit be before a justice of the peace, and judgment obtained, and the execution issued thereon be returned not satisfied, a transcript of such judgment may be taken to the Circuit Court and spread upon the records thereof, and execution issued thereon as in other cases.[7]

[1] Sec 5, act 1874, as amended
[2] Sec 5, 1874, as amended Downey v O'Donnell, 92 Ill 559
[3] Sec. 11, act 1874, as amended
[4] Sec 37, act 1874, as amended
[5] Culver v Fleming 61 Ill 498
[6] Baptist Church v Andrews, 87 Ill. 172.
[7] Sec 38, act 1874, as amended

4 In case of several contractors' liens on the same land, any one
having such lien and fearing that there is not enough due the
original contractor to pay all, can bring suit for a general settlement
and distribution *pro rata* of what is coming to the original contractor among those entitled to it.[1]

5. In case of abandonment of the contract by the original contractor, he not only can, but must proceed as is especially provided
for such cases[2]

These are all statutory, wholly, and in addition to his right
of action at law against the contractor who employed him,
who is his primary debtor, and against whom he can proceed at the
same time he pursues his other statutory methods for relief — such
action being as independent of the statute as ever, in no wise cur-
tailed or interfered with by it[3]

§ 210. **Petition of sub-contractor.** — The petition of the sub-
claimant to enforce his lien must set out, the terms of the contract
of the owner with the original contractor; that the sub-contract was
within the power of the original contractor to make so as to bind
the owner's property ; that a sufficient sum is due the original contractor to pay the petitioner; set out his contract, if he has one, or
state what it was; that he has performed it, or what he did, and
when he begun and completed his work, or delivery of materials,
that he has given the notice pursuant to the statute, and when he gave
it, and set it out in the petition ; or that the original contractor has
given the owner notice of petitioner's claim pursuant to the statute,
as the case may be ; then, as the petition of the original contractor,
the amount yet due and unpaid and when it became due, a description of the property subject to the lien, the owner's interest therein,
and such other facts as may be necessary to a full understanding of
the rights of the parties[4]

§ 211. **Where he sues for general settlement.** — If there are
several liens of sub-claimants upon the same premises, and any person having such lien shall fear that there is not a sufficient amount
coming to the original contractor to pay all such liens, such owner,
or any one or more persons having such liens, may file his or their

[1] Sec 39, act 1874 as amended
[2] Sec 45, act 1874 as amended, Schultz v Hav, 62 Ill 157, Biggs v Clapp, 74
id 335, Mehrle v Dunne, 75 id 239; Doyle v. Munster, 27 App 130, Conklin v
Plant, 34 id 264
[3] Sec 7. *ante*
[4] Thomas v Industrial University, 71 Ill 310, sec 37 act 1874 as amended,
sec 5 act 1874 as amended, Marski v. Simmerling, 46 App 531, Havighorst v.
Lindberg 67 Ill 463

sworn bill or petition in the Circuit Court of the proper county, stating such fact, and such other facts as may be sufficient to a full understanding of the rights of the parties. The contractor and all persons having liens upon, or who are interested in the premises, so far as the same are known, or can be ascertained by the claimant or petitioner, upon diligent inquiry, shall be made parties. Upon the hearing the court shall find the amount coming from the owner to the original contractor, and the amount due to each of the persons having liens. The owner can file such bill whether sued or not, where two or more claim the fund that is owing[1]

If the amount so found to be coming to the contractor, shall be sufficient to pay such liens in full, the court shall order the same so paid[1]

In case the amount so found to be coming to the original contractor from the owner is insufficient to pay all the liens in full, it shall be divided between the persons entitled to such liens *pro rata*, in proportion to the amounts so found due to them respectively[1]

The premises may be decreed to be sold for the payment of such liens as in other cases[1]

§ 212 **When original contractor abandons** — Where an original contractor has failed to complete and abandoned his contract, the sub contractor must proceed in a different way

He can file his petition in any court of record against the owner and contractor, setting forth the nature of the claim, the amount due, as near as may be, and the names of the parties employed on such house, or other improvement subject to liens, and notice of such suit shall be served on the persons therein named[2]

This petition is not required to set out the original contract, nor to allege that there is any thing due the original contractor. The section of the statute applicable thereto does not proceed on the theory that there is any thing due the original contractor, but that the owner is liable for so much as the work and material are reasonably worth, according to the original contract price, deducting rightful payments and damages for failure to complete[3]

Where, in an action under this section, it was alleged that after the materials were furnished by the petitioner, and had been used in the building, but before the same was completed, D (the original contractor) abandoned the work and surrendered to M (the owner),

[1] Sec 39, act 1874, as amended, Newhall v Kastens, 70 Ill 156, Hellman v. Schneider 75 id 422
[2] Sec 45, act 1874 as amended Conklin v Plant, 34 App 264
[3] Doyle v Munster, 27 App 130, Mehrle v Dunne, 75 Ill 239

and that said unfinished building was, at the time of the abandonment, reasonably worth a large sum over and above the aggregate of amounts paid thereon, and of any damages sustained by reason of non-fulfillment of the original contract for erecting said building, which sum was greater than the amount petitioner claimed, the petition was held good[1]

§ 213. **Petition, general practice** — There is no peculiar rule of pleading especially and only applicable to petitions for mechanic's liens, other than the general rules of chancery practice,[2] the averment of facts showing statutory rights and performance of statutory duties, the only allegations peculiarly essential in these pleadings

The rights sought to be enforced being wholly statutory, a party, to avail himself of the statute, must show by his pleadings that his case comes clearly within its provisions, must, by their averments, bring himself strictly within its terms, and show his right to the lien against those made defendants[3]

The petition should contain the necessary averments to show not only the sum of money that is due the plaintiff,[4] but that the debt is created by the performance of such labor as is secured by the statutory lien.[5]

An architect cannot recover for services not *per se* architectural, nor as superintendent, unless employed as such, nor a superintendent for labor outside of a superintendent's duties, and the petition must aver employment for and performance of such services.[5]

The petition must allege that the materials were bought, furnished for,[6] and used in the building sought to be charged with the lien,[7] not merely that they were furnished to the contractor and used in the construction of it.[8]

It is equally incumbent on the materialman or mechanic, in order to bring himself within the statute, to show affirmatively on the face of the proceedings that his claim is such as the statute confers a lien for, and that all the formalities for acquiring and fixing that lien have been complied with by doing the work or furnishing the material within the statutory time, filing the claim or serving the notice in like manner, making the payments per contract due within

[1] Doyle v Munster, 27 App 130. Mehrle v Dunne, 75 Ill 239
[2] Benner v Schmidt, 44 App 304. Portones v Holmes, 33 App. 312
[3] Cook v Heald, 21 Ill 425. McLurken v Logan, 23 id 79, Sutherland v. Ryerson, 24 Ill 518. Crowl v Nagle 86 Ill 437.
[4] Kinney v Hudnut 2 Scam 472
[5] Adler v World's Pastime Co, 126 Ill 373, 26 App 528.
[6] Secs 70-72 *ante*
[7] Secs 107, 108. *ante*
[8] Croskey v Corey, 48 Ill. 442.

the statutory period, and setting forth those dates, and not for antagonistic creditors to show the reverse[1]

Time is the important part of the statutory requirement. No other lien is allowed to exist without formal record evidence, and the time when the contract was made, when the work or delivery of material was begun, and ended, when payment was agreed upon, or by law its promise implied, are matters the court must pass upon as statutory or not. Hence the necessity of the petition setting forth these times instead of averring in an argumentative way, performed as the statute required, etc. It is just this statutory performance the court must pass upon from the facts alleged and proved[2]

The filing of the claim or serving of the notice within the statutory time after the last payment was due, or cause of action accrued, is a material issuable fact, and must be averred, or the petition will not show a cause of action.[3] It is not enough to aver the filing of the claim with the clerk of the Circuit Court by an original claimant, or the service of notice on the owner by a sub-claimant without an averment of the time when, for a filing at the wrong time is as inefficient as if not filed at all.

Where suit was brought on a note, in which was written "above sum due for work at my mill," and the petition alleged that the note was given for so much work done on the defendant's mill, it was held that the petition was insufficient, and a demurrer thereto should be sustained. That it did not appear whether the note was given in pursuance of that contract, or upon a subsequent agreement, neither did it appear when the work was performed, nor at what time, by the terms of the original contract, it was to be paid for. The note, from anything that appeared, might have been given years after the work was done, and should have been paid for. All of which were fatal defects.[4] It is not sufficient simply to aver that notes sued on were given for the amount due for work on, or materials used in, improvements on the maker's land. The petition must contain a statement of the cause of action, the time when the contract was made, what the contract was, within what time it was to be per-

[1] Brady v Anderson 24 Ill 111 Burkhart v Reisig id 530, Phillips v Stone, 25 id 67, Columbus Machine Mfg Co v Dorwin, id 153 Scott v Keeling, 25 id 316, C. & St L R R v Cauble, 85 id 555, 4 App 133 McDonald v Rosengarten, 35 id 71, 134 Ill 126, Boals v Intrup, 40 App 62
[2] Cook v Heald, 21 Ill 425, Cook v Vreeland, 21 id. 431, Brady v Anderson, 24 id. 111, Burkhart v Reisig, 24 id 530
[3] Boals v Intrup 40 App 62, Shinn v Matheny 48 id 135, McDonald v Rosengarten, 35 id 71, 134 Ill 126 Campbell v Jacobson, 145 id 389, 46 App 287
[4] Logan v. Dunlop, 3 Scam 189

formed, when what it obligated to do was commenced, when it was completed, and when payment was to be made, and show clearly on its face a right in plaintiff to recover[1]

The complainant must set out the contract, not only to show that he is entitled to the benefit of the act, but to apprise all parties interested of the nature and character of his claim.[1]

§ 214. **If note taken it must be surrendered before decree.** — And where suit is brought in a case where a note has been given the action cannot be maintained without a return and cancellation of the note[2] Even a stipulation that the notes at the time of the filing of the bill were due and unpaid, and were dated and due for the amounts as charged, will not obviate the necessity of their production, surrender and cancellation at the time of the trial.[a] Where the plaintiff does not produce the note and offer to cancel the same, judgment should be for the defendant.[2]

The fact that a party seeking to enforce a lien, took the note of the person for whom the work was done for the work and traded it off, and the note was not produced on the trial and offered to be surrendered, nor any excuse shown for its non-production, would warrant a judgment for the defendant.[b] The taking of the note, unless so intended and understood between the parties, is not a payment of the debt; and where it is taken for the accommodation of the debtor who is in default and unable to pay, and with the understanding that it is to be negotiated, the act of negotiating the same adds no force to the act of taking it, nor does the further act of proceeding to judgment thereon by the holder[c]

In either case the lien creditor before he can have his decree, must be in control of the note or judgment, so allege, and offer to surrender or cancel the same.[2]

§ 215. **Petition must set out nature of contract.** — The plaintiff will be held to just what contract he sets out, and his claim governed by the law applicable to the kind of contract sued upon.[3] If he avers an express contract, he cannot recover on an implied, or one partly expressed and partly implied[3] And the construction on ex-

---

[1] Muller v Smith, 3 Scam 544; Logan v Dunlop, id 189, Kinney v Hudnut, 2 Scam 472

[2] Clement v Newton, 78 Ill 427,[b] Chisholm v Williams 128 id 115. Kankakee Coal Co. v Crane Bros Mfg Co , id 627,[a] Bavard v McGraw, 1 Bradw 134 [c]

[3] Austin v Wohler 5 Bradw 500,[b] Adler v World's Pastime Co , 26 App 528 Belanger v Hersey 90 Ill 70,[a] Carroll v. Crane 4 Gilm 563, Rowley v James, 31 Ill 298 Grundeis v Hartwell, 90 id 324, Driver v Ford, id 595, Douglas v McCord, 12 Bradw 278, Ruggles v. Blank, 15 id 436.

press contracts and the averments necessary in suits thereon are the same under the present act, as under the act of 1845 [a]

If the contract is attached as an exhibit, and there is a discrepancy between that contract so attached and the description of it in the petition, the exhibit governs [1]

Where the petition alleged the contract to be an express contract and in writing, the proof showed it to be part written, part oral, but the contract was set out *in extenso*, it was held that the error in stating the legal effect was mere surplusage, would be rejected as such, and not condemned for variance [2]

In all cases the petitioner is confined to his own theory of his case, and cannot recover upon another, though it be proved and a proper case for relief. Although a good case appear in the evidence, yet if variant to that in the petition, the petition will be dismissed [3] The allegation and the proof must correspond, and a variance in the case stated, and the case proved will be fatal to the petitioner, no matter what the merits of the case are He cannot make one case by his pleading, another by his proof — however strong that proof may be [3]

The following cases will illustrate wherein a variance between the allegations of the petition and the proof was held to be fatal and barred recovery on the suit, as brought

Petition, alleged materials were furnished on an implied contract Proof, payment to be $50 cash, balance in thirty days Held, an express contract, variance fatal [4]

Allegation to be paid in April Proof, to be paid on delivery; variance fatal [5]

Allegation, that the work was to be paid for on completion Proof, to be paid for on a certain stipulated time, December 25, 1855; variance fatal [6]

Allegation, 155 days, labor, to commence December 27, 1859, end June 25, 1860 Proof, commenced before Christmas, 1st to 15th of December, and continued until after July 1st, 1860, variance fatal [7]

Allegation, to build for $185, and complete January 6, 1857. Proof, built for $125, and completed March 1, 1857, variance fatal. [8]

---

a Note 3 page 144
b Note 3, page 144
1 Benner v Schmidt, 44 App 304
2 Ruggles v Blank 15 Bradw 436
3 Tracy v Rogers 69 Ill 662 Belanger v Hersey, 90 id 70.
4 Randolph v Onstott 58 Ill 52
5 Van Court v Bushnell, 21 Ill 624
6 Bush v Connelly 33 Ill 447
7 Martin v Eversal, 36 Ill 222
8 Stein v. Schultz, 23 Ill 646

Allegation, hardware sold to E A. R at the usual market price Proof, sold to E. A R & Co , certain lines at a certain discount, nails at wholesale market price , variance fatal [1]

But an allegation that labor was to be paid for when done, materials on delivery, is sustained by proof that no time of payments was specified, or agreed upon, for the law implies a promise to pay on performance [2]

Nor can the petitioner depart from his action on a contract of any sort and recover on a *quantum meruit*, no matter how much the evidence may show he is justly entitled to it [3] Nor can he sue as a sub-contractor and recover as original contractor.[4]

This variance must be objected to on the trial to be availed of, and the court will allow an amendment on the trial to obviate variance without a continuance, unless it is made to appear that the opposite party is taken by surprise.[5]

§ 216 **Must show completion within time limited by statute.** —A petition on an express contract, which avers that payments were to be made in installments of ten per cent from time to time, as work progresses, and fully made when the work was completed, and the work was to be completed within three years, is substantially good   The statute does not require a contract to state a particular date and day to make it valid as a lien, but simply provides that the time for completion shall not be extended for a longer period than three years from the commencement of work, or delivery of materials, nor the time of payment beyond one year from the time fixed for completion [6]

A statement of the gross amount due, the aggregate amount of credits, the net balance due and unpaid, was held sufficient ; th the amount due according to the contract was $13,248.94, on which there had been paid $6,550.02, leaving a balance due of $6,705 92 and interest thereon, according to a bill rendered and approved by the defendant, substantially sufficient as to the sum due.[6]

§ 217 **Must show architect's certificate where contract requires.**—Where the contract makes the architect's certificate a condition precedent, it must allege that the same was obtained, waived or excused in some manner recognized by law.[7]

---

[1] Peck v Standert 1 Bradw 228
[2] Brady v Anderson, 24 Ill 111; Claycomb v Cecil, 27 id 497
[3] Carroll v Crane, 4 Gilm 563, Kimball v Cook, 1 id 423
[4] Douglas v McCord, 12 Bradw 278
[5] Grundeis v Hartwell 90 Ill 324, Driver v. Ford, id 595
[6] Reed v Boyd, 84 Ill 66
[7] Wolf v. Michaelis, 27 App. 336, adv , 33 id. 645, McAuley v Carter, 22 Ill 53

Where a party wishes to attack an architect's certificate on the ground of fraud or mistake, the facts constituting such fraud or mistake must be properly set out in the pleading, or no proof can be introduced in regard thereto

In the absence of some allegation that the architect either issued or refused to issue the certificate required, or statement of any matter of excuse for failure to secure such certificates, the petition would be insufficient, and no evidence touching same could be admitted Where there was no such allegation, and parol evidence was offered to show that the certificate had been issued, it was held that there was no foundation laid for the admission of such evidence, and its admission was erroneous [1]

Unless the contract requires the contractor to give the owner notice of having obtained the architect's certificate, suit may be brought without giving such notice, and no allegation thereof is necessary in the petition [1]

§ 218 **Performance.**—The petition must allege that the plaintiff has completed and performed his contract [2] It must truly describe the contract entered into, and what was done under it. If no time was fixed for performance, the law will imply a reasonable time, and if done in a year, the lien attaches It is not necessary, by express words, to negative that part of the statute (section 3) which sets forth excepted cases in which no lien can exist, but only by affirmative description of the contract, and of acts done in performance of it, show what the whole case is, and if, when so shown, nothing repugnant to the provisions of that section appears, the lien attaches [3]

Where a contract required a contractor to furnish the material and complete the building, but contained a clause that the owner was to pay a third party a certain sum by assuming bills for lumber for the building, and to a certain extent, and the balance of such sum when such third party completed the carpenter work, a petition by such contractor for a mechanic's lien, which set out these facts, and averred that the third party furnished the lumber and finished the carpenter work, and that the plaintiff furnished the material and completed the balance of the work, and that the entire work was completed and accepted by the owner, showed a performance of the contract by the petitioner, and was sufficient to entitle him to a lien [4]

[1] Wolf v Michaelis, 27 App 336, adv , 33 id 645, McAuley v Carter 22 Ill 53.
[2] Warren v Harris, 2 Gilm 307, Hobart v Reeves, 73 Ill 527, Reed v Boyd, 84 id 66
[3] Portones v. Holmes 33 App 312
[4] Hobart v Reeves, 73 Ill. 527

§ 219 Estoppel, if relied on, facts set out must show.—If ownership by estoppel is relied upon, it must be alleged and the facts constituting such estoppel must be set out.[1] If the contract was made by agent, agency must be averred.[1]

Where it appears the wife was the owner of the land, and had the evidence of her title on record, and the petition alleged a contract with the husband, that he was in possession and exercising acts of ownership over the land, and that the wife was personally cognizant of the work and labor bestowed, and the making of the improvements thereon, the facts stated in the petition were held insufficient. If it intended to bind the wife by way of estoppel, the facts to be relied upon should have been alleged, and if it was intended to bind her by the acts of her husband as her agent, such agency should have been alleged. If he acted in his own name, but the wife was the undisclosed principal, such should be alleged.[1]

§ 220 Interest, if desired, must be shown.—If under the contract specific sums are agreed to be paid, interest need not be claimed, that follows as an incident of the debt,[3] otherwise it should be claimed in the petition. If not claimed it can only be recovered from the date of the filing the petition.[4]

§ 221 Must give description. Petition.—The petition must contain a description of the premises, which are subject to the lien.[5] A correct description in the petition will cure an erroneous description in the contract, as where it is described in the contract · Lot 1, block 2, Smith's subdivision, north-west quarter, north-east quarter, section 18, town 39, range 14; in the petition, lot 1, block 2, S F Smith's subdivision, north-east quarter, north-east quarter, section 18, town 39, range 14.[6]

When the contract is made the lot or land to be improved may be fully understood and considered by both parties, yet not described in the contract. The land with reference to which the contract is made, if not described in it, may be proved by parol evidence.[7]

While the title to realty cannot be proved by parol generally, in these cases admissions in the pleading are sufficient proof thereof,

[1] Geary v Hennessy, 9 Bradw 17, Campbell v Jacobson, 145 Ill 389
[2] Wilson v Schuck, 5 Bradw 572
[3] Heiman v Schroeder 74 Ill 158; Downey v O'Donnell, 92 id 559
[4] Mills v Heeney, 35 Ill 173, Prescott v Maxwell, 48 id 82, Race v Sullivan, 1 Bradw 94
[5] Sec 5, act 1874, as amended
[6] Clark v Manning, 90 Ill 380.
[7] Burns v Lane, 23 App 504

and if the allegation of ownership of the property described is not denied by the defendant, it is taken as confessed and true.[1]

Where the contract was for the improvement of lots owned by L in the town of Waverly, the petition alleged L owned lots 11 and 12 in block 7 in Waverly, and the answer did not deny owner-ship of the lots. Held, in absence of proof, that L owned other lots, and on proof that he did own these, and they were built upon, the allegation was sufficient.[2]

This description should be sufficiently accurate for the officer's deed in event of the sale to convey it, for parties investigating with a view of purchase to identify and locate, and to give notice so as to create a *lis pendens* lien[3]

A house situated in a tract of twelve acres in part of the north-west quarter of section 13, town 28, range 1, included in that por-tion known as William Campbell's addition to Galena, and the house designated as Argyle Cottage, in which the defendant now resides, was held to be insufficient, so indefinite that the premises could not be located[4]

A description which would be insufficient, as — Certain three acres lying in the south-east corner of the south-west quarter, north-west quarter, section 22, town 15, range 10 — may be made good if attendant circumstances are averred to help fix the precise location, which by the aid of extrinsic evidence would enable any one to locate the precise premises, as where the above description was fur-ther qualified by stating that, " the defendant is now owning and in possession of said land, as he has ever been since the time above mentioned, and in his own right is now holding, and has been so holding under a title bond for said land made by W B W "[5]

A mill at Marseilles, where the owner had no other mill, for machinery placed therein was held sufficient[6]

The number of the lot, block and street number, are sufficient, though the congressional subdivision is omitted

No 181 South Leavitt street, Chicago, lots 8 and 19, block 1, Bank's subdivision, of lot 9, block 11, Rockwell's addition to Chicago, was held sufficient, and the objection to omission of con-gressional subdivision to be a frivolous objection[7]

---

[1] Lavery v Brooke, 37 App 51
[2] Lombard v Johnson, 76 Ill 599
[3] Watson v Gardner, 119 Ill 312
[4] Turney v Saunders, 4 Scam 527
[5] Quackenbush v Carson, 21 Ill 99
[6] Strawn v Cogswell, 28 Ill 457
[7] Buckley v. Boutellier, 61 Ill 293

Where the material is to be used in a house in process of construction, the necessity of description in the contract is less strict

Where it was alleged the machinery was bought to be used in a mill then being built by the defendant, and the defendant was not engaged in building any other mill, it was held sufficient.[1]

If the same building cover more than one lot and is under one roof, it must be averred that the labor was done, contract made or materials furnished to so improve these lots, and if so proved, the lien will extend to all, the same as one[2]

But a correct description in the petition will not cure a defective description in the claim filed, and the lien extends only to the property described in the claim

§ 222 **By whom suit must be brought.** — This statute does not change the relations of parties to contracts The proper parties to bring an action *in assumpsit* on matters arising out of the contract, if no lien existed, are the proper parties to enforce the claim of lien. The suit must be by parties in interest against the owner, but parties must have a joint interest to maintain a joint action.[3]

Where a contract was made in the name of one of the parties for the benefit of both, the petition, being governed by the rules of equity, may be in the names of both.[4]

Several original parties, however, cannot join in a proceeding to enforce a mechanic's lien, unless they are jointly entitled to such lien Where persons were partners, and as such contracted to build a house, and upon a settlement a note was given to one of the parties for a certain portion of the price, and to the other two for the residue, the interest of the one who received the note to himself alone thereby became severed from the other two, and they could not, therefore, join in a proceeding to enforce their mechanic's lien, but had to proceed separately, according to their respective rights, as fixed upon the settlement.[5]

§ 223. **Partnership** — The constant changes occurring from death, disagreement, or the voluntary and friendly changes in plans of parties, as well as the formation of such after and in the midst of undertakings, present the same questions in regard to liens as other contracts Neither the formation nor dissolution of a partnership

[1] Power v McCord, 36 Ill 214
[2] Orr v N W Mut Life Ins Co , 86 Ill 260 Seiler v Schaeffer, 40 App 71
[3] Lombard v Johnson, 76 Ill 599
[4] Roberts v Gates 64 Ill. 374
[5] Bush v Connelly 33 Ill 447

could have any other effect upon contracts for building than those for
other purposes.

Where work is being done for a partnership, its dissolution does
not affect the lien on the property. If the firm orders improvements on the land of one, the claim is a lien upon the land as well
as a debt of the firm.[1]

Where, after contract, the partnership is dissolved, and the remaining member continues on, in and completes the work, the partnership character continues in him so far as to enable enforcement of
the lien and collection of the debt. If one dies, the survivor can
prosecute the lien in the name of the firm for the use and benefit of
himself.

It has been held that where one makes a contract to furnish materials and takes in a partner for future work, only, and they continue
to fill the contract, that a judgment could not be rendered for one
for what was due him, for the firm for what was due it in the same
action. Justice Walker dissented, and held there was an implied
contract with the firm. This is unquestionably the case under the
law at present, but would require proceedings from filing claim to
final action to be separate.[2]

The individual should sue for the amount due him, the firm for
the amount due it, having, in the same way, previously filed claims
or served notice, as their position as original or sub-contractor required. It would be the safer course for the new partnership, by
arrangement between themselves, to have the one who originally
made the contract complete it in his own name, and enforce the lien
in the same manner.

§ 224. **Who must be made parties defendant.**—In proceedings
under this act, all persons interested in the subject-matter of the
suit, or in the premises intended to be sold, may, on application to
the court wherein the suit is pending, be made or become parties at
any time before final judgment.[3]

Parties in interest, within the meaning of this act, shall include all
persons who may have any legal or equitable claim to the whole or
any part of the premises upon which a lien may be attempted to be
enforced under the provisions of this act.[4]

When any defendant resides or has gone out of the State, or on
due inquiry cannot be found, or is concealed within this State, so

[1] Croskey v. N. W. Mfg Co., 48 Ill. 481
[2] Roberts v. Gates, 64 Ill. 374
[3] Sec. 12, act 1874, as amended
[4] Sec. 13, act 1874, as amended.

that process cannot be served upon him, the complainant or petitioner may cause notice to be given to him in like manner and upon the same conditions as provided in suits in chancery [1]

For the purpose of bringing all parties in interest before the court, the court shall permit amendments to any part of the pleadings, and may issue process, make all orders requiring parties to appear, and requiring notice to be given, that are or may be authorized in proceedings in chancery, and shall have the same power and jurisdiction over the parties and subject, and the rules of practice and proceedings in such cases shall be the same as in other cases in chancery, except as is otherwise provided in this act [2]

If other liens or incumbrances exist by mortgage, judgment or otherwise, the parties holding them must be made parties, or their rights cannot be affected [3]

Failing by the exercise of reasonable diligence to ascertain whom they are, they may be described and proceeded against as unknown holders of such notes or securities, as in other cases in chancery, and their rights adjudicated in the same manner. [4]

Where previous trust deeds or mortgages exist, the *cestui que trust*, as well as trustees, must be made a party, or he will not be bound by any decree that may be obtained [5] But if the *cestui que trust* is made a party, the trustee not, and he allows a trial on the merits of the case, without objecting to the non-joinder of the trustee, he and those claiming under him will be bound by the decree rendered [6]

§ 225 **Active trust. Cestui que trust not necessary party.**—
Where the trust is an active one, imposing on the trustee the duty of receiving, controlling and managing the trust fund for the benefit of the *cestui que trust*, the rule is different, and such trustee only may be made a party; but where the trustee is interposed between borrower and lender merely for the purpose of enabling the lender to obtain payment through the exercise by the trustee of the

[1] Sec 7, act 1874, as amended
[2] Sec 9, act 1874, as amended
[3] McLagan v Brown, 11 Ill 519, Kelly v Chapman, 13 id 530, Steigleman v McBride, 17 id 300, Williams v Chapman, id 423, Raymond v Ewing, 26 id 329, Radcliff v Noyes, 43 id 318 Lomax v Dore, 45 id 379 Clark v Moore, 64 id 273, Mehrle v Dunne 75 id 239, Dunphy v Riddle, 86 id 22, Crowl v Nagle, id 437, Clark v Manning, 90 id 380, 95 id 580, Price v Hudson, 125 id 285, Rene v Sullivan, 1 Bradw 94, Ridenour v Shideler, 5 id 190, Lamb v Campbell, 19 id 272
[4] Phoenix Mut Life Ins Co v Batchen, 6 Bradw 621, Bannon v Thayer, 124 Ill 421 24 App 428, Columbia B & L Asso 25 id 429
[5] Note 5, sec 224: Paddock v Stout, 121 Ill 571, 22 App 65
[6] Bennit v Star Mining Co , 119 Ill 9

powers conferred upon him by the mortgage or deed of trust, and the trustee can only be called upon to act in case of default of the borrower in performing the conditions of the trust deed, both the trustee and *cestui que trust* are necessary parties[1]

§ 226. **Heirs.** — Where the owner dies, his heirs, having a direct interest in the land, as well as executor or administrator, are necessary parties

§ 227 **Defunct corporations not necessary parties.** — Where a corporation, with whom a contract was made to erect a building, ceases to exist, as a church, and it becomes disorganized, it is not necessary to make such body a defendant on petition to establish a mechanic's lien[2]

§ 228 **Unpaid claimants necessary parties** — A sub-claimant seeking to enforce a lien as against the owner for labor or materials, is required to make all unpaid persons parties, who have done work or furnished materials for such building, defendants ; also, subsequent purchasers, mortgagees, judgment-creditors, and any others who have record liens of any nature upon the property, no matter when their rights attached to the property. If it appears from the record there are such who have not been made parties, the decree will be reversed on appeal[3]

Those whose claims are not yet due and for that reason unable to institute suit, are necessary parties, and where such suit is brought by another, may come in whether made parties or not, and be allowed their claims with a reduction of interest from the time allowed to when due[4]

§ 229. **Those not made parties not cut off** — Where a purchaser contracted for the erection of a house, but previously conveyed the property to a trustee to secure the balance of the purchase money, the mechanic filed a bill to enforce his lien, making the purchaser alone a party, and obtained a decree under which the mechanic became the purchaser at the judicial sale, subsequently the trustee sold the premises under the trust deed, and A became the purchaser. It was held the sale under the mechanic's lien decree did not affect the interests of the trustee or *cestui que trust*, inasmuch as they were not made parties, and the title of A. was superior, claiming

---

[1] McGraw v Bayard, 96 Ill 146
[2] Jennings v Hinkle, 81 Ill 183
[3] Mehrle v Dunne 75 Ill 239 note 5 sec 224
[4] Sec 16, act 1874 as amended, Cox v Keiser 15 Bradw 432, Sharkey v Miller, 69 Ill 560, McGraw v Bayard, 96 id 146, North Pres Church v Jevne, 32 id 214

under a prior lien to that of the mechanic All persons interested
in the premises should have been made parties to the proceeding to
enforce the lien.[1]

A sale under a decree to which a person in interest is not made a
party is a nullity as to him The same rule prevails as judgment-
creditors[2] If a prior incumbrancer is not made a party, the subsequent lienholder takes subject to his claim.[3]

Where a purchaser under a prior judgment was not made a party
to proceedings to enforce a mechanic's lien, it was held that a subsequent sale under the mechanic's lien decree conferred no title on
the purchaser, and an action in ejectment by the latter could not be
maintained.[3]

Where suit is brought to cancel a deed for fraud against one who
has built on the property conveyed, and suits are pending by
mechanics to enforce liens for such building, those mechanics are
indispensable parties to the proceeding, and it is improper for the
court to proceed with the case until they are made such and their
interests ascertained[4]

Where the petition alleges the husband has an interest in the land
and the demurrer, being general, admits it, he is a necessary party[5]

§ 230 **Improper parties.** — Those who have been paid,[6] the wife,
where only the husband's own fee or his dower estate in her property
is sought to be subjected to the lien,[7] and the landlord, where only
the tenant's estate is sought to be subjected to the lien,[8] are not only
unnecessary, but improper parties In such case the wife has no
estate to entitle her to become a party, either on her own or other
application, nor can her interest be affected if she be made a party
and defaults.[7]

The same rule prevails as to the landlord.[8]

§ 231. **Those acquiring interest pendente lite proper, but not
necessary parties.** — A new party acquiring interest *pendente lite*
is a proper, but not necessary party,[9] and may, if he please, make

[1] Lomax v Dore, 45 Ill. 379, Kelly v Chapman, 13 id 530, McLagan v. Brown,
11 id 519
[2] Clark v. Moore, 64 Ill 273
[3] McLagan v Brown, 11 Ill 519, Williams v Chapman, 17 Ill 423
[4] Radcliff v Noyes, 43 Ill 318
[5] Greenleaf v Beebe, 80 Ill 520
[6] McLagan v Brown, 11 Ill 519 Kelly v Chapman, 13 id 530· North Presbyterian Church v Jevne, 32 id 214, Lomax v Dore, 45 id 379, McGraw v
Bayard, 96 id 146
[7] Gove v Cather, 23 Ill 634, Schnell v Clements, 73 id 613 (What is known
at common law as estate by curtesy is dower in Illinois.)
[8] Judson v Stephens, 75 Ill 255
[9] Phœnix Mut Life Ins. Co v Batchen, 6 Bradw 621.

himself a party by supplemental bill He cannot by petition pray to be admitted as a party defendant Where he is made a defendant, his position is the same as his assignor, and he can avail himself of the answer of his assignor.[1]

§ 232 **Amendments.** — For the purpose of bringing all parties in interest before the court, the court shall permit amendments to any part of the pleadings, and may issue process, make all orders requiring parties to appear, and requiring notice to be given, that are or may be authorized in proceedings in chancery, and shall have the same power and jurisdiction over the parties and subject, and the rules of practice and proceedings in such cases shall be the same as in other cases in chancery, except as is otherwise provided in this act.[2]

A material and substantial amendment of the petition within ten days of the commencement of the term entitles the defendant to a continuance, and it is error in the court to refuse it.[3]

An amendment to obviate variance, or for other reason, may be made on the hearing If the opposite party is surprised thereby, a continuance should be allowed him.[4]

§ 233 **When a new cause of action.** — An amendment of a petition, although technically it may set out a new contract, will not expose the cause of action to the bar of the statute limiting the time for filing a petition.[5]

Where suit was brought in the name of a firm, and the petition set out a contract with the firm, the amendment set out a contract with the individual member of that firm, who, after its dissolution, made the contract, and also material changes in the description of the contract in the original petition, making it technically a different contract, but the same cause of action against the same parties was set out in the amendment, and the contract therein was the same one upon which the action was originally intended to be brought; the court held that such amendment was not a commencement of the suit; that there was an error in the recital of the contract in the first instance; that it did not differ in principle from any other amendment of a pleading by which an error in the description of a contract is corrected; that the suit was commenced on the date of filing the original petition; that in applying the statute of limitations the iden-

[1] Lunt v Stephens, 75 Ill 507
[2] Sec 9 act 1874 as amended
[3] Link v Architectural Iron Works, 24 Ill 551
[4] Downey v O Donnell 92 Ill 559, Driver v Ford, 90 id 595, Martin v Eversal, 36 id 222, Littlefield v Schmoldt, 24 App 624
[5] Phœnix Mut Life Ins Co v Batchen, 6 Bradw. 621.

tity of the original and amended petitions is not to be determined by rigid and technical rules, but is a matter in the discretion of the court[1]

So where there is a suit by a firm, change of firm who carry out the contract, all parties agreeing, and a new petition by the new firm, the first suit filed was held to be the commencement of the suit[2]

§ 234. **Summons, service of, personal.** — Upon the filing of such bill or petition, summons shall issue and service thereof be had, as in suits in chancery[3] The fact that the summons is at law, the case is on the chancery side of the docket is no ground of objection[4]

In case alias summons be issued, only the names of those not served need be included[4]

§ 235 **Service by publication.** — When any defendant resides or has gone out of the State, or on due inquiry cannot be found, or is concealed within this State, so that process cannot be served upon him, the complainant or petitioner may cause notice to be given to him in like manner, and upon the same conditions as provided in suits in chancery[5] Service by publication is equal to personal service[6]

Publication is governed by chancery practice, and may be made by the clerk on proper affidavit, an order of court not being necessary therefor, and judgment *in personam* may be rendered against one summoned by publication[7]

§ 236. **Appearance by solicitor.** — Where defendants appear by solicitor, neither summons nor publication is necessary,[8] but where one is not served, such appearance is regarded as only for those served[9]

The object of service of process or publication is to bring parties before the court Where all of the defendants appear it is immaterial whether they have been served, or publication has been made, as they are in court by appearance Where the record recites that the parties came by their solicitors, it will be presumed that all, and not a part only, of the parties entered their appearance, as well those as those who have not been served[8]

---

[1] Phœnix Mut Life Ins Co v Batchen, 6 Bradw 621
[2] Work v Hall, 79 Ill 196
[3] Sec 6, act 1871 as amended
[4] Reed v Boyd, 84 Ill 66
[5] Sec 7, act 1874, as amended
[6] Gould v Garrison, 48 Ill 258
[7] James v Hambleton, 42 Ill 308
[8] Radcliff v Noyes, 43 Ill 318, see *per contra*, note 9
[9] Gardner v Hall, 29 Ill 277

§ 237. **Answer.**—The answer must be under oath unless the petitioner waives the requisition therefor.[1]

Where the answer is sworn to, it has weight as evidence so far as responsive to the petition, the same as the testimony of a witness,[2] and is not equal to,[3] but must be overcome by two witnesses, or one and strong corroborating circumstances.[4]

Where the oath is waived, though sworn to, it is not evidence, and has no other weight than answer not sworn to.[4]

To be used as evidence it must be responsive to the allegations of the petition, fully so, but no more.[5] Answer of set-off is not responsive, nor payment to a third party, unless averred and sworn to be at the request of the plaintiff.[6] It is not evidence where it sets up a defense, and should be objected to, and answer of no means to determine the correctness of the items charged, and, therefore, deny them, is evasive, such mental reservation as equity abhors, and equal to admission of the facts charged. Nor is on information and belief sufficient to make it evidence.[6] New matter set up in the answer is regarded as surplusage and mere pleading and cannot be used as evidence.[6]

§ 238. **Damages cannot be recovered.**—It cannot be made a cross bill for damages. Such can be set up as matter for defense only.[7]

After the defendant has answered the allegations of the petition, there is no objection to stating new matter in defense, entitling him to such relief as he would be entitled to on a cross bill, nor need such be detached from his answer. It is not vicious to reply in the same paper to one plea and demur to another, or in the same manner to plead to one count and demur to another.[8]

If an owner be apprehensive that the lien suit is brought to cloud his title and force him to settle an illegal claim, and that the same might be dismissed, allowing the claim filed with the clerk to remain as a cloud on the title until the period for foreclosing same had

---

[1] Sec. 10, act 1874, as amended, Kimball v Cook, 1 Gilm 123
[2] Kimball v Cook, 1 Gilm 423, Morrison v Stewart, 24 Ill 24 Moore v Smith, id 513, Gregg v Renfrews, id 621, Martin v Eversal, 36 id 222, Tracy v. Rogers, 69 id 662, L S & M S R R v McMillan 84 id 208
[3] Morrison v Stewart, 24 Ill 24
[4] Clark v Boyle, 51 Ill 104, Tracy v Rogers. 69 id 662
[5] Lake Shore & M S R R v McMillan, 84 Ill 208.
[6] Gregg v Renfrews, 24 Ill 621
[7] Garrett v Stevenson, 3 Gilm 261
[8] Cunningham v Ferry, 74 Ill 426
[9] McCarthy v Neu, 93 Ill 455
[10] Thielman v Carr, 75 Ill 385

158   MECHANIC'S LIEN LAW.

passed, he could make his answer a cross bill to clear such cloud
from his title, prevent the aggravation of delay by such dismissal
and force the trial of the case

§ 239 **Cross bills not necessary in mechanic's lien proceeding.**—Where other lienholders are made parties, their answers are
in the nature of cross bills and should set forth their rights as original
petitions, though it is not necessary to make them cross bills [1] When
brought before the court, all are actors, whether plaintiff or defendant, their rights are statutory and subject to the same strict construction in their adjudication [2]

The proceedings under the statute is to subject the property, not
to the payment of the petitioner's claim alone, but to make it a fund
for the satisfaction of all the liens established, and a party, under
his answer, whether brought into the court by service, or who inter-
venes, is required to prove his claim, and, when proved, is entitled
to share in the fund. It is not necessary for such defendant to file
a formal cross bill Such co-claimant, as a prior incumbrancer, may
make his answer a cross bill and ask affirmative relief [1]

The fact of a lienholder or claimant being made a party defendant by a plaintiff in a suit to enforce a mortgage or lien does not
release him from the obligation of setting forth his claim in his answer
as fully as in an original petition An answer by a mechanic setting
up the claim of his lien while not a cross bill, is in the nature of one.
He can make it a cross bill against the plaintiff, or any co-defendant [3]
He is at liberty to defeat the claim of the original petitioner, whether he
be incumbrancer or lien claimant, if he choose, and can thereby better
secure his own claim, or increase his proportional share of the common fund arising from the sale of the property, or from what is due
from the owner by decreasing the number of claims and claimants
who can share in it.[4] Therefore, his own cause of action should be
set forth with sufficient breadth and particularity to sustain the case,
if they be defeated In these proceedings, to a large extent, every
claimant of a mechanic or other lien upon or interested in the property, is an Ishmael, every claimant an antagonist Any lien claimant can interpose the same objections to a co claimant's lien that the
owner could, can even attack an incumbrance or lien where the
owner would be estopped to do so The collection of his own debt
is what each one is after, and, if by defeating any, or all other

[1] Thielman v Carr, 75 Ill 385
[2] Sutherland v Ryerson 24 Ill 518.
[3] Culver v. Elwell, 73 Ill 536
[4] Sec 18, act 1874, as amended

claims, he can better achieve this end, the statute gives him the privilege to do so [1]

§ 240. **Assignee of incumbrance must aver he held same at time the suit was begun** —The holder of trust deed or mortgage notes must aver that he held such at the time of the institution of the action [2] If the assignee of a mortgage indebtedness would protect himself under a proceeding for mechanic's lien, he must show that at the time of the institution of proceedings to enforce the lien he was in possession of the securities [2] In the absence of such proof, it will be presumed that they remained in the hands of the assignor until after the date of filing the petition for a lien [3]

§ 241 **Incumbrancer cannot by answer set up claim for materials furnished.**—Where a mortgagee sets up a claim for materials furnished, he must do so by cross bill, and not merely set up same in his answer setting up his mortgage claim [3] If the mortgage does not provide for repairs to be made by the mortgagee, his rights to recover therefor rest on the statute, as that of any other person, and must be so set forth to recover, by proper pleading, as well as be acquired by all the preceding steps necessary for an original or sub-claimant, whichever he may be [4]

§ 242 **Limitations must be pleaded** —If he be a prior or subsequent incumbrancer and seeks to make his a preferred claim to that of the petitioner, by reason of the limitations running in his favor, because not made a party in time, he must plead such to avail [5]

So where a trustee, but not the *cestui*, is made a party within the statutory period, and objection is not in any way set up in the lower court, it cannot be enforced on appeal, as the statute of limitations should have been pleaded or insisted upon, by the answer, to have entitled the party to the benefit of it [6]

§ 243. **Defense, how set up.**—There are no particular rules for setting up matters of defense The answer should set up the facts which the defendant relies upon therefor He may traverse the allegation of doing the work or furnishing the materials, the amount claimed; or set up that the work was not done in the period stated, or allowed by the statute, or waived by taking other security, or payment, or release, or damages in consequence of delay in, or de-

---
[1] Sec 18, act 1874, as amended
[2] Austin v Wohler, 5 Bradw 300, Phoenix Mut Life Ins Co v Batchen, 6 id 621
[3] Howett v Selby, 54 Ill 151
[4] Seiler v Schaefer, 40 App 71
[5] Gardner v Hall, 29 Ill 277
[6] Barstow v McLachlan 99 Ill 641

fective manner of the work " The pleadings should show whether
the issue be one of fact or of law

§ 244 **Defendant may buy outstanding title** — The defense
may depend entirely upon the claim set up, not upon the party's
original position who sets it up. There is no obstacle to the purchase by the defendant of a superior title to that of the complainant
from a person not a party, and the setting up of such title to defeat
the complainant's equities, though the party doing so is, as to his
other particular and personal claim, bound by the *lis pendens* [1]

A contract was made November 10, 1883, completed December
4, 1883, notes given, the last maturing in seven months, July 7,
1884, and suit to enforce the lien was brought December 27, 1884,
wherein one Dwen was made a party as holding some claim as purchaser, mortgagee, judgment creditor or otherwise   October 5,
1886, Dwen answered, claiming title in fee and pleading limitation
by reason of failure to bring suit within six months after maturity
of claim.   January 8, 1884, Darlow recovered judgment against
the owner, February 25, 1884, purchased the property in question
under said judgment; December 28, 1885, assigned the certificate
of purchase to Dwen, and the premises not being redeemed, the
sheriff executed a deed therefor to Dwen, January 12, 1886   The
court held, that as to Darlow's judgment the limitation began to
run July 7, 1884; that he not being made a party in time, the lien
was barred as to him; that Dwen, though a party, could assert the
rights of his assignor, Darlow, conferred upon him by his purchase.[1]

Between original contractor and owner plea of set-off, counter-
claim or other defense is allowable.   Between sub-contractor on the
one side, and original contractor *in personam* and owner *in rem*,
the original contractor can set up any matter of defense that he
could in a common-law action against him alone, and if he prove an
excess of indebtedness in his favor, recover a judgment against the
sub-contractor, but the owner could not.   The contractor would
have the right to make any defense that he could in any other ordinary action: the owner can only defeat the lien.

§ 245. **Averments in case of abandonment.** — In case of abandonment where the owner relies on the fact that the sums he has
paid the contractor before he abandoned the work, and the cost of
completing the building, amount to more than the contract price,
he must aver in his answer that the sum paid the contractor was due
when it was paid; that the aggregate liens sought to be foreclosed

---

[1] Douglas v Davies, 23 App 618

exceed the amount which was to be paid the contractor, and that the sum paid out by him after the abandonment by the contractor was paid to complete the building according to the terms of the contract[1]

The owner is not compelled to pay any thing to a sub-contractor when he is compelled to exhaust the original contract-price to complete the building, and such is a complete defense to the asserted liens,[2] except the ten per cent provided for by section 33 in favor of laborers.

§ 246. **Averments as to non-ownership.**—Where the ground had been built on without defendant's authority, is a good defense, but that defendant is not the owner of the ground at the time of institution of the action, without the allegation that he was not at the time the contract was made, would be bad[3]

§ 247. **Plea in abatement not good.** — Plea of other action in abatement is not good. In such case the proper method is to move to consolidate the causes[4]

§ 248. **Replication must be general.**— The plaintiff shall reply to the answer of the defendant and this pleading concludes the issues.[5] The general replication puts the entire answer in issue[6]

The owner should have opportunity to reply to the answers of parties brought in, for such are in the nature of cross-bills, and it is error to force him to trial without allowing opportunity to do so[7]

As in chancery cases, no rejoinder can be filed, the replication must, of course, be general, and hence if the answer sets up new matter, which requires to be admitted or avoided, or otherwise specially replied to, it must be done by amending the bill, and inserting the new matter in the charging part, and then explaining it, as in ordinary chancery cases.

Where a defendant filed a rejoinder to the plaintiff's replication and the plaintiff demurred thereto, it was held that the case stood on the bill, answer and replication; that the demurrer was filed to a paper that did not properly belong to the record; that in that state of the pleadings the court should have proceeded to the trial of the case[6]

---

[1] Biggs v Clapp 74 Ill 335, Morehouse v Moulding, id 322, Culver v Elwell 73 id 536
[2] Schultz v Hay, 62 Ill 157
[3] Austin v Wohler, 5 Bradw. 300.
[4] Thielman v Carr 75 Ill 385
[5] Sec 10, act 1874, as amended
[6] Shaeffer v Weed, 3 Gilm 511, Kimball v Cook, 1 id 423
[7] Culver v Elwell, 73 Ill 536, see, also, Linnemeyer v. Miller, 70 id, 344; Person v. Smith, 30 App 103

§ 249. Demurrer as in other chancery causes — Demurrers, general or special, under this statute may be availed of as in any other action, should be framed as in general practice, have the same effect, and are burdened with the same consequences. A general demurrer to the whole complaint cannot be sustained if it be good in part.

Where the statutory grounds for a lien, filing of the claim, giving of the notice, or lack of other facts sufficient to constitute a cause of action or ground of defense are omitted, a demurrer is the proper method to reach these defects, without the delay, cost and vexation of answer and trial.

Where the petition is for work or labor for which the statute does not give a lien, or by a party to whom a lien is not allowed, as a sub-claimant of a sub-claimant, a demurrer would be fatal   And some formal objections which might be fatal on demurrer are regarded as waived after pleading to the merits of the case.

Where a bill of review was brought, which was insufficient and defective in failing to bring before the court a complete copy of the bill and decree sought to be reviewed, and the defendant failed to demur to the same, it was held advantage could not be taken of the defect on appeal [1]

If the petition does not state a time for completion and payment, and is not demurred to, but answered, a trial is had and the proof shows that the time for completion and payment are within the statutory period, it is too late to object to such defects in the court appealed to   Such defects should be demurred to in the lower court.[2]

If a prior incumbrancer is not made a party, the defendant should demur to the bill, if he thinks such a necessary party   A demurrer for want of proper parties must show on its face the specific ground of demurrer.   Claiming in an answer in a general way the advantages of a demurrer will not present the question of want of proper parties.[3]

Failing to aver the filing of the statement with the clerk of the Circuit Court is a fatal omission in a petition by an original claimant and reached by a general demurrer.[4]

[1] Judson v Stephens, 75 Ill. 255
[2] Brown v. Lowell, 79 Ill 484, Warren v Harris, 2 Gilm 307, Heiman v Schroeder, 74 Ill. 158.
[3] Portones v. Badenoch, 132 Ill 377
[4] Boals v Intrup. 40 App 62, Shinn v. Matheny, 48 id. 135; Campbell v Jacobson, 46 id 287, 145 Ill. 389

A petition will not be demurrable because it does not show the parties for whom the building was erected to be the owners of the land, since under the law the interest, whatever it may be, of a party in possession who makes the improvement, may be sold, a purchaser taking the title as against him [1]

A demurrer on the ground that other suit at law is pending in the same or other court between the same parties and for the same cause of action is improper ; and also where parties in pending suits to foreclose a lien intervene in another for the same purpose. The proper course in the latter case being a motion to consolidate the different suits [2]

A demurrer to a cross-bill for damages is properly sustained. Such are recoverable only at law, not in suits under this act [3]

§ 250. **Suits on chancery docket** — Suits instituted under the provisions of this act must be placed upon the chancery docket, and stand for trial as other suits in chancery [4] The trial may be by the court, or by a jury under the direction of the court, as the court may direct, or the parties agree, [5] and oral evidence may be heard, as well as other, by the court, though trying as a chancery case

The finding of the jury is merely advisory, which the court may disregard, set aside, or correct, if incompatible with the testimony. This action is of the court's own motion, and doing or not doing, is not error to appeal from [6]

When there are several lien claimants entitled to participate in the fund, in order to find the amount due each claimant, if it be provided that a jury shall pass upon them, it is the better practice to submit each claim to a distinct jury, as if it were a separate proceeding; but where there are few claimants, and there is no complication, it would not probably be objectionable to submit all the claims to the same jury. [7]

§ 251. **Consolidation of cases.** — Contrary to general chancery practice, which is opposed to the consolidation of different cases having different parties and involving different rights, where there are different lien suits by the original and sub-claimant against the owner, both relating to the same subject matter, the court should

---

[1] Steigleman v McBride 17 Ill 300.
[2] Thielman v Carr, 75 Ill 385
[3] McCarthy v Neu, 93 Ill 455
[4] Sec. 8, act 1874 as amended
[5] Sec 10, act 1874, as amended
[6] Sharkey v Miller, 69 Ill 560· Kimball v Cook, 1 Gilm 423, Garrett v Stevenson, 3 id 261, Schnell v Clements, 73 Ill. 613.
[7] Power v. McCord, 36 Ill 214

order the same consolidated, and where such suits are pending in different courts, the court will on motion order all consolidated, and either transfer the suit before it to the other court, or order suits there transferred to it [1]

§ 252 **Trial should be prompt.**— Parties whose issues are made up are entitled to be promptly heard, whether others who assert distinct claims are ready for trial or not.[2]

In no case shall the want of preparation for trial of one claim delay the trial in respect to others, but trial shall be had upon issues between such parties as are prepared, without reference to issues between other parties; and when one creditor shall have obtained a decree or judgment for the amount due, the court may order a sale of the premises on which the lien operates, or a part thereof, so as to satisfy the judgment, provided, that the court may, for good cause shown, delay making any order of sale or distribution until the rights of all parties in interest are ascertained and settled by the court.[2]

§ 253. **Decree** —The court's remedial power is predicated solely upon the existence of a statutory lien, exercised only upon statutory ground.

The court must first decree a lien. If no lien is decreed there can be no decree for any thing [3]

Where property becomes divested of a mechanic's lien by reason of a sale under a prior incumbrance, so that it cannot be sold to satisfy the mechanic's demand against his employer, no decree should be entered, except for a dismissal of the petition. In such case it is error to render any decree against the party for whom the work was done or materials furnished [a]

Where a contract is made with the owner of real estate for the furnishing of materials and labor to improve the property, pending a bill to foreclose a prior mortgage on the same premises, a decree and sale under the bill will cut off all rights of the mechanic or materialman for a lien, and a bill to enforce the lien would have to be dismissed.[a]

The decree is the final administration of this general assignment *in rem*, or wrecked estate, enforced on the contract and under the statute. It should adjudge, therefore, the existence of contract rela-

[1] Thielman v Carr, 75 Ill 385, Schnell v Clements, 73 id 613
[2] Sec 20, act 1874, as amended
[3] Green v. Sprague, 120 Ill 416ᵃ; Martin v Swift, id 488, O'Brien v Graham, 33 App 546, Sprague v. Green, 18 id. 476, Swift v. Martin, 20 id. 515, 27 id. 117.

tions between the parties and their statutory performance[1] It should show from what time this lien attached. For a decree giving a lien prior to the date of the contract is erroneous[2] If, however, third parties are not affected thereby, this is not cause for reversal[2] The petition, proof and decree must correspond[3] Being a final administration of the estate affected, it must partition some among all those interested in it according to their interests, turn it into money, by which alone this can be done, give a clear title against all parties to the action to whomsoever pays that money for it, and ascertain and settle the interests of all parties before it, before ordering sale, or the decree will be erroneous[4] If it appears by the pleadings, or is disclosed, that there are parties interested who are not made parties, a decree without having them made parties and settling their interests is erroneous[4] It is no error to find the amount due one party and not order a sale of the property until other interests are adjusted[5]

The correct practice is not to render a decree until the rights of all claimants are found and determined.[5] It is improper to find the amount due one claimant, and decree a sale, without passing upon the rights of other claimants who have been made parties, and who may be entitled *pro rata* to the proceeds[a] If some of the incumbrances be prior, some junior to the mechanic's liens, the decree should declare the order of their payment.[6] The statute contemplates that all parties interested in the property shall be made parties. This makes it the duty of the court to adjudicate upon the rights of all parties, and direct the application of the proceeds of the sale to be made to such in proportion to their several amounts, and that the sale may convey an unclouded title[6]

Where there are conflicting claims to priority of payment out of the proceeds of the land about to be sold to satisfy the liens upon it, the court, in order to prevent the danger of sacrificing the property by discouraging creditors from bidding, should determine the priorities, and it is error merely to decree a sale and direct the proceeds to be brought into court without so doing[4]

---

[1] Seiler v Schaefer, 40 App 74, N P Church v Jevne, 32 Ill 214
[2] Nibbe v. Brauhn, 24 Ill 268
[3] Seiler v. Schaefer, 40 App 74, North Pres Church v Jevne, 32 Ill 214
[4] Power v. McCord, 36 Ill 214a Martin v Eversal, id. 222, Radcliff v Noyes, 43 id 318, Lomax v Dore, 45 id 379, Tracy v Rogers, 69 id 662 Lunt v. Stephens 75 id 507, Race v Sullivan, 1 Bradw 94 Ogle v Murray, 3 id 343, Clark v Manning, 4 id 649, 90 Ill 380, Miller v Ticknor, 7 Bradw 393.
[5] Sec. 20, act 1874, as amended, Martin v Eversal, 36 Ill 222
[6] Croskey v Corey, 48 Ill 442, Lunt v Stephens, 75 id. 507

Where the petition against two parties sought a discovery of their interests, and neither answered or filed any defence, and, in consequence, defaults were entered against them, the decree was held not erroneous, because it did not state the respective interests of the parties If a cloud be thus cast upon the title of a party who has neglected to make a discovery of his interest, he must bear the consequences of his own *laches*.[1]

§ 254. **Apportionment. Distribution of proceeds.** — The court in its decree must not only settle all interests and priorities, but apportion the proceeds of the sale in accordance therewith. This apportionment must be *pro rata*,[2] after decreeing the payment in full of labor claims[3]

Before distributing the proceeds of the sale, the court must require proof to be taken and ascertain therefrom, the value of the land prior to the improvements, the value added by the improvements, and as the prior mortgagees have a preferred lien on the land, the mechanics on the improvements, the decree should direct the payment of the proceeds on that basis, that portion arising from the sale of the land, first to the prior mortgagees, if any surplus, then to the mechanics, and *per contra* as to that portion arising from sale of the improvements[4] and the surplus, if any, after all is paid, to the owner.[5]

Though it be apparent when the sale is ordered that the property will not sell for enough to pay all claims, the court cannot decree otherwise. For instance, in such case it cannot decree the surplus, after payment of the prior mortgagees, to the claimants, or any of them.[6] It may not in the decree direct the disposition of the surplus, but reserve that direction for further order.[7]

This requirement which makes it obligatory on the court to distribute the proceeds, does not render it necessary that the decree should determine at first in what proportion such proceeds should be paid. The fund would still remain under the control of the court, and might by a subsequent order be directed to be paid over to the

[1] Gould v Garrison, 48 Ill 258
[2] Sec 15, act 1874, as amended, Buchter v Dew, 39 Ill. 40, Tracy v Rogers, 69 id. 662, Mehrle v Dunne, 75 id 239, Lunt v Stephens, id. 507, Ogle v Murray, 3 Bradw. 343
[3] Sec 34, act 1874, as amended
[4] Secs 156-161, *ante,* N. P Church v. Jevne, 32 Ill 214, Croskev v. N W Mfg Co , 48 id 481, Dingledine v Hershman, 53 id 280, Grundeis v Hartwell, 90 id 324, Miller v. Ticknor, 7 Bradw 393
[5] N P. Church v Jevne, 32 Ill. 214, Woodburn v Gifford, 66 id 285, Hickox v Greenwood, 94 id 266, Powell v Rogers, 105 id 318, adv , 1 Bradw 631, Phœnix Mut Life Ins Co v Batchen, 6 id 621
[6] Phœnix Mut Life Ins Co v. Batchen, 6 Bradw 621.
[7] Kelly v Chapman, 13 Ill 500

parties as they should show themselves entitled to it [1], [2]. A decree ordering the payment to a mere lien creditor of the entire surplus proceeds after satisfying other lien creditors is erroneous. This surplus belongs to the owner. He should be ascertained and it be ordered to be paid over to him. The fact that there was evidence tending to show that the property was not worth enough to satisfy the liens will not change the rule. What the property will bring at a sale cannot be known judicially, until a sale is made [1]. So, where there is a subsequent mortgage, the decree should direct that the surplus be paid to the mortgagee, or held subject to further order of the court.[3]

Where a decree enforcing a mechanic's lien under which a party to the record has acquired title by purchase, has been reversed and a decree entered foreclosing a prior mortgage on the same property, and ordering a sale, it is error to direct that the surplus arising from the sale, after the payment of the lien debt and the mortgage debt, be brought into court. Such surplus should be ordered to be paid to the purchaser under a prior sale, to apply upon the improvements made by him upon the premises, when the original owner and debtor makes no defense and claims nothing.[3]

§ 255. Value of both land and improvements must be found.

-- Finding the value of improvements only, not of the land is, erroneous; that of both must be found. Where F. held a first, G., a second mortgage, and after both the improvements were made, and the court ordered the property sold, out of the proceeds to pay, first, the mechanic, then F., then G., the decree was reversed, and it held that the value of both land and improvements should be found, that F. had a first lien on the land, second on the improvements, G., a second lien on the land, third on the improvements, the mechanic a first lien on the improvements and a lien on the land after both F. and G., and in accordance with such priorities the proceeds of the sale should be apportioned [4]

Proof as to value of property for apportionment may be taken after sale,[5] but such proof as to the value of the land should be confined to its value at the date of the contract regardless of such sale [6]

§ 256. Judgment for deficiency only. — There should be no

[1] Phœnix Mut Life Ins Co v Batchen, 6 Bradw. 621
[2] Kelly v Chapman, 13 Ill 530
[3] Rogers v Powell 1 Bradw 631, Powell v Rogers, 105 Ill 318
[4] Grundeis v Hartwell 90 Ill 324 North Pres Church v Jevne, 32 id 214.
[5] Croskey v N W Mfg Co 48 Ill 481
[6] Sec 17, act 1874, as amended.

decree for a personal judgment, except for what deficiency may
exist after the sale of the property. In a proceeding by original or
sub-claimant to enforce a lien, it is error to order a general execution before the property is sold. That writ is only issuable for the
balance that the sale fails to realize,[1] and must be ordered against
those liable at law for the debt.[2]

§ 257 **Rights of sub-sub-claimant in fund.** — The court may
adjust the rights of all parties before it,[3] and though a sub-claimant
of a sub-claimant has no lien and cannot maintain action against any
other than his employer for his debt, if the fund belonging to his
employer be in the hands of the court it may order him paid out
of that fund, if he be a party and ask such relief[4]

§ 258 **Only out of what due original paid sub-contractor.** —
Where suits are by original and sub-claimants, the decree should
direct payment to be made to the sub-claimants out of the amount
found due the original contractor up to the limit of such amount.[6]
Where the suit by a sub-contractor is against the owner personally,
judgment is enforceable only by general execution, not by special
execution against the specific improved property.[6]

§ 259. **Various tracts in same suit.** — If the suit be against different tracts, though between the same parties, or where the buildings are separate and distinct and susceptible to division, the decree
should not be *in solido*, but for the sale of each tract for what was
due for labor done, materials furnished on each respectively.[7]

Where the lien is sought against several separate buildings, the
decree must be against each for the value of the work and materials
on it, and not against all for the aggregate value of the work and
materials on all [a]

Where there are several houses on several lots, and various claims
on each, each house and lot must be sold for what is due on it alone,
not one sold for what is due on others beside it[8] If the lots are
contiguous, and the entire block is compact, forms one building

---

[1] Bouton v McDonough County, 84 Ill 384, First Baptist Church of Chicago v.
Andrews, 87 id 172, Green v Sprague, 120 id. 416, Martin v Swift, 120 id 488.
As to judgment on stipulation, see Johnson v Estabrook, 84 id. 75.
[2] Race v Sullivan, 1 Bradw 94
[3] Henderson v Connelly 123 Ill 98, 23 App 601
[4] Newhall v Kastens, 70 Ill 156
[5] Schnell v Clements, 73 Ill 613
[6] Secs 37-38, act 1874, as amended, First Baptist Church v Andrews, 87 Ill 172;
Powell v Rogers, 105 id 318
[7] Steiglemen v McBride, 17 Ill 300 (a) Culver v Elwell, 73 id 536,(a) Major v.
Collins, 11 Bradw 658, Van Lone v Whittemore, 19 id 447
[8] McGraw v. Bayard, 96 Ill 146, Bayard v. McGraw, 1 Bradw 134.

under one roof, it is proper to decree the lien against the entire block [1]

If more than one building be on the entire tract of land, the contracts be between the same parties, though made and to be completed at different times, the decree may be against the land for both debts, need not be separate for each [2]

Where one contract was made July 30, 1872, to commence August 2, 1872, be completed June 1, 1873, the other October 30, 1872, to be completed May 1, 1873, the same parties contracting, the buildings to be on the same tract of land, a decree to sell the entire property was held proper. [2]

§ 260. **Must not sell improvements without land.** — It is improper to decree a sale of the house and not of the ground, or to pay a part of the debts, [3] but not for the owner's interest, instead of the land, nor for the sale of his leasehold interest [4]

Where the petition alleges that the work was done for the equitable owner, and the legal owner is made a party, and the court decree's a sale, the purchaser gets a good title to the whole property [5]

The court may direct the sale of the estate of all parties before it having such an interest in the property as is affected by the lien. But it is not compelled to do so. The better practice is not to do so, if the object of the statute — payment of the debt — can be attained by decreeing a sale of the interests of those parties only who owe the debt for which the lien attached. [6]

§ 261. **Must show it against right property.** — The decree must show that it is against the right property. If, for instance, the suit be to enforce liens for four houses built on five lots, it must show on what lots they were built [7]

§ 262. **Decree for sub-contractor must be against both original contractor and owner.** — The decree, where suit is against the owner and original contractor, must be against both, not against the owner alone, and not to render any finding against the original contractor in such cases is error. [8]

§ 263 **Must show materials were bought for property subject to decree.** — It must show that the material was bought for

[1] Orr v N W Mut Life Irs Co, 86 Ill 260, James v Hambleton, 42 id 308, Culver v Ellwell, 73 id 536
[2] St Louis Nat Stock Yards v O'Reilly, 85 Ill 546
[3] North Pres. Church v Jevne, 32 Ill 214
[4] Kidder v Aholtz, 36 Ill 478, Reed v Boyd, 84 id 66
[5] Lewis v Rose, 82 Ill 574
[6] Secs 21-22, act 1874, as amended, Kidder v Aholtz, 36 Ill 478.
[7] Maxwell v Koeritz, 35 App 300
[8] Culver v Elwell, 73 Ill 536
22

the lot against which the lien is decreed [1] But where the petition showed the defendant owned certain described lots, and the contract which was made part of the petition, showed the plaintiff was to furnish the materials for a house on defendant's lots in the same town, without describing them, and the petition claimed a lien on the lots described; the answer did not deny such ownership, and the proof showed the building upon the lots of defendant, but did not show he owned any other lots, it was held sufficient to authorize a decree for the sale of those lots in enforcement of the liens [2]

§ 264. **Defaults.**—If defendants do not answer on or before the day set for trial, default can be properly taken without waiting for second call of the docket, and setting it aside is wholly discretionary with the court ; [3] and the court may impose such conditions as it sees fit, if it does set it aside , [4] it cannot open the decree to allow set-off of other debt not connected with the matter [5]

Where a discovery of the interest of the parties defendant is sought, and they default, the whole property may be sold. [5]

Where the petition alleges that the house improved or built is upon a leasehold interest, and the owner of the fee is made a party and defaults, a decree ordering a sale of the house and leasehold interest is good [6]

Nor is a rule to plead necessary, before entering default and judgment *pro confesso*, when the defendant is summoned by publication [7]

If a demurrer is overruled, the court may properly render a decree *pro confesso* without ruling defendant to answer. [8]

A default admits only what the petition properly alleges, and no more If that petition omits any essential averment, it can be taken advantage of by motion in arrest of judgment, or on appeal. If, for instance, the petition omits to allege that the debt sued for was due and unpaid at the time of filing the same, the decree will be reversed on appeal. Such allegation is indispensable. [9] And if the petition aver no facts upon which a lien could be predicated, a default will not authorize a decree for a lien. [10]

---

[1] Croskey v Corey, 48 Ill 442.
[2] Lombard v Johnson, 76 Ill 599
[3] Thielmann v Burg, 73 Ill 293
[4] Freibroth v Mann, 70 Ill. 523
[5] Gould v Garrison, 48 Ill 258, Van Pelt v Dunfo l, 58 id 145, Fitzhugh v. Smith, 62 id 486, Topping v Brown, 63 id 349
[6] Reed v Boyd 84 Ill 66
[7] James v Hambleton 42 Ill 308
[8] Roach v Chapin, 27 Ill 194
[9] Thielmann v Burg, 73 Ill 293, Cronan v Frizell, 42 id 319.
[10] Seiler v Schaeffer, 40 App. 74.

§ 265 **Decree pro confesso is discretionary with court.**—
A decree *pro confesso* is, however, discretionary with the court, it
may require proof of the matters set forth in the petition[1]

Where exceptions to answer are sustained, and the remainder of
the answer presents no material issue, and the defendant makes no
further answer, a decree *pro confesso* is proper[2]

A default cannot be taken where the answer of the mortgagee is
on file. Decree in such case is erroneous, and will be reversed;[3]
nor can a decree be taken against the wife on default where the suit
is for a lien on the husband's property.[4]

Pendency of affidavit, and motion thereon for bond for costs, is
no excuse for not filing answer, and when not filed in proper time,
on account of the pendency thereof, default may be properly taken.[4]
Affidavit for costs is not favored, and the oath of the two parties in
regard thereto is held equal.[5]

§ 266. **Sale must be in accordance with decree.**— The officer
making the sale under the decree must conform strictly to it as to
time, terms of sale, mode of advertising, and interest of the party
to be sold[6]

If the sale is not made in pursuance of the decree, the court may
set it aside and order another sale   The sale may be by special
execution directed to the sheriff or a master.[7]

§ 267. **Sale to party to record set aside on reversal of
decree.**— Title acquired by sale under an erroneous decree is
divested by a reversal thereof, unless the property is bought by a
stranger without notice, and the court may vacate its decretal sale
as long as the property is held by a party to the proceedings.[8] But
the sale cannot be set aside where the purchaser is one not a party
to the record   The stranger to the proceedings who buys at a judicial sale is protected, if the court having jurisdiction orders the sale,
whatever irregularities may exist in those proceedings.[9] The court
has jurisdiction to set aside a sale as long as the title continues in
the parties to the proceedings. Being set aside, any claim may be
contested *de novo* [10]

---

[1] Thielmann v Burg, 73 Ill. 293, Cronan v Frizell, 42 id 319.
[2] Work v Hall, 79 Ill. 196
[3] Younger v Louks, 7 Bradw. 280
[4] Gove v Cather, 23 Ill 634
[5] Hamilton v Dunn, 22 Ill 259
[6] Gould v Garrison, 48 Ill 258
[7] Kelly v Chapman, 13 Ill 530, Lubliner v Yeomans, 65 id 305
[8] Powell v Rogers, 105 Ill 318
[9] Dingledine v. Hershman, 53 Ill 280, Topping v Brown, 63 id 349.
[10] Clark v. Moore, 64 Ill. 273.

§ 268 **When court may set decree aside.**—The court may set aside its decree to enforce a superior or equal lien,[1] but after a decree cannot incorporate evidence not heard or offered on the hearing [2]

It is improper for a court on its own motion to set aside a decree of a former term [3]

An amendment to a petition and a decree thereon after a trial of a mechanic's lien suit, *nunc pro tunc*, without notice, is improper The probability of it working injustice is sufficient to secure a reversal [4]

§ 269. **When bound by erroneous decree.**—The party who procures a decree is bound by its terms, where he allows others to act on the faith of it

Where, a grantor reserved a lien for purchase money and the decree ordered the property sold subject thereto, and the notes of the vendor were purchased on the faith of such decree giving them a prior lien to the mechanic's lien, it was held the mechanic could not take advantage of the error in his own decree.[5]

Where after finding the value of the land and the improvements and decreeing the property to be sold it was ordered that the prior mortgage be paid first out of the proceeds, and the mechanic's lien claimants allowed the property to be sold as the decree ordered, it was held, that after the making of such sale it was too late to object to such order of payment. The only relief in such case would be to order a resale of the property   In this case, a stranger having purchased, it was held neither a resale could be ordered, nor could the prior mortgagees so paid be compelled to refund any portion of what was paid them, as they had bid in the property on the faith of that decree [6]

§ 270 **Costs.**— The statute controls the matter of costs, and the rule regarding costs in chancery does not apply in lien cases.[7] By the statute, as between original parties, creditors claiming liens, and the person against whom the lien is intended to be enforced, the costs abide the event of the suit, and must be adjudged in favor of the successful party, and the costs as between the creditors aforesaid, in contests relative to each other's claims, shall be subject to the order of the court, and the same rule prevails in respect to costs growing out of proceedings against and between incumbrances [7]

---

[1] Clark v Moore, 64 Ill 273
[2] L S & M S R R v McMillan, 84 Ill. 208.
[3] Bush v Connelly, 33 Ill. 447
[4] Littlefield v. Schmoldt, 24 App 624.
[5] Wood v Rawlings, 76 Ill 206
[6] Dingledine v Hershman, 53 Ill 280
[7] Sec 27, act 1874, as amended, Kipp v. Massin, 15 Bradw. 300

Where an abstract of testimony was ordered on appeal, and instead of such abstract the testimony in full was given, the costs of printing the same were not allowed for, ·but compelled to be borne by him who incurred it.[1]

Where the amount of the judgment was reduced on appeal and otherwise the case affirmed, each party was required to pay half the costs[2]

§ 271 **Bill of review. Writ of error** — A bill of review may be brought for error on the face of the decree, or for new matter discovered since the decree, and that could not fairly have been used when the decree was rendered. This bill must give a copy of the entire record, except the evidence.[3] Upon a petition to enforce a mechanic's lien, to which prior incumbrancers by mortgage were made parties, the decree found the value of the premises before the erection of the improvements, and their value with the improvements, for the making of which the mechanic's lien accrued, and then declared the rule of distribution so that the prior mortgages should first be paid out of the proceeds of a sale of the premises, to the extent of their value without the improvements, and upon a sale being made the proceeds of the sale were distributed according to the rule thus declared Upon a bill of review afterward filed by those claiming the mechanic's lien, alleging there was error in that decree in regard to the rule of distribution, it was held, even though there was error in that respect, it could not, equitably, be corrected upon a bill of review so as to compel the prior incumbrancers to refund any portion of what they had received, because the sale under the decree being allowed to stand, they would have no opportunity under a different rule of distribution limiting their proportion of the proceeds of the sale, to protect their interests by making the property bring a higher price The only equitable mode of correcting such error in the original decree, if one existed, would be to set aside the sale and order a resale.[4]

While a decree dismissing a bill of review to impeach a decree for error upon the face of the proceedings, might be pleaded in bar of a writ of error to reverse the same decree, yet if it is not so pleaded, and the original decree is reversed and the cause remanded, the decree on the bill of review cannot be held any bar in the original case, or to a proper distribution of the money arising from a sale of the premises among the several creditors having liens[5]

---

[1] Kelly v Kellogg 79 Ill 477.
[2] Wolfe v Stone, 20 Ill 174
[3] Judson v Stephens, 75 Ill 255
[4] Judson v. Stephens, 75 Ill 255, Moore v Bracken, 27 id 23.
[5] Powell v Rogers, 105 Ill. 318, adv , 1 Bradw. 631

The doctrine of *res adjudicata* embraces not only what has been determined in the former suit, but also extends to any other matter properly involved, and which might have been raised and determined in it   Therefore, a decree on the merits is conclusive as to all defenses that might have been interposed.[1]

The conclusive effect of a former adjudication sometimes applies to persons not parties to the record, and who have not acquired rights *pendente lite*.   Persons on whose behalf and under whose direction a suit is prosecuted or defended in the name of some one else, will be equally concluded by the judgment or decree in such suit, and parol evidence may be introduced to show that such party is bound by the decree, that he conducted or managed the case, employed counsel, etc[2]

As bills of review and writs of errors are governed in cases under this statute by the rules of general practice, their further presentation is needless in this treatise.

§ 272. **Appeals.**—The rules and practice in appeals are the same in cases arising under this law as in those taken in other civil actions, except that the rule in chancery that the record must show on its face the facts necessary to support the decree does not apply in lien cases.[3]

It is the duty of the party who complains of the verdict or decree to preserve the evidence in the records, either by bill of exception, certificate of the judge, or other approved manner[3]   Where the evidence is not preserved the decree is presumed to be correct[3] Appeals can be taken only on errors affecting the party appealing

Our courts have held that it has been so repeatedly decided that a party cannot complain of error that does not affect him, that citation of authority is unnecessary[4]

Where a party submits to a trial in a case arising under one section, as section 37, he cannot raise the point above that the case should have been tried under the provisions of another section, as section 45[5]

§ 273. **Original contractor may appeal from lien decree.**— The original contractor has a right to appeal from a decree establishing the lien of a sub-contractor and is really the party in interest[6]

---

[1] Powell v Rogers, 105 Ill 318 adv , 1 Bradw, 691
[2] Bennitt v Star Mining Co , 119 Ill 9; 18 App 17
[3] Kelly v Chapman, 13 Ill 530; Ross v Derr, 18 id. 245, Drennan v. Huskey, 31 App 208 Kidder v Aholtz, 3d Ill. 478, Croskey v N W Mfg. Co , 48 id 481, Jennings v Hinkle 81 id. 183, Lewis v Rose, 82 id 574
[4] McGraw v Storke 44 App 311
[5] Conklin v Plant, 34 App 264
[6] Swift v. Martin, 20 Bradw 515, Martin v. Swift, 120 Ill. 488.

§ 274 **Defective pleadings aided by verdict.** — A petition which fails to aver when work was to be completed and money to be paid is bad on demurrer, but if answer is put in and the case tried, and the proof shows that the time for completion and payment was within the statutory period, it is too late to raise the objection on appeal [1]

Where the statements in a pleading, although imperfect and insufficient in themselves, are yet of such a character as to lead the court to believe that all must have been proved on the trial that should have been stated in the pleadings to procure the verdict, then the defective pleading is aided by intendment after verdict, and the court may render judgment. A verdict will aid a defective statement of title, right or cause of action, but cannot make good a defective right or cause of action. This implication is never raised, except where there is a verdict, can never aid defective pleading where there is a judgment by default.[2] A motion based on the fact that the petition did not contain sufficient averments to constitute a cause of action, that the time for performance was not within the time limited by the statute, and in arrest of judgment, was overruled on appeal after a verdict on answer and trial had been rendered [a]

§ 275. **Want of proper parties will reverse decree.** — Where it appears there were other persons entitled to liens who were not made parties for this reason alone, the decree will be reversed.[3]

§ 276. **Variance must be objected to in trial court.** — Where a bill is erroneously dismissed upon the merits of the case, the decree will not be sustained above on the ground of variance between the allegations and the evidence, when no objection to such variance was made in the court below. Unless judgment is upon default, the objection to variance must be made in the trial court to be availed of above [4]

§ 277. **Powers of upper court.** — The upper court can review the evidence, reform the verdict and amend the decree, and where against the weight of the evidence, that court may either correct, reform or reverse.[5]

---

[1] Brown v Lowell, 79 Ill 484

[2] Warren v Harris, 2 Gilm 307,(a) Heinan v. Schroeder, 74 Ill 158, Morrison v Stewart. 24 id 24

[3] Mehrle v Dunne, 75 Ill 239, Radcliff v Noyes, 43 id 318, Race v Sullivan, 1 App. 94.

[4] Driver v Ford, 90 Ill. 595

[5] Wolf v Stone, 20 Ill 174, Nibbe v Brauhn, 24 id. 268, Moore v Bracken, 27 id 23, Lubliner v Yoemans, 65 id 305 Adams v Russell, 85 id 64, Jacoby v. Scougale, 26 App 46, Koeritz v Neimes, id 562, Albrecht v Kraisinger, 44 id 313

But the record of the lower court cannot be altered, amended or in anywise changed in the upper court Where the decree or judgment is for more than claimed in the petition, or for too large a sum, *remittur* cannot be allowed in the upper court to rectify the error; the case must be reversed.[1]

---

[1] Beese v. Becker, 51 Ill. 82.

APPENDIX.

THE
MECHANIC'S LIEN LAW
OF THE
STATE OF ILLINOIS.

Act of 1874, as Amended and in Force March 1, 1894.

CHAPTER 82 OF THE REVISED STATUTES OF ILLINOIS

SECTION 22 When part may be sold.
   23. Manner of making sale
   24. Redemption
   25. Deficiency of proceeds of sale, execution in case of; excess, to
        whom paid
   26. Representatives, death of parties in interest
   27. Costs
   28. Limitation as to filing claim of original contractor
        As to suit after filing

SUB-CONTRACTORS.

29 Liens of sub-contractors, mechanics, workman, etc
    Limits thereof, limit of owner's liability, exception
30 Notice to owner by sub-contractor, form of, excuse of.
31 Notice to owner, copy of sub-contract to be attached
    Limitation for service of, clerk's fees
32 Notice to non resident; publication of; posting of
33 Lien limited to amount owner owes contractor at date notice served,
    exception in favor of laborer, limitation as to laborer's notice
34 Owner's privilege to retain and pay money after notice, preference
    to laborers
35 Contractor to make statement to owner, requisites for and of state-
    ment sub-contractor to make statement to contractor, requisites,
    penalty for failure of either
36 Repealed, amendment, June 16, 1887
37 Suit to enforce lien by sub-contractor, when can be brought, how,
    action at law by against owner and contractor
38 Judgment before justice of the peace, when transcript of may be
    filed, execution thereon
39 Proceedings for general settlement, interpleader.
40 How liens and claims cut off in such proceedings
41 How judgment on liens stayed in such proceedings.
42, 43, 44 repealed   Amendment, June 16, 1887
45 Failure to complete contract by original contractor, requisites and
    manner of sub-contractor's suit in case of, owners liability in
    case of
46 Payments of owner to original contractor, when wrongful.
47. Limitation as to suit of sub-contractor to enforce lien
48, 49, 50 Liens of others not mechanics
51 Repeal of previous acts, etc , see act 1874, Appendix, page
52 Suit to be commenced by lien claimant within thirty days on de.
    mand of owner, or interested party.
53. Circuit Court clerk's duties with regard to claims for lien filed,
     abstract, fee
54. Neglect to satisfy lien paid, penalty

----

48. Hotels, inns, boarding-houses, lien of
49 Stable keepers and others, lien for keep of horses, carriages and
    harness
50. Agisters and keepers of domestic animals, lien of

SECTION 1. **Original contractors, to whom and when lien is given; area covered by lien.**—*Be it enacted by the People of the State of Illinois, represented in the General Assembly,* That any person who shall, by contract, express or implied, or partly expressed or partly implied, with the owner of any lot or piece of land, furnish labor or materials, or services as an architect, or superintendent, in building, altering, repairing or ornamenting any house or other building or appurtenance thereto on such lot, or upon any street or alley, and connected with such building or appurtenance, shall have a lien upon the whole of such tract of land or lot, and upon such house or building and appurtenance, for the amount due to him for such labor, material or service.

(Section 1, act 1845, page 214, section 1, amendment February 18, 1861, extended to implied contracts, page 218, act February 14, 1863, improvements beyond lot line, page 219, compare sections 1, acts 1825, page 205, 1833, pages 205-6)

§ 2. **To what estates and interests liens of original and subcontractors extend**—The lien provided for in sections 1 and 29 of this act shall extend to an estate in fee, for life, for years, or any other estate, or any right of redemption, or other interest, which such owner may have in the lot or land at the time of making the contract

(Section 17, act 1845, page 216)

§ 3. **Time for completion after commencing performance of contract; classes of contracts; time for payment**—When the contract is expressed, no lien shall be created under this act, if the time stipulated for the completion of the work or furnishing materials is beyond three years from the commencement thereof, or the time of payment beyond one year from the time stipulated for the completion thereof. If the work is done or materials are furnished under an implied contract, no lien shall be had by virtue of this act, unless the work shall be done or materials be furnished within one year from the commencement of the work or delivery of the materials

(Section 2, act 1845, page 214, section 1, amendment February 18, 1861, page 218)

§ 4. **Claim for lien by original contractor; requisites thereof; when, how, and in what court he can bring suit.**—Every creditor or contractor who wishes to avail himself of the provisions of this act shall file with the clerk of the Circuit Court of the county in which the building, erection, or other improvement to be charged with the lien is situated, a just and true statement or account or demand due him, after allowing all credits, setting forth the time when such material was furnished or labor performed, and containing a correct description of the property to be charged with the lien, and verified by an affidavit. Any person having filed a claim for a lien, as provided in this section, may bring a suit at once to enforce the same by bill or petition in any court of competent jurisdiction in the county where the claim for a lien has been filed.

(Amendment, May 31, 1887   In force July 1, 1887, page 236, sections 3, 4, act 1845, page 214, see sections 28, page 184, 53, page 190)

§ 5 **Pleading; requisites of bill or petition** —The bill or petition shall contain a brief statement of the contract on which it is founded, if expressed, or if the work is done or materials are furnished under an implied contract, the bill or petition shall so state, and shall show the amount due and unpaid, a description of the premises which are subject to the lien, and such other facts as may be necessary to a full understanding of the rights of the parties.

(Section 4, act 1845, page 214)

§ 6 **Summons; how served.**—Upon the filing of such bill or petition, summons shall issue and service thereof be had, as in suits in chancery

(Sections 4, 6, act 1845, page 214, Revised Statutes of Illinois, section 8, chap. 22)

§ 7. **Publication; service of process on non-resident, etc** — When any defendant resides or has gone out of the State, or on due inquiry cannot be found, or is concealed within this State, so that process cannot be served upon him, the complainant or petitioner may cause notice to be given to him in like manner and upon the same conditions as provided in suits in chancery

(Section 9, act 1845, page 215, Revised Statutes of Illinois, section 12, chap 22)

§ 8 **Docket; trial** —Suits instituted under the provisions of this act shall be placed upon the chancery docket, and stand for trial as other suits in chancery.

(Section 6, act 1845, page 214)

§ 9 **Practice; powers of court.**—For the purpose of bringing all parties in interest before the court, the court shall permit amendments to any part of the pleadings, and may issue process, make all orders requiring parties to appear, and requiring notice to be given, that are or may be authorized in proceedings in chancery, and shall have the same power and jurisdiction of the parties and subject, and the rules of practice and proceedings in such cases shall be the same as in other cases in chancery, except as is otherwise provided in this act

(Section 5, act 1845, page 214)

§ 10 **Practice ; answer ; replication ; trial.**—Defendants shall answer the bill or petition under oath, unless the oath is waived by the complainant or petitioner, and the plaintiff shall except or reply to the answer as though the proceeding was in chancery The answer shall be regarded as the plea of the defendant, and by replication thereto an issue or issues shall be formed, which shall be tried by the court, or by a jury under the direction of the court, as the court may direct or the parties agree.

(Section 7,   ' 1845, page 215)

§ 11. **Breach of contract by owner ; recovery for partial performance ; quantum meruit.**—When the owner of the land shall have failed to perform his part of the contract by failing to advance to the contractor moneys justly due him under the contract at the time when the same should have been paid to the contractor, or has failed to perform his part of the contract in any other manner, and by reason thereof the other party shall, without his own default, have been prevented from performing his part, he shall be entitled to a reasonable compensation for as much thereof as has been performed in proportion to the price stipulated for the whole, and the court shall adjust his claim and allow him a lien accordingly.

(Amendment June 22, 1891 In force July 1, 1891, page 241, section 13, act 1845, page 215)

§ 12 **Persons interested ; how and when made, or may become parties ; new parties.**—In proceedings under this act, all persons interested in the subject-matter of the suit, or in the premises intended to be sold, may, on application to the court wherein the suit is pending, be made or become parties at any time before final judgment.

(Section 10, act 1845, page 215)

§ 13 **Who are parties in interest.**—Parties in interest, within the meaning of this act, shall include all persons who may have any legal or equitable claim to the whole or any part of the premises upon which a lien may be attempted to be enforced under the provisions of this act.

(Section 21, act 1845, page 217)

§ 14. **No preference to first contractor.**—Upon questions aris ing between different creditors, having liens under this act, no preference shall be given to him whose contract was first made.

(Section 11, act 1845, page 215)

§ 15. **Proceeds of sale; application of pro rata**—The court shall ascertain the amount due each creditor, and shall direct the application of the proceeds of sales to be made to each in proportion to their several amounts.

(Section 12, act 1845, page 215)

§ 16. **Claims not due, etc**—Parties entitled to liens under this act, whose claims are not due or payable at the time of the commencement of suit by any other party, shall be permitted to become parties to the suit, and their claim shall be allowed, subject to a reduction of interest from the date of judgment to the time such claim is due or payable

(Section 15, act 1845, page 215)

§ 17. **Incumbrances; apportionment.**—No incumbrance upon land, created before or after the making of the contract under the provisions of this act, shall operate upon the building erected or materials furnished, until the lien in favor of the person doing the work or furnishing the materials shall have been satisfied ; and upon questions arising between previous incumbrances and creditors, the previous incumbrance shall be preferred to the extent of the value of the land at the time of making the contract, and the court shall ascertain, by jury or otherwise, as the case may require, what proportion of the proceeds of any sale shall be paid to the several parties in interest

(Section 20, act 1845, page 217)

§ 18. **Adverse claimants; issues between.** — Parties claiming may contest each other's rights, as well with respect to amount due, as with respect to their right to the benefit of the lien hereby created ; and upon all questions made by parties, the court shall require issues of law or fact to be formed so as to bring about a speedy decision thereof.

(Section 19, act 1845, page 216)

§ 19. **Fraudulent incumbrances; disposition of**—Any incumbrance, whether by mortgage, judgment or otherwise, charged and shown to be fraudulent in respect to creditors, may be set aside by the court, and the premises made subject to the claim of the complainant or petitioner, freed and discharged from such fraudulent incumbrance

(Section 22, act 1845, page 217)

§ 20. **Trials; parties ready not to be delayed; decrees; sales.**—In no case shall the want of preparation for trial of one claim delay the trial in respect to others, but trial shall be had upon issues between such parties as are prepared, without reference to issues between other parties; and when one creditor shall have obtained a decree or judgment for the amount due, the court may order a sale of the premises on which the lien operates, or a part thereof, so as to satisfy the judgment *Provided*, that the court may, for good cause shown, delay making any order of sale or distribution until the rights of all parties in interest are ascertained and settled by the court.

(Section 16, act 1845, page 216)

§ 21 **What estate to be sold; disposition of proceeds.**—Whatever right or estate such owner had in the land at the time of making the contract, may be sold, and the proceeds of sale applied according to the provisions of this act.

(Section 17, act 1845, page 216)

§ 22. **When part may be sold.**—If any part of the premises can be separated from the residue, and sold without damage to the whole, and if the value thereof is sufficient to satisfy all the claims proved in the cause, the court may order a sale of that part.

(Section 14, act 1845, page 215)

§ 23. **Manner of making sale.**—The sale shall be made in the same manner as other sales of real estate under decrees in chancery.

(Revised Statutes of Illinois, section 48, chap. 22; section 16, chap 77)

§ 24. **Redemption.**—Upon all sales under this act, the right of redemption shall exist in favor of the same persons, and may be made in the same manner as is or may be provided for redemption of real estate from sales under judgments and executions at common law.

(Section 1, act March 30, 1869, page 224, Revised Statutes of Illinois, chap 77, sections 18–27)

§ 25. **Deficiency of proceeds of sale ; execution in case of; excess, to whom paid.** — If, upon making sale of any premises under this act, the proceeds of such sale shall not be sufficient to pay the claims of all parties, according to their rights, the judgment shall be credited by the amount of such sale, and execution may issue in favor of any creditor whose claim is not satisfied, for the balance due, as upon a judgment in actions of debt or *assumpsit,* and in case of excess of sales over the amount of judgment, such excess shall be paid to the owner of the land, or to the person who may be entitled to the same, under the direction of the court.

(Section 26, act 1845, page 217)

§ 26 **Personal representatives ; death of parties in interest.**— Suits may be instituted under the provisions of this act, in favor of administrators or executors, and may be maintained against the representatives in interest of those against whom the cause of action accrued, and in suits instituted under the provisions of this act, the representatives of any party who may die pending the suit, shall be made parties

(Section 18. act 1845, page 216)

§ 27. **Costs.** — The cost of proceeding, as between creditors claiming liens and the person against whom the lien is intended to be enforced, shall abide the event of the suit; and the costs, as between creditors aforesaid, in contests relative to each other's claim, shall be subject to the order of the court, and the same rule shall prevail in respect to costs growing out of proceedings against and between incumbrances.

(Section 27, act 1845, page 218.)

§ 28. **Limitation as to filing claim of original contractor; as to suit after filing** — No creditor shall be allowed to enforce a lien created under the provisions of this act as against or to the prejudice of any other creditor, or incumbrancer or purchaser, unless a claim for a lien shall have been filed with the clerk of the Circuit Court, as provided in section four of this act, within four months after the last payment shall have become due and payable. Suit shall be commenced within two years after filing such claim with the clerk of the Circuit Court, or the lien shall be vacated.

(In force July 1, 1887, amendment May 31. 1887. page 236, prior act, 1879, page 236, section 24, act 1845, page 217)

SUB-CONTRACTORS.

§ 29 **Liens of sub-contractors, mechanics, workman, etc.; limits thereof; limit of owner's liability; exception.** — Every sub-contractor, mechanic, workman, or other person, who shall hereafter, in pursuance of the purposes of the original contract between the owner of any lot or piece of ground, or his agent and the original contractor, perform any labor or furnish any materials in building, altering, repairing, beautifying or ornamenting any house or other building or appurtenance thereto, on such lot or on any street or alley, and connected with such building or appurtenance, shall have a lien for the value of such labor and materials upon such house or building and appurtenances, and upon the lot or land upon which the same stands, to the extent of the right, title and interest of such owner at the time of making the original contract for such house or the improvement; but the aggregate of all the liens hereby authorized shall not exceed the price stipulated in the original contract between such owner and the original contractor for such improvements. In no case shall the owner be compelled to pay a greater sum for or on account of such house, building or other improvements than the price or sum stipulated in said original contract or agreement, unless payments be made to the original contractor, or to his order, in violation of the rights and interests of the persons intended to be benefited by section thirty-five of this act: *Provided*, if it shall appear to the court that the owner and contractor fraudulently, and for the purpose of defrauding sub-contractors, fixed an unreasonably low price in their original contract for the erection or repairing of such building, then the court shall ascertain how much of a difference exists between a fair price for the labor and materials used in said building or other improvements and the sum named in said original contract Said difference shall be considered a part of the contract and be subject to a lien, but in no case shall the original contractor's time or profits be secured by this lien, only so far as the sum named in the original contract or agreement

(Amendment June 16, 1887, page 238, prior, section 1, act 1863, page 219, section 1, act 1869, page 224)

§ 30 **Notice to owner by sub-contractor: form of; excuse of.** —The person performing such labor, or furnishing such materials, shall cause a notice, in writing, to be served on such owner or his agent, substantially in the following form ·

24

To   : You are hereby notified that I have been employed by   to (here state whether to labor or furnish material, and substantially the nature of the undertaking or demand) upon your (here state the building and where situated, in general terms), and that I shall hold the (building or, as the case may be), and your interest in the grounds liable for the amount that (is or may become) due me on account thereof.

Date.   Signature.

Provided, Such notice shall not be necessary where the sworn statement of the contractor provided for in section thirty-five of this act shall serve to give the owner true notice of the amount due, and to whom due.

(In force July 1, 1887, amendment June 16, 1887, page 238, prior, act 1869, section 2, page 225)

§ 31 Notice to owner; copy of sub-contract to be attached; limitation for services of; clerk's fees.— If there is a contract in writing between the original contractor and the sub-contractor, a copy of such sub-contract, if the same can be obtained, shall be served with such notice and attached thereto, which notice shall be served within forty days from the completion of such sub-contract, or within forty days after payment should have been made to the person performing such labor or furnishing such material.

(Section 2, act 1869, page 225)

§ 32. Notice to non-resident owner; clerk's fees; publication of; posting of.— In all cases where the owner cannot be found in the county in which said improvement is made, or shall not reside therein, the person furnishing labor or materials shall file said notice in the office of the clerk of the circuit court, who shall enter, in a book to be kept for that purpose, alphabetically, the names of the owners, and opposite thereto the names of the persons claiming liens, for which the clerk shall receive a fee of fifty cents A copy of said notice shall be published in some newspaper printed in said county, for four successive weeks after filing such notice with the clerk as aforesaid. If, however, there is no paper published in said county, then the claimant of the lien shall post notices in four of the most public places in the vicinity of said improvement.

(Section 3, act 1869, page 225)

§ 33. Lien limited to amount due or to become due contractor at date notice served; exception in favor of laborer; limitations as to laborer's notice.—No claim of any sub-contractor, me-

chanic, workman or other person, shall be a lien under section
twenty-nine of this act, except so far as the owner may be indebted
to the contractor at the time of giving such notice, as aforesaid, of
such claim, or may become indebted afterward to him as such contractor : *Provided,* however, the claim of any person for mechanical
or other labor, under section twenty-nine of this act, shall be a lien
for twenty days from the last day's work performed by such person,
to an amount equal to ten per cent of the proportionate value of the
contract completed up to the date of said last day's work ; *Provided,*
such notice is served within twenty days from the day when such
last day's work was performed by such person serving such notice,
and the owner or his agent may retain for said twenty days such
ten per cent out of any money due to or to become due the contractor : And *provided* further, this ten per cent shall not be
construed as in addition to any per cent that may be held back in
pursuance of the terms of the contract between the owner and the
original contractor.

(In force July 1, 1891, amendment 1891, page 241)

§ 34. **Owner's privilege to retain and pay money after notice;
preference to laborers.**— When the owner or his agent is notified
as aforesaid he may retain from any money due or to become due
the original contractor an amount sufficient to pay all demands that
are or will become due such sub-contractor, mechanic, workman, or
other person so notifying him, and may pay over the same to the
persons entitled thereto. In case the amount due the original contractor and the ten per cent in section thirty-three provided, is not sufficient to pay such persons so entitled in full, he shall first pay all claims
for mechanical and other labor in full, if the amount due the contractor and the said ten per cent is sufficient, if not, then *pro rata,*
but if more than sufficient, the balance shall be divided and paid to
such other persons, *pro rata,* in proportion to the amounts due
them respectively at the time of such payment All payments so
made shall, as between such owner and contractor, be considered the
same as if paid to such original contractor.

(In force July 1, 1891, amendment of 1891, page 242, section 35, amendment
1887, page 239)

§ 35. **Contractor to make statement to owner; requisites for
and of statement; sub-contractor to make statement to contractor; requisites; penalty for failure of either.** — The original contractor shall, as often as requested in writing by the owner,
lessee, or his agent, make out and give to such owner, lessee, or his

agent, a statement of the number of persons in his employ, and of the sub-contractors, or other persons, furnishing labor or material, giving their names, and how much, if any thing, is due or to become due to each of them for work done or material furnished, which statement shall be made under oath, if required of him by such owner, lessee, or agent, in which case the sub-contractor shall, as often as requested in writing by the contractor or his agent, make out and give to the contractor a statement of the number of persons in his employ, or sub-contractors or other persons furnishing material, giving their names and how much, if any thing, is due to each of them, which statement shall be made under oath, if required by such contractor, and, if any contractor or sub-contractor shall fail to furnish such statement within five days after demand, made as aforesaid, he shall forfeit to such owner or contractor the sum of $50 for every offense, which may be recovered in an action of debt before a justice of the peace.

(In force July 1, 1891   Amendment 1891, page 241, compare amendment 1887, section 35, page 239)

§ 36. Repealed.
(Amendment, June 16, 1887, page 240.)

§ 37 Suit to enforce lien by sub-contractor; when can be brought; how; action at law by against owner and contractor.
— If the money due to the person giving such notice shall not be paid within ten days after service thereof, as aforesaid, or within ten days after the money shall become due and payable, and any money shall then be due from such owner to the original contractor, then such person may file his petitition and enforce his lien, in the same manner as is hereinbefore provided in case of original contractors, or he may sue the owner and contractor jointly for the amount due him, in any court having jurisdiction of the amount claimed to be due, and a personal judgment may be rendered therein as in other cases.

(Section 5, act 1869. page 226)

§ 38. Judgment before justice of the peace; when transcript of may be filed; execution thereon. — If execution issued on a judgment obtained before a justice of the peace shall be returned not satisfied, a transcript of such judgment may be taken to the Circuit Court and spread upon the records thereof, and execution issued thereon as in other cases.

(Revised Statutes of Illinois, sections 95, 97, chap 79 , act 1869, section 5, page 226.)

§ 39. **Proceedings for general settlement; interpleader.** — If there are several liens, under section twenty-nine, upon the same premises, and the owner, or any person having such lien, shall fear that there is not a sufficient amount coming to the contractor to pay all of such liens, such owner, or any one or more persons having such lien, may file his or their sworn bill or petition in the Circuit Court of the proper county, stating such fact, and such other facts as may be sufficient to a full understanding of the rights of the parties. The contractor and all persons having liens upon, or who are interested in the premises, so far as the same are known to or can be ascertained by the claimant or petitioner, upon diligent inquiry, shall be made parties. Upon the hearing, the court shall find the amount coming from the owner to the contractor, and the amount due to each of the persons having liens; and in case the amount found to be coming to the contractor shall be insufficient to discharge all the liens in full, the amount so found in favor of the contractor shall be divided between the persons entitled to such liens *pro rata*, in proportion to the amounts so found to be due them, respectively. If the amount so found to be coming to the contractor shall be sufficient to pay such liens in full, the same shall be so ordered. The premises may be decreed to be sold for the payment of such liens as in other cases.

§ 40 **How liens and claims cut off in such proceedings.** — All persons who shall be duly notified of such proceeding, and who shall fail to prove their claims, whether the same be in judgment against the owner or not, shall forever lose the benefit of and be precluded from their liens and all claims against the owner

§ 41 **How judgment on liens stayed in such proceedings.** — Upon the filing of such bill or petition, the court may, on the motion of any person interested, stay any further proceedings upon any judgment against the owner on account of such lien.

(Sections 42, 43, 44, repealed, amendment June 16, 1887, page 240.)

§ 45 **Failure to complete contract by original contractor; requisites and manner of sub-contractor's suit in case of; owner's liability in case of.** — Should the original contractor, for any cause, fail to complete his contract, any person entitled to a lien as aforesaid may file his petition in any court of record, against the owner and contractor, setting forth the nature of his claim, the amount due, as near as may be, and the names of the parties employed on such house or other improvements subject to liens; and

notice of such suit shall be seived on the persons therein named;
and such as shall appeal shall have their claims adjudicated, and decree shall be enteied against the owner and oiiginal contractor for
so much as the work and materials shall be shown to be reasonably
worth accoiding to the oiiginal contract price, first deducting so
much as shall have been iightfully paid on said original contiact by
the owner, and damages, if any, that may be found to be occasioned
the owner by ieason of the non-fulfillment of the oiiginal contiact;
the balance to be divided between such claimants in propoition to
their respective interests, to be ascertained by the court.   The
premises may be sold as in other cases under this act.

(Section 7, amendment 1869, page 226)

§ 46. **Payments of owner to original contractor; when wrongful.** — No payments to the original contractor or to his oider shall
be regarded as rightfully made, if made in violation of the rights
and interests of the persons intended to be benefited by this act.

(Amendment April 5, 1869, section 8, page 226)

§ 47 **Limitation as to suit of sub-contractor to enforce lien.**
— No petition shall be filed or suit commenced to enfoice the lien
created by section twenty-nine, unless the same is commenced within
three months from the time of the performance of the sub-contract,
or doing the work or furnishing materials, as aforesaid : *Provided*,
if any delay in filing such petition or commencing suit is caused in
consequence of the amount not being due the original contractor,
the time of such delay shall not be reckoned.

(Amendment April 5, 1869, section 9, page 226)

§§ 48, 49, 50. **Liens of others not mechanics.**
§ 51. **Repeal of previous acts, etc.**

(See act 1874, page 235)

§ 52. **Suit to be commenced by lien claimant within thirty
days, on demand of owner or interested party.**—Upon the written demand of the owner or his agent, or any person interested in
the real estate, served on the person or his agent claiming the lien,
requiring suit to be commenced to enforce the lien, suit shall be
commenced within thirty days thereafter, or the lien shall be forfeited.

(Amendment May 31, 1887   In force July 1, 1887, page 237)

§ 53 **Circuit Court clerk's duties with regard to claims for
lien filed; abstract; fee.**—The clerk of the Circuit Court where

such lien shall be filed shall indorse on every such claim for a lien filed, the date of filing, and make an abstract thereof in a book kept for that purpose and properly indexed, containing the name of the person filing the lien, the amount of the lien, the date of filing, the name of the person against whom the lien is filed, and a description of the property charged with the lien, and for which the person filing the lien shall pay one dollar to the clerk.

(Amendment May 31, 1887. In force July 1, 1887, page 237.)

§ 54. **Neglect to satisfy lien paid ; penalty.**—Whenever a lien has been claimed by filing the same with the clerk of the Circuit Court, and is afterward paid, the person filing the same shall acknowledge satisfaction thereof in the proper book in such office in writing, and on neglect to do so for ten days after the claim has been paid, he shall forfeit to the owner the sum of twenty-five dollars

(Amendment May 31, 1887. In force July 1, 1887, page 238.)

---

§ 48 **Hotels, inns, boarding-houses ; lien of.**—Hotel, inn and boarding-house keepers shall have a lien upon the baggage and other valuables of their guests or boarders brought into such hotel, inn or boarding-house by such guests or boarders, for the proper charges due from such guests or boarders for their accommodations, boarding and lodgings, and such extras as are furnished at their request

§ 49. **Stable-keepers and others ; lien for keep of horses, carriages and harness.**—Stable-keepers and any persons shall have a lien upon the horses, carriages and harness kept by them for the proper charges due for the keeping thereof and expenses bestowed thereon at the request of the owner, or person having the possession thereof.

§ 50. **Agisters and keepers of domestic animals ; lien of.**—Agisters and persons keeping, yarding, feeding or pasturing domestic animals shall have a lien upon the animals agisted, kept, yarded or fed, for the proper charges due for the agistering, keeping, yarding or feeding thereof.

WAGES OF EMPLOYEES.

AN ACT TO PROTECT EMPLOYEES AND LABORERS IN THEIR CLAIMS FOR WAGES.

APPROVED June 15, 1887   In force July 1, 1887

SECTION 1   Claims for wages to the extent of fifty dollars preferred
Claimant's statement, requisites of
Within what time must be presented
Duty of officer, person or court
Parties interested may contest

SECTION 1. *Be it enacted by the People of the State of Illinois, represented in the General Assembly:* That hereafter, when the property of any company, corporation, firm or person shall be seized upon by any process of any court of this state; or when their business shall be suspended by the action of creditors, or be put into the hands of a receiver or trustee, then in all such cases, the debts owing to laborers or servants, which have accrued by reason of their labor or employment to an amount not exceeding fifty dollars to each employee, for work or labor performed within six months next preceding the seizure or transfer of such property, shall be considered and treated as preferred debts, and such laborers or employees shall be preferred creditors, and shall be first paid in full; and if there be not sufficient to pay them in full, then the same shall be paid to them *pro rata*, after paying costs. Any such laborer or servant, desiring to enforce his or her claim for wages due under this act, shall present a statement under oath showing the amount due after allowing all just credits and set-offs. the kind of work for which such wages are due, and when performed, to the officer, person or court charged with such property. within ten days after the seizure thereof on any execution or writ of attachment, or within thirty days after the same may have been placed in the hands of any receiver or trustee; and thereupon it shall be the duty of the person or court receiving such statement to pay the amount of such claim or claims to the person or persons entitled thereto (after first paying all costs occasioned by the seizure of such property) out of the proceeds of the sale of the property seized: *Provided,* that any person interested may contest any such claim or claims or any part thereof by filing exceptions thereto, supported by affidavit, with the officer having the custody of such property, and thereupon the claimant shall be required to reduce his claim to judgment before some court having jurisdiction thereof, before any part thereof shall be paid

(Session Laws 1887, page 308.)

25

LIENS UPON RAILROADS.

AN ACT TO PROTECT CONTRACTORS, SUB–CONTRACTORS AND LABOR-
ERS IN THEIR CLAIMS AGAINST RAILROAD COMPANIES, OR
CORPORATIONS, CONTRACTORS OR SUB–CONTRACTORS.

SECTION 1. **For fuel, ties, material, supplies, labor, etc.**—*Be it enacted by the People of the State of Illinois, represented in the General Assembly* That all persons who have furnished, or who shall hereafter furnish to any railroad corporation now existing, or hereafter to be organized under the laws of this State, any fuel, ties, materials, supplies, or any other article or thing necessary for the construction, maintenance, operation or repair of such roads, by contract with said corporation, or who shall have done and performed or shall hereafter do and perform any work or labor for such construction, maintenance, operation or repair by like contract, shall be entitled to be paid for the same as part of the current expenses of said road, and in order to secure the same, shall have a lien upon all the property, real, personal and mixed, of said railroad corporation as against such railroad, and as against all mortgages or other liens which shall accrue after the commencement of the delivery of said articles, or the commencement of said work or labor. *Provided*, suit shall be commenced within six months after such contractor or laborer shall have completed his contract with said railroad corporation, or after such labor shall have been performed or material furnished.

§ 2. **Liens of sub-contractor, materialman, laborer, etc.** — Every person who shall hereafter, as sub-contractor, materialman or laborer, furnish to any contractor with any such railroad corporation any fuel, ties, materials, supplies, or any other article or thing, or who shall do and perform any work or labor for such contractor in conformity with any terms of any contract, express or implied, which such contractor may have made with any such railroad corporation, shall have a lien upon all the property, real, personal and mixed, of said railroad corporation : Provided, such sub-contractor, materialman or laborer shall have complied with the provisions of this act; but the aggregate of all liens hereby authorized shall not, in any case, exceed the price agreed upon in the original contract to be paid by such corporation to the original contractor : *And, provided, further*, that no such lien shall take priority over any existing lien.

§ 3. **Notice of claim of lien ; form of; when lien attaches.** — The person performing such labor, or furnishing such material, shall cause a notice, in writing, to be served on the president or secretary of such railroad corporation, substantially as follows, viz. :

To   president, (or secretary, as the case may be), of the   You are hereby notified that I am (or have been) employed by   as a laborer (or have furnished supplies, as the case may be), on or for the   and that I shall hold all the property of said railroad (or railway, as the case may be), company to secure my pay

If there shall be a contract in writing between the original contractor and sub-contractor, materialman or laborer, a copy of such contract, if the same can be obtained, shall be served with such notice and attached thereto, which notice shall be served at any time within twenty days after the completion of such sub-contract, or such labor : *Provided*, that no lien shall attach in favor of any person performing such labor or furnishing material until such notice shall have been served as above, or filed for record as hereinafter provided

§ 4 **When notice filed with circuit clerk ; copy to be mailed ; duties of clerk ; fees.** — If neither the president or the secretary of such railroad corporation shall reside or can be found in the county in which the sub-contract was made, or labor performed, the laborer, or person furnishing labor or material, shall file said notice in the office of the clerk of the Circuit Court; and the clerk of the Circuit Court shall file and keep a record of said notice, and cause a copy of the same to be mailed to the president or secretary of said company, for which he shall receive the sum of twenty-five cents, and said clerk shall keep a list of the names of the persons so claiming lien, and the names of the corporation against which such liens are claimed.

§ 5. **When suit may be brought ; in what court ; against what parties ; transcripts of justice's judgments.**—If the money due the person having given notice as aforesaid, shall not be paid within ten days after the money shall become due and payable, then

such person may commence suit therefor, in any court having jurisdiction of the amount claimed to be due, against the corporation with
which the original contract was made; or he may commence suit, as
aforesaid, against such railroad corporation and original contractor
jointly, and execution to issue as in other cases.   If execution, issued
on judgment obtained before a justice of the peace, shall be returned
not satisfied, a transcript of such judgment may be taken to the Circuit Court, and spread upon the records thereof, and shall have all
the force and effect of judgments obtained in the Circuit Court, and
execution issued thereon as in other cases.

§ 6. **Costs, attorney's fees in claimant's favor.** — Whenever
any suit, so brought, shall be determined in favor of the plaintiff,
the court shall allow, if before a justice, $5, if in a court of record,
$20, attorney's fees to be taxed as costs.

§ 7. **Failure of original contractor to complete contract; sub-
contractor's suit in case of; clerk's duties.** — Should the original
contractor in any case fail to complete his contract, any person entitled to a lien, as aforesaid, may file his petition in any court of
record, in any county through which the road may be constructed,
against the railroad corporation and the contractors, setting forth the
nature of his claim, and the amount due as near as may be, [and] the
fact that the contractor has failed to complete his contract.   The
clerk of said court shall thereupon cause a notice to be published for
four successive weeks in a newspaper printed in the county, setting
forth that said petition has been filed, and the time when the writ
issued on the same shall have been made returnable, and all persons
entitled to liens under this act may enter their appearance and inter-
plead in said cause, and have their claims adjudicated, and it shall
be the duty of the court, in case the petitioner or claimants, or either
of them, establish their claims, to enter a decree against said corporation and original contractor, for the amount to which the persons
so establishing their claims are respectively entitled, and such decree
shall have the same force and effect as decrees in other cases.

§ 8. **Limitation as to lien.** — The lien hereby created shall continue for three months from the time of the performance of the sub-
contract, or doing of the work or furnishing the material as aforesaid, except when suit shall be commenced, by petition as aforesaid,
and in such cases all liens shall be barred by decree entered in such
cause

§ 9 **Repeal of act of February 22, 1861.**—In force July 1, 1872.
(Session Laws, 1871-2, page 279)

Demand of Owner or Agent to Contractor under Section 35.

To   ... .

I hereby request that you make out and give to me a statement (under oath)[1] of the number of persons in your employ, and of the sub-contractors, or other persons, furnishing labor or material, giving their names, and how much, if any thing, is due or to become due to each of them for work done or material furnished to you in the performance of your contract with me to[2]   . . . .

on my property, situated as follows (legal description of lot or tract of land)

Dated ... ., 18..

[3](Signature)   ....

(Make in duplicate and preserve copy)

---

[1] Under oath may be required or not, omit if not so required
[2] Here insert what to be done
[3] Where agent makes request, the signature should be

J S.,
by A B , *Agent.*

Contractor's Statement to Owner under Section 35.

To   . ...

The following is a statement of the number of each and all the persons in my employ and of the sub-contractors or other persons furnishing labor or material, giving their names, and how much, if any thing, is due or to become due to each of them for work done or for material furnished

NAMES	Amounts due	Amounts to become due	What for
	$	$	

Total number of persons above named .   , all of whom have been or are employed by me, and who have furnished or are furnishing material or labor in and about the performance of my contract with you, for[1] ... .., your[2] ...   , described as follows

.. ..

....

situated on (here give legal description of lot or tract of land)

....

....…... ....

....

....

Dated .. .., 18..

(Signature.) ....

Subscribed and sworn to before me, this }
.......day of ... .. , A. D , 18. , }
            ....
                        Notary Public.
(Make in duplicate and preserve copy)

---

[1] State what to do.   [2] House, building or what

Demand of Contractor to Sub-Contractor under Section 35.

To .. . . :

I hereby request that you make out and give to me a statement (under oath[1]) of the number of persons in your employ and of the sub-contractors or other persons furnishing labor or material, giving their names, and how much, if anything, is due to each of them for work done or material furnished to you in the performance of your contract with me to[2] ... .

... ·   ....

. .. · ....

under my contract with (name of owner) on the following described premises (location and legal description)

.. .. · ... .

· . ...

....

· ·   · · · · ....

Dated..... . , 18

(Make in duplicate and preserve copy.)

[3](Signature) . . ..

---

[1] Under oath may be required or not, omit if not so required.
[2] State what to do
[3] Where agent makes request the signature should be

J. S.,
by A. B., *Agent.*

Sub-Contractor's Statement to Contractor under Section 35.

To. ....

The following is a statement of the number of each and all the persons in my employ, and the sub-contractors and other persons furnishing material, giving their names, and how much, if any thing, is due to each of them

NAMES.	Amount due	What for
	$	

Total number of persons above named . ., all of whom have been or are employed by me, or have furnished or are furnishing materials or labor in and about the performance of my contract with you for[1] . . . . . , under your contract with[2] .. .., for[3] . . .. on the following described premises.

....

...., ...

....

....

Dated........, 18 .

(Signature.) ....

Subscribed and sworn to before me, this }
....day of ...., A. D., 18 ., }

....,
Notary Public.

(Make in duplicate and preserve copy.)

[1] State what to do.   [2] Owner.   [3] What to do

Verification of Original Contractor's Claim for Lien.

STATE OF ILLINOIS, } ss
    ... County, }

IN THE CIRCUIT COURT OF ... .COUNTY, ILLINOIS.

.... ·   ·   .. · · ·
       vs   } *Claim for lien.*
·   ·   · ... ..

..   · ...   .   ·   ·   ·   ... .
     .   ., being first duly sworn on oath, says that   ... .
·   ·   ...   . ·   ·   ..... · .
w .. employed by..   ... . ·   ... ..
to furnish   ...... ·   ..   ..   ·   ..... ·   ..
and did so furnish same in (building, altering, repairing or ornamenting a house
or other building as the case may be), on the following described real estate,
to wit

....·....... . .

....· ... ·   ... .

. ... · .. ..   ·   · ...   .   ·

.. ·   ·   .... ·   ... ..   ·   ... .

upon which real estate said   ..   .. ·   ·   .. ...
hereby claim a lien for the amount due h . as hereinafter mentioned

Affiant further says that "Exhibit A," hereto annexed and made part hereof,
is true as set forth, and is a just and true statement of the account or demand
due from said... ..   .. ·   ·   ..   · ..
to said   ... ... · ... ·   .. ·   ... ·   ·
for such   ·   ·   · ... ·   ·   ·   . ·
that the same were purchased for and used in the construction of such improvement, and the items thereof furnished on the dates in said exhibit mentioned That there is now due and owing to said   ..... ·   ..
from said . . ..   ·   ·   ·   .... ·   ·
dollars on such account, after allowing all just credits, deductions and set-offs.

                        (Signature)........ ....

Subscribed and sworn to before me, }
   this . day of .. .., A D. 18 . }

              .. · .. .. ,
                Notary Public.

(This affidavit may be made by agent or employee of, as well as by, owner.)
26

Notice of Sub-Contractor to Owner.

To (1).... ... .

You are hereby notified that I have been employed by (2) ... .
to (3) ... . .upon your (4) . . . , and that I shall
hold the said property .. .. and your interest in the grounds
liable for the amount that (5) .. ..

Date ....

(Signature.) ....

Write

At (1) the owner's name

At (2) the original contractor's name

At (3) what was to be done if to furnish materials, what sort — brick, lumber,
hardware, etc , or contract work — masonry, carpentry, plaster 'g. etc , or what
the labor was, substantially as the case is

At (4) the description of the property House situated No .., and. .
street, or on such a tract of land or lot — the legal description thereof

At (5) is or may become due on account thereof, as the case may be

(Make in duplicate and preserve copy.)

This notice can be served on the day the sub-contract is made, and binds the
owner from the date of service.

Demand of Owner or Party Interested in the Property on Lien Claimant to Bring Suit Under Section 52.

To ....:

I hereby demand that, within thirty days from this date, you commence suit
to enforce the mechanic's lien that you claim on the following described property

....

....

Date, ...

(Signature.) ....

(Make in duplicate and preserve copy.)

If by agent, sign

A B,
by J. S., *Agent.*

Notice for Labor.

To .. ..

You are hereby notified, that I have been employed by .. .., to labor ... . upon your building, described as follows:

. . ..

...., ...

.... and that I shall hold the building, and your interest in the ground, liable for the amount that (1) .. .   due me on account thereof

Dated this ... .. day of ... , A D , 18 .

... ...

(1) If the claim is due, insert the word "is ; " if not due, the words "may become."

The above notice can be served at any time after employment and will secure whatever may be coming to the mechanic or laborer thereafter

————

The following notice should be served if the work is done, and the mechanic or laborer wishes to secure his lien on ten per cent of the proportionate value of the contract completed, according to the provisions of section 33, and must be served within twenty days after the last day's work :

To . ...

You are hereby notified, that I have been employed by ... ., to labor ... ... upon your building, described as follows:

....

..../..... . .. .

That my last day's work thereon was done on the . . .. day of ..... , A. D , 18. , and that I shall hold the building, and your interest in the ground, liable for the amount, ... dollars, that is due me on account thereof.

Dated this .. ... day of ......, A. D , 18

(Signature.) ....

(Make either notice in duplicate and keep copy.)

Waiver and Release of Lien for Material or Labor.

STATE OF ILLINOIS, ⎰
 . .. *County,* ⎱ *ss :*

.... 18. .

TO ALL WHOM IT MAY CONCERN

Whereas, .. , the undersigned ....

ha been employed by . . . . to furnish
(*services, labor, or material, and of what class or character*) . . . .

. .. .

for the building known as No . , situated on..... . .. . .

(*the legal description of the land*) .. ..

... .

....

owned by (*name of the owner*) . ...

Now, therefore, know ye, that.... ... ., the undersigned, for and in consideration of . .. .dollars, and other good and valuable considerations, the receipt whereof is hereby acknowledged, do . hereby waive and release any and
all lien, or claim, or right of lien on said above described building and premises,
under "An act to revise the law in relation to liens, approved March 25, 1874,
and all amendments thereto," on account of labor or materials, or both, furnished
(or which may be furnished[1]) by the undersigned to or on account of the said
(*name of contractor, owner, or person who employed or purchased material for
claimant releasing*) for said building or premises

Given under . hand and seal. this . day of ..... 18 ..

(Signature). . ... [SEAL]

[1] Omit, if intention to release lien for only for what has been done or furnished
(Make in duplicate and preserve copy)

The different acts and amendments thereof passed by the Legislature of the State of Illinois with respect to Mechanics' Liens, but not now in force, inserted for interpretation of previous decisions.

ACT OF 1825 — MECHANICS.

An Act for the Benefit of Mechanics, etc.

Section 1. *Be it enacted by the People of the State of Illinois, represented in the General Assembly:* That in all cases hereafter, when any contract shall be made between the proprietor or proprietors of any tract of land or town lot, on the one part, and any person or persons on the other part, for the erecting or repairing any house, or other building, mill, or machinery, of any description whatever, or their appurtenances; or for furnishing labor or materials for the purpose aforesaid; and every other person who may have furnished materials, which shall have been used in the construction of such house, building, or mill, whether by special agreement, or otherwise; the person or persons who shall, in pursuance of such contract, have furnished labor or materials, for such purpose, or who shall have furnished such materials as aforesaid, shall respectively have a lien, to secure the payment of the same, upon such house, or other building, mill, or machinery, and on the lot or tract of land on which the same shall stand or be erected *Provided,* That no such lien shall continue in force for more than three months from the time when payment should have been made, by virtue of any such contract, by which any such lien shall be claimed, unless within that time a suit shall have been commenced for the purpose of enforcing such contract.

(Approved January 13, 1825)
(Revised Code of Laws, 1828, page 106)

ACT OF 1833 — MECHANICS.

An Act for the Benefit of Mechanics.

Section 1. *Be it enacted by the People of the State of Illinois, represented in the General Assembly:* That in all cases, hereafter, where any contract shall be made between the proprietor or proprietors of any tract of land or town lot, on the one part, and any person or persons on the other part, for the erecting or repairing any house or other building, mill, or machinery of any description whatever, or their appurtenances, or for furnishing labor or materials for the purposes aforesaid, and every other person who may have furnished materials, which may have been used in the construction of such house, building or mill, whether by special agreement or otherwise, the person or persons who shall, in pursuance of such contract, have furnished labor or materals for such purpose, or who shall have furnished such materials as aforesaid, shall respectively have a *lien*, to secure the payment of the same, upon such house or other building, mill, or machinery, and on the lot or tract of land on which the same shall be erected

§ 2   When any person or persons shall wish to avail himself, her self, or themselves, of the benefit of such *lien*, he, she, or they shall commence his, her, or their action in any court having jurisdiction of the same, within three months from the time payment should have been made by virtue of any such contract, by which such lien shall have been claimed : And if such suit be commenced in the Circuit Court, it shall be by bill or petition, describing, with common certainty, the tract of land, town lot, building, mill, or machinery, upon which said lien is intended to be made to operate, and also the nature of the contract, or indebtedness; which bill or petition shall be filed in the clerk's office of the proper county, and docketed by the clerk on the common-law appearance docket.   The courts trying such causes shall be governed by the same rules of evidence that are now observed in suits at law, and give judgment according to the justice and equity of the case.

§ 3. The clerk of the court, when judgment has been had, under the provisions of this act, on application, shall issue a special execution, directed to the sheriff of the proper county, describing the property upon which said lien is made to operate, and out of which said judgment and costs are to be collected, or so much thereof as said property will bring ; and no other property of the said defendant, in any suit as aforesaid, shall be bound for the payment of such judgment, unless the claimant hold collateral security for the payment of the same.

§ 4. Any person or persons, wishing to avail himself, herself, or themselves of the benefit of the *lien*, under this act, by suit before a justice of the peace, shall, upon the commencement of such suit, file an account setting forth, with common certainty, the property upon which said lien is intended to be made to operate, and whether it is for work and labor done, or materials furnished ; and upon the trial of said cause, the justice of the peace trying the same, shall hear the proof, and if it shall appear that the defendant in such cause is indebted to the plaintiff, he shall give judgment for the amount so due, and, on application of the plaintiff, said justice of the peace shall give a transcript of the judgment, and certify the same to be for work and labor done, or materials furnished (as the case may be), and also a description of the property subject to such *lien* which transcript and certificate shall be filed in the clerk's office of the county in which said judgment shall have been rendered, and when filed it shall have the same effect as a judgment of the Circuit Court, and execution shall issue in the same manner, and have the same effect as an execution issued upon a judgment rendered in the Circuit Court, under this act: *Provided*, that either of the parties in such suit shall have the same right to appeal that is, or hereafter may be allowed from the judgment of justices of the peace in other cases.

§ 5. All acts and parts of acts, coming within the purview of this act, are hereby repealed

This act to take effect from and after its passage.

(Approved February 22, 1833)
'Revised Laws of Illinois, 1833, page 447)

ACT OF 1839-40.

AN ACT TO PROVIDE FOR SECURING TO MECHANICS AND OTHERS LIENS FOR THE VALUE OF LABOR AND MATERIALS.

SECTION 1. *Be it enacted by the People of the State of Illinois, represented in the General Assembly:* That any person who shall, by contract with the owner of any piece of land or town lot, furnish labor or materials for erecting or repairing any building, or the appurtenances of any building on such land or lot, shall have a lien upon the whole tract of land or town lot, in the manner herein provided, for the amount due to him for such labor or materials

§ 2. The lien shall extend to all work done and materials furnished under the provisions of the contract, whether the kind or quantity of work, or amount to be paid, be specified or not: *Provided*, that the time of completing the contract shall not be extended for a longer period than three years, nor the time of payment beyond the period of one year from the time stipulated for the completion thereof.

§ 3. When any sum due by such contract shall remain unpaid after the same is payable, the creditor may, upon bill or petition to the Circuit Court of the county in which the land or lot lies, obtain an order for the sale thereof, and for applying the proceeds of such sale to the discharge of his demand; and the filing of the bill or petition in the clerk's office, and suing out a summons thereon, shall be deemed the commencement of the suit

§ 4 The bill or petition shall contain a brief statement of the contract on which it is founded, and of the amount due thereon, with a description of the premises which are subject to the lien, and all other material facts and circumstances necessary to a full understanding of the rights of the parties, and shall be considered as the foundation of the plaintiff's action; and upon the filing of which with the clerk, a summons shall issue thereon against all persons made parties as is required upon filing bills in chancery.

§ 5 For the purpose of bringing all parties in interest before the court, the court shall have power to permit amendments to any part of the pleadings, and to issue process, make all orders requiring parties to appear, and requiring notice to be given by publication in newspapers, that are or may be authorized in proceedings in chancery; and the court shall have the same power and jurisdiction over the parties and subject that are or may be conferred upon courts in chancery in respect to proceedings before that court

§ 6. Suits instituted under the provisions of this act shall be placed upon the common-law docket, and shall stand for trial at the term of the court to which the summons is made returnable. The summons shall be served by the sheriff as other process; but if not served ten days before the return thereof, the cause shall be continued, unless the parties agree to a trial at that term of the court.

§ 7. Defendants, in proceedings under this act, shall answer the bill or petition under oath; and the plaintiff shall except or reply to the answer as though the proceeding was in chancery; the answer shall be regarded as the plea of the defendant, and by the replication thereto, an issue or issues shall be formed, which shall be tried by the court or by a jury under the direction of the court, as the court may direct or the parties agree.

§ 8. Every defendant served with process ten days before the return day thereof, shall answer the bill or petition on or before the day on which the cause shall be set for trial on the docket, and the issue or issues in the cause shall be made up under the direction of the court, and oral testimony shall be received as in cases at law.

§ 9. Notice given to parties by publication in newspapers, under the direction of the court, shall be equivalent to personal service of such notice.

§ 10 In proceedings under this act, all persons interested in the subject-matter of the suit, or in the premises intended to be sold, may, on application to the court wherein the suit is pending, become parties at any time before final judgment

§ 11 Upon questions arising between different creditors, no preference shall be given to him whose contract was first made.

§ 12. Upon the trial of causes under this act, the court shall ascertain the amount due each creditor, and shall direct the application of the proceeds of sales to be made to each in proportion to their several amounts.

§ 13. When the owner of the land shall have failed to perform his part of the contract, and by reason thereof the other party shall, without his own default, have been prevented from performing his part, he shall be entitled to a reasonable compensation for as much thereof as he has performed in proportion to the price stipulated for the whole, and the court shall adjust his claim accordingly

§ 14 If any part of the premises can be separated from the residue and sold without damage to the whole, and if the value thereof should be sufficient to satisfy all the claims proved in the cause, the court may order a sale of that part.

§ 15. Parties entitled to liens under the provisions of this act, whose claims are not due or payable at the time of the commencement of suit by any other party, shall be permitted to become parties to the suit, and their claims shall be allowed, subject to a reduction of interest from the date of judgment to the time such lien is due or payable.

§ 16. In cases under this act, where there are several claimants, the issue of law and fact, or either, may be tried separately, and in no case shall the want of preparation for trial to one claim delay the trial in respect to others; but trials shall be had upon issues between such parties as are prepared, without reference to issues between other parties: and when one creditor shall have obtained a verdict or judgment for the amount due, the court may order a sale of the premises on which the lien operates or a part thereof, so as to satisfy the judgment: *Provided*, that the court may, for good causes shown, delay making any order of sale until the rights of all parties in interest shall be ascertained and settled by the court.

27

§ 17. If the person who procures work to be done, or materials furnished, has an estate for life only, or any other estate less than a fee simple in the land or lot on which the work is done, or materials furnished, or if such land or lot, at the time of making the contract, is mortgaged, or under any other incumbrance, the person who procures the work or materials shall nevertheless be considered as the owner within the meaning of this act, to the extent of his right and interest in the premises, and the lien herein provided for shall bind his whole estate and interest therein, in like manner as a mortgage would have done, and the creditor may cause the right of redemption, or whatever other right or estate such owner had in the land at the time of making the contract, to be sold, and the proceeds of sale applied according to the provisions of this act.

§ 18. Suits may be instituted under the provisions of this act in favor of administrators or executors, and may be maintained against the representatives in interest of those against whom the cause of action accrued; and in suits instituted under the provisions of this act, the representatives of any party who may die pending the suit, shall be made parties as though it was a suit in chancery.

§ 19. Upon proceedings under this act, parties claiming may contest each other's rights as well with respect to amount due, as with respect to their right to the benefit of the lien hereby created; and upon all questions made by parties, the court shall require issues of law or fact to be formed, so as to bring about a speedy decision thereof.

§ 20. No incumbrance upon land created before or after the making of a contract, under the provisions of this act, shall operate upon the building erected, or materials furnished, until the lien in favor of the person doing the work or furnishing the materials, shall have been satisfied; and upon questions arising between previous incumbrances and creditors, under the provisions of this act, the previous incumbrance shall be preferred to the extent of the value of the land at the time of making the contract, and the court shall ascertain by jury or otherwise, as the case may require, what proportion of the proceeds of any sale shall be paid to the several parties in interest.

§ 21. Parties in interest, within the meaning of this act, shall include all persons who may have any legal or equitable claim to lands or lots upon which a lien may be attempted to be enforced under the provisions of this act.

§ 22. Creditors who file bills or petitions under this act, may contest the validity of incumbrances, as well in regard to amount as to their justice; and any incumbrance, whether by mortgage, judgment or otherwise, charged and shown to be fraudulent in respect to such creditor, or in respect to creditors generally, may be set aside by the court, and the premises made subject to the claim of the creditor freed and discharged from such fraudulent incumbrance.

§ 23. In proceedings under this act, the courts are vested with all the powers of courts of chancery, and shall be governed by the rules of proceeding and decision in these courts, so far as that power may be necessary to carry into full and complete effect the provisions hereof, and so far as those rules of proceeding and decision are applicable to cases and questions presented for adjudication and decision

§ 24. No creditor shall be allowed to enforce the lien created under the provisions of this (act), as against or to the prejudice of any other creditor or any incumbrance, unless suit be instituted to enforce such lien, within six months after the last payment, for labor or materials, shall have become due and payable.

§ 25. Nothing contained in this act shall be construed to prevent any creditor from maintaining an action at law upon his contract, in like manner as if he had no lien for the security of his debt.

§ 26. If upon making sale of any premises under this act, the proceeds of such shall not be sufficient to pay the claims of all parties according to their rights, the judgment shall be credited by the amount of such sale, and execution may issue in favor of any creditor whose claim is not satisfied for the balance due, as upon a judgment in actions of debt or *assumpsit;* and in cases of excess of sales over the amount of judgment, such excess shall be paid to the owner of the land, or to the person who may be entitled to the same, under the direction of the court.

§ 27 The costs of proceeding under this act, as between creditors claiming liens and the person against whom the lien is intended to be enforced, shall abide the event of the suit and the costs, as between the creditors aforesaid, in contests relative to each other's claims, shall be subject to the order of the court, and the same rule shall prevail in respect to costs growing out of proceed (proceedings) against and between incumbrances.

§ 28. The act entitled "An act for the benefit of mechanics, approved February 22, 1853," is hereby repealed; but rights acquired and liabilities incurred, under that act, shall not be affected by the repeal thereof. This act shall take effect on the first day of May next.

This bill having been laid before the council of revision, and ten days not having intervened before the adjournment of the General Assembly, and the said bill not having been returned with the objections of the council on the first day of the present session of the General Assembly, it has become a law.

Given under my hand this 10th day of December, 1839.

A. P. FIELD,

Secretary of State.

(Laws of Illinois, 1839-40, page 147.)

ACT OF 1845.

CHAPTER LXV.

LIENS.

SECTION 1. Any person who shall, by contract with the owner of any tract or piece of land or town lot, furnish labor or materials for erecting or repairing any building, or the appurtenances of any building on such land or lot, shall have a lien upon the whole tract of land or town lot, in the manner herein provided, for the amount due to him for such labor or materials.

§ 2. The lien shall extend to all work done and materials furnished under the provisions of the contract, whether the kind or quantity of the work, or amount to be paid, be specified or not provided, That the time of completing the contract shall not be extended for a longer period than three years, nor the time of payment beyond the period of one year, for the time stipulated for the completion thereof.

§ 3 When any sum due by such contract shall remain unpaid after the same is payable, the creditor may, upon bill or petition to the Circuit Court of the county in which the land or lot lies, obtain an order for the sale thereof, and for applying the proceeds of such sale to the discharge of his demand; and the filing of the bill or petition in the clerk's office, and suing out a summons thereon, shall be deemed the commencement of the suit

§ 4. The bill or petition shall contain a brief statement of the contract on which it is founded, and of the amount due thereon, with a description of the premises which are subject to the lien, and all other material facts and circumstances necessary to a full understanding of the rights of the parties, and shall be considered as the foundation of the plaintiff's action; and upon the filing of which with the clerk, a summons shall issue thereon against all persons made parties, as is required upon filing bills in chancery.

§ 5 For the purpose of bringing all parties in interest before the court, the court shall have power to permit amendments to any part of the pleadings, and to issue process, make all orders requiring parties to appear, and requiring notice to be given by publication in newspapers that are or may be authorized in proceedings in chancery, and the court shall have the same power and jurisdiction over the parties and subject that are or may be conferred upon courts in chancery in respect to proceedings before that court.

§ 6 Suits instituted under the provisions of this chapter shall be placed upon the common law docket, and shall stand for trial at the term of the court to which the summons is made returnable. The summons shall be served by the sheriff as other process; but if not served ten days before the return day thereof the cause shall be continued, unless the parties agree to a trial at that term of the court.

§ 7. Defendants, in proceedings under the provisions of this chapter, shall answer the bill or petition under oath, and the plaintiff shall except or reply to the answer as though the proceeding was in chancery, the answer shall be regarded as the plea of the defendant, and by the replication thereto an issue or issues shall be formed, which shall be tried by the court or by a jury under the direction of the court, as the court may direct or the parties agree

§ 8. Every defendant served with process ten days before the return day thereof shall answer the bill or petition on or before the day on which the cause shall be set for trial on the docket, and the issue or issues in the cause shall be made up under the direction of the court, and oral testimony shall be received as in cases at law.

§ 9 Notice given to parties by publication in newspapers, under the direction of the court, shall be equivalent to personal service of such notice.

§ 10. In proceedings under this chapter, all persons interested in the subject-matter of the suit, or in the premises intended to be sold, may, on application to the court wherein the suit is pending, become parties at any time before final judgment.

§ 11. Upon questions arising between different creditors, no preference shall be given to him whose contract was first made.

§ 12. Upon the trial of causes under the provisions of this chapter, the court shall ascertain the amount due each creditor, and shall direct the application of the proceeds of sales to be made to each in proportion to their several amounts

§ 13. When the owner of the land shall have failed to perform his part of the contract, and by reason thereof the other party shall, without his own default, have been prevented from performing his part, he shall be entitled to a reasonable compensation for as much thereof as he has performed in proportion to the price stipulated for the whole, and the court shall adjust his claim accordingly

§ 14. If any part of the premises can be separated from the residue and sold without damage to the whole, and if the value thereof should be sufficient to satisfy all the claims proved in the cause, the court may order a sale of that part.

§ 15. Parties entitled to liens under the provisions of this chapter, whose claims are not due or payable at the time of the commencement of suit by any other party, shall be permitted to become parties to the suit, and their claims shall be allowed, subject to a reduction

of interest from the date of judgment to the time such claim is due
or payable

§ 16. In cases under the provisions of this chapter, where there
are several claimants, the issue of law and fact, or either, may be
tried separately, and in no case shall the want of preparation for
trial to one claim delay the trial in respect to others ; but trials
shall be had upon issues between such parties as are prepared, without reference to issues between other parties ; and when one creditor shall have obtained a verdict or judgment for the amount due,
the court may order a sale of the premises on which the lien operates, or a part thereof, so as to satisfy the judgment : *Provided*,
that the court may, for good causes shown, delay making any order
of sale until the rights of all parties in interest shall be ascertained
and settled by the court.

§ 17. If the person who procures work to be done, or materials
furnished, has an estate for life only, or any other estate less than a
fee simple in the land or lot on which the work is done, or materials furnished, or if such land or lot, at the time of making the
contract, is mortgaged, or under any other incumbrance, the person
who procures the work or materials shall nevertheless be considered
as the owner within the meaning of this chapter, to the extent of
his right and interest in the premises , and the lien herein provided
for shall bind his whole estate and interest therein in like manner
as a mortgage would have done : and the creditor may cause the
right of redemption, or whatever other right or estate such owner
had in the land at the time of making the contract, to be sold, and
the proceeds of sale applied according to the provisions of this
chapter

§ 18. Suits may be instituted under the provisions of this chapter
in favor of administrators or executors, and may be maintained
against the representatives in interest of those against whom the
cause of action accrued; and in suits instituted under the provisions of this chapter, the representatives of any party who may die
pending the suit, shall be made parties as though it were a suit in
chancery.

§ 19. Upon proceedings under the provisions of this chapter, parties claiming may contest each other's rights as well with respect to
amount due as with respect to their right to the benefit of the lien
hereby created ; and upon all questions made by parties, the court
shall require issues of law or fact to be formed, so as to bring about
a speedy decision thereof.

§ 20. No incumbrance upon land created before or after the making of a contract under the provisions of this chapter, shall operate upon the building erected or materials furnished, until the lien in favor of the person doing the work or furnishing the materials shall have been satisfied: and upon questions arising between previous incumbrances and creditors, under the provisions of this chapter, the previous incumbrance shall be preferred to the extent of the value of the land at the time of making the contract, and the court shall ascertain by jury or otherwise, as the case may require, what proportion of the proceeds of any sale shall be paid to the several parties in interest.

§ 21. Parties in interest, within the meaning of this chapter, shall include all persons who may have any legal or equitable claim to lands or lots upon which a lien may be attempted to be enforced under the provisions of this chapter

§ 22 Creditors who file bills or petitions under the provisions of this chapter, may contest the validity of incumbrances, as well in regard to amount as to their justice, and any incumbrance, whether by mortgage, judgment or otherwise, charged and shown to be fraudulent in respect to such creditor, or in respect to creditors generally, may be set aside by the court, and the premises made subject to the claim of the creditor freed and discharged from such fraudulent incumbrance.

§ 23 In proceedings under the provisions of this chapter, the courts are vested with all the powers of courts of chancery, and shall be governed by the rules of proceeding and decision in these courts, so far as that power may be necessary to carry into full and complete effect the provisions hereof, and so far as those rules of proceeding and decision are applicable to cases and questions presented for adjudication and decision.

§ 24 No creditor shall be allowed to enforce the lien created under the provisions of this chapter, as against or to the prejudice of any other creditor or any incumbrance, unless suit be instituted to enforce such lien, within six months after the last payment, for labor or materials, shall have become due and payable.

§ 25 Nothing contained in this chapter, shall be construed to prevent any creditor from maintaining an action at law upon his contract, in like manner as if he had no lien for the security of his debt.

§ 26. If, upon making sale of any premises under this chapter, the proceeds of such sale shall not be sufficient to pay the claims of

28

all parties, according to their rights, the judgment shall be credited
by the amount of such sale, and execution may issue in favor of any
creditor, whose claim is not satisfied, for the balance due, as upon
a judgment in actions of debt or assumpsit; and in case of excess
of sales over the amount of judgment, such excess shall be paid to
the owner of the land, or to the person who may be entitled to the
same, under the direction of the court.

§ 27. The costs of proceeding under the provisions of this chapter, as between creditors claiming liens and the person against whom
the lien is intended to be enforced, shall abide the event of the suit,
and the costs, as between creditors aforesaid, in contests relative to
each other's claims, shall be subject to the order of the court, and
the same rule shall prevail in respect to costs growing out of proceedings against and between incumbrancers.

Approved March 3, 1845.

AMENDMENT OF FEBRUARY 18, 1861.

AN ACT TO AMEND CHAPTER SIXTY-FIVE OF THE REVISED STATUTES
OF 1845, ENTITLED "LIENS."

SECTION 1. *Be it enacted by the People of the State of Illinois,
represented in the General Assembly,* That chapter sixty-five of the
Revised Statutes of 1845, entitled "Liens," shall be held to include
implied as well as expressed contracts, under which labor or materials
are furnished, at the request of any owner of land or town lot, for
erecting or repairing any building or the appurtenances of any building on such land or town lot, where no price is agreed upon or no
time is expressly fixed for the payment of such labor, or for the furnishing of such labor or materials: *Provided,* that the work is done
or materials furnished within one year from the commencement of
said work or the commencement of furnishing said materials.

§ 2. This act shall take effect and be in force from and after its
passage

(Approved February 18, 1861)
(Public Laws of Illinois, 1861, page 179.)

ACT OF FEBRUARY 22, 1861.

AN ACT IN RELATION TO THE LIENS OF OPERATIVES AND OTHERS ON THE PROPERTY OF RAILROAD CORPORATIONS WITHIN THIS STATE.

SECTION 1 *Be it enacted by the People of the State of Illinois, represented in the General Assembly,* That all persons who may have furnished or who shall hereafter furnish to any railroad corporation existing under the laws of this State, any fuel, ties, materials, supplies, or any other article or thing, necessary for the construction, maintenance, operation or repair of such roads, by contract with said corporation, or who shall have done and performed, or shall hereafter do and perform any work or labor for such construction, maintenance, operation or repair, by like contract, shall be entitled to be paid for the same as part of the current expenses of said road, and, in order to secure the same, shall have a lien for three months after the right of action accrues upon all the property, real, personal and mixed, of said railroad corporation, as against all mortgages or other liens which accrued after the commencement of the delivery of said articles or the commencement of said work or labor

§ 2. In case within the three months, heretofore limited, the party furnishing such article or thing, or performing such work or labor, shall commence suit for the recovery of such debt, in any court of record, then the lien hereby created shall continue until the same has been decided by said court; and, if the judgment be against said corporation, until an execution thereupon issued shall be satisfied or released by the plaintiff

§ 3. This act to take effect and be in force from and after its passage.

(Approved February 22, 1861)
(Public Laws of Illinois, 1861 page 142.)

ACT OF FEBRUARY 14, 1863.

AN ACT FOR THE BETTER SECURITY OF MECHANICS ERECTING BUILDINGS IN THE STATE OF ILLINOIS

SECTION 1. *Be it enacted by the People of the State of Illinois, represented in the General Assembly,* That every sub-contractor, mechanic, workman or other person, who shall hereafter, in conformity with the terms of the contract between the owner of any lot or piece of ground, or his agent, and the original contractor, perform any labor or furnish any materials in building, altering or repairing any house or other building, or in any street or alley, and connected with such building or appurtenance to any house or other building, in the counties of Cook, Alexander, Union, Peoria, Williamson, Bureau, Putnam, Marshall, Woodford, Pulaski, Edgar, Marion, Franklin, Henry, Fulton and De Kalb, in this State, shall have a lien for the value of such labor and materials upon such house or building and appurtenances, and upon the lot of land upon which the same stand, to the extent of the right, title and interest at that time existing of such owner, in the manner and to the extent hereinafter provided; but the aggregate of all the liens authorized by this act to be created shall not exceed the price stipulated in the contract between such owner and the original contractor to be paid for such improvement, and nothing in this act contained shall oblige such owner to pay a greater sum for or on account of such house or building than the price or sum agreed and stipulated to be paid in and by such contract.

§ 2 The person performing such labor or furnishing such materials shall cause to be drawn up specifications of the work by him contracted to be performed or materials to be furnished, and stating the price or prices agreed to be paid therefor, and shall file them, or, if there be a contract in writing, a true copy thereof, in the office of the clerk of the Circuit Court of the county wherein the said house or other building is situated, and serve notice of such filing on such owner or his agent, within twenty days after making of such contract or commencing the performing of such labor or the furnishing of said materials. Said clerk shall provide a book, which shall be called the "Mechanics and Laborers' Lien Docket," in which he shall enter, alphabetically, the names of the owners, and opposite to them the names of the contractors or laborers, or other persons claiming a lien, and the lot or street on which said work is to be done, or materials furnished, and the time of filing such specifications or copy of such contract; and such clerk shall, in each case, receive the sum of twenty-five cents

§ 3. The lien created by this act shall take effect from the time of filing the specifications or contract, as provided by section two of this act, and the service of the notice of the filing thereof in said section provided, and shall continue in full force for the period of one year thereafter.

§ 4. Any person performing such labor or furnishing such materials, as mentioned in preceding sections of this act, and claiming a lien therefor by virtue of this act, shall, within thirty days after such labor has been performed or such materials have been furnished, produce and deliver to such owner or his said agent a statement, in writing, signed by himself and said contractor, specifying how much is due to such person for such labor done or materials furnished; or in default of so doing shall take the necessary legal proceedings against the contractor to procure an accounting and settlement of the amount due or owing for such labor or materials; which proceeding may be instituted in any court having jurisdiction of the amount claimed to be due, and shall, in all respects, be conducted like other suits at law; and shall serve the owner of said premises, or his agent, with a copy of the summons and notice of the amount claimed; and the service of such summons and notice shall, during the pendency of said suit, be a bar to the recovery by the contractor from the owner of the amount claimed in said summons and notice, together with interests and costs thereon. And in case such person shall fail to produce and deliver such statement, or take the necessary legal proceedings to adjudicate and settle such claim, within said period of thirty days, to compel such accounting and settlement between himself and such contractor, and serve said owner, or his said agent, with a copy of the summons and notice aforesaid, or shall fail to prosecute the proceedings so taken with effect and without unreasonable delay to final judgment, he shall forever lose the benefit and be precluded of his said lien The amount of any judgment which may be recovered by any such person for any such labor and materials, or the amount which by written statement, to be signed by them as aforesaid, shall be specified to be due to such person from such contractor, shall be paid by such owner, or his agent, to such person; and when so paid, shall be deemed to be a payment of such amount by the said owner on the contract, made with the said owner or his said agent And if such owner, or his said agent, shall refuse or neglect to pay such sum, after being served with such statement or a transcript of the docket of the judgment, for ten days after being requested so to do, then the person owning or holding such statement or transcript of such judgment may file in the Circuit Court of the county where the property, building or premises are situated, his petition against such owner, for an order or decree to sell said premises, building or property; which said petition shall contain a brief statement of the facts, and allege, under the oath of the petitioner: 1st. That the defendant is the owner of the property, premises or building, or state the nature of his interest therein, as near as may be, and describing the same. 2d. The nature, as near as may be, of the contract between the owner and the original contractor, and the kind of buildings and improvements contracted to be made. 3d The nature and amount of the work done, or materials furnished by the petitioner, and the fact that such owner or his agent has been duly served with a copy of the statement of the amount due to the petitioner, signed by such petitioner and the contractor, or a copy of the transcript of a judgment in favor of such petitioner and against such contractor, for such work and labor done or materials furnished, and the refusal of such owner or his agent to pay the same, as required by the provisions of this act. And upon the filing of such petition, duly verified, the clerk of said court shall issue a summons, as now provided by law in cases of mechanics' liens, which summons shall be served as now provided by law; and said case shall be docketed and stand for trial, and the same proceedings shall be had in respect thereto as are now provided by law in cases of mechanics' liens

§ 5. On the trial of said cause, if the court shall be satisfied that the petitioner has complied with the requirements of this act, and taken the necessary steps to perfect his said lien, as hereinbefore provided, then said court shall enter judgment for the amount of said statement, signed as aforesaid by said petitioner and said contractor, or for the amount of the transcript of said judgment in favor of such person against said contractor, and decree or order that the same be a lien upon the said premises or lot of said owner to the extent hereinbefore provided, and that the same be sold to satisfy such judgment, together with the costs of such proceedings; and execution may issue on such judgment, and costs shall be awarded and taxed, and the same proceedings be had upon said judgment and the execution issued thereon as are now provided by law in cases of mechanic's liens.

§ 6. Whenever any suit shall be brought by any contractor, subcontractor, laborer, or person furnishing material, as hereinbefore provided, to enforce a lien, as provided by this act, or by the law of *lien*, as it now exists in this State, or the contractor shall sue upon the contract, the owner may file his petition, as the cause so brought, stating who has liens upon the premises; and the proceedings in said cause shall be stayed until all the parties having such liens are brought before the court; and when all the parties interested shall be brought before the court, the court shall cause the rights of all the parties to be adjusted and render judgment according to the rights of the parties, and cause the proper division of the amount due from the owner to be made ratably among said sub-contractors, laborers and persons furnishing materials until they are fully paid (should there be sufficient due from the owner to pay the same), and the balance, if any, to the contractor, and if the owner shall desire to have said claims adjusted, he may file his petition in the Circuit Court, stating the facts, and summon all parties interested as contractors, sub-contractors, laborers or materialmen, and upon the hearing therein, the court shall determine the amount due from the owner and the amount due to each of the other parties respectively, and distribute the amount due from the owner, as hereinbefore specified

The provisions of this act shall apply to the counties of Cook, Alexander, Union, Peoria, Williamson, Bureau, Putnam, Marshall, Woodford, Pulaski, Edgar, Marion, Franklin, Henry, Fulton and De Kalb, and to no other part of the State, and this act shall take effect and be in force from and after its passage.

(Approved February 14. 1863)

(Public Laws of Illinois, 1863, page 57)

(This act was extended to Adams county, February 16, 1865; Session Laws, 1865, page 91.)

(To the counties of Lake, McHenry, Boone, Winnebago, Peoria, Marshall, Stark, Putnam, Knox, Mason, Fulton, Kane, DuPage, Will, Coles, St Clair and Hancock, March 7, 1867 Session Laws 1867, page 133)

(To Douglas county, March 30, 1869)

(To McLean, De Witt and Macon counties, March 31, 1869 Session Laws, 1869, page 258)

(Repealed in the enactment of April 5, 1869)

AMENDMENT, FEBRUARY 14, 1863.

An Act to Amend Chapter Sixty-five of the Revised Statutes of 1845, Entitled " Liens."

SECTION 1. *Be it enacted by the People of the State of Illinois, represented in the General Assembly.* That when any person or persons shall furnish labor or materials for erecting or repairing any building or superstructure, or the appurtenances thereof, in accordance with the existing lien laws of this State, or any that may be enacted during the present session of the General Assembly, and such building, superstructure or appurtenance shall extend over and beyond the line of the lot upon which the main building or superstructure is erected, or shall furnish materials or perform any

labor outside of the lot line subject to be ordered by any incorpo
rated city within this State, such person or persons shall have a lien
upon said lot in the manner provided by the existing statutes for
the amount due for such labor or materials.

§ 2 This act to be in force from and after its passage.

(Approved February 14, 1863)
(Public Laws of Illinois, 1863, page 71)

ACT OF MARCH 30, 1869.

An Act to Provide for the Redemption of Property sold under Mechanics' Lien.

Section 1. *Be it enacted by the People of the State of Illinois,
represented in the General Assembly,* That, hereafter, there shall
exist in favor of the same persons, and in the same manner as is or
may be provided for redemption of real estate from sales under
judgments and executions at common law, the right to redeem real
estate sold under any decree obtained under the provisions of chapter sixty-five of the Revised Statutes, or any act amendatory thereof,
from such sales.

(Approved March 30, 1869)
(Laws of Illinois, 1869, page 258.)

ACT OF APRIL 5, 1869 — MECHANICS' LIEN.

An Act Amendatory of the Mechanics' Lien Law of this State

Section 1. *Be it enacted by the People of the State of Illinois,
represented in the General Assembly,* That every sub-contractor,
mechanic, workman, or other person who shall hereafter, in conformity with the terms of the contract between the owner or lessee
of any lot or piece of ground, or his agent, and the original contractor, perform any labor or furnish any materials in building, altering, repairing, beautifying or ornamenting any house or other building, or in any street or alley, and connected with such building, or
appurtenance to any house or other building in this State, shall have
a lien for the value of such labor and materials upon such house or
building and appurtenances, and upon the lot of land upon which
the same stands, to the extent of the right, title and interest of such
owner or lessee at the time of the making the original contract for

such house or the improvements. But the aggregate of all the liens hereby authorized shall not exceed the price stipulated in the original contract between such owner or lessee and the original contractor for such improvements, in no case shall the owner or lessee be compelled to pay a greater sum for or on account of such house, building or other improvement, than the price or sum stipulated in said original contract or agreement.

§ 2 The person performing such labor or furnishing such materials shall cause a notice, in writing, to be served on such owner or lessee, or his agent, substantially in the following form. "To   .
You are hereby notified that I am (or have been) employed by
            , as a laborer (or have furnished materials, or am about to furnish materials) on or for your house or building, and that I shall hold the house, building, and your interest in the ground liable for my services thereon (or materials furnished) " If there shall be a contract, in writing, between the original contractor and the subcontractor, a copy of such sub-contract, if the same can be obtained, shall be served with such notice and attached thereto, which notice shall be served within twenty days from the completion of such sub contract, or within twenty days after payment should have been made to the person performing such labor or furnishing such material

§ 3. In all cases where the owner or lessee cannot be found in the county in which said improvements shall be made, or shall not reside therein, the person furnishing labor or materials shall file said notice in the office of the clerk of the Circuit Court, and the clerk of the Circuit Court shall enter, in a book to be kept for that purpose, alphabetically, the names of the owners or lessees, and opposite thereto the names of the persons claiming liens, for which the clerk shall receive a fee of fifty cents A copy of said notice shall be published in some newspaper, printed in said county, for four successive weeks after filing such notice with the clerk as aforesaid. If, however, there shall be no paper published in said county, then the claimant of lien shall post four notices in four of the most public places in the vicinity of said improvement for four weeks

§ 4 The original contractor shall, as often as requested, in writing, by the owner or lessee, or his agent, make out and give to him a statement of the number of persons in his employ, and subcontractors, giving their names and the rate of wages or terms of contract, and how much, if any thing, is due to them, or any of them, which statement shall be made under oath, if required

§ 5. And if the money due to such person shall not be paid within ten days after service of said notice as aforesaid, or within ten days after the money shall become due and payable, then such person may commence suit therefor in any court having jurisdiction of the amount claimed to be due against the owner or lessee and contractor jointly; execution to issue thereon as in other cases If execution, issued on judgment obtained before justice of the peace, shall be returned not satisfied, a transcript of such judgment may be taken to the Circuit Court and spread upon the records thereof, and have all the force and effect of judgments obtained in Circuit Courts, and execution issue thereon as in other cases

§ 6 Whenever any suit shall be brought by any laborer, the court shall allow, if before a justice of the peace, five dollars, and in courts of record, twenty dollars attorney fees, if judgment shall be given against the defendant, which fees shall be a part of the costs in suit

§ 7 Should the original contractor, for any cause, fail to complete his contract, any person entitled to a lien, as aforesaid, may file his petition in any court of record against the owner or lessee and contractor, setting forth the nature of his claim, the amount due, as near as may be, and the names of the parties employed on such house or other improvement subject to liens, and notice of such suit shall be served on the persons therein named, and such as shall appear shall have their claims adjudicated, and decree shall be entered against the owner or lessee and original contractor for so much as the work and material shall be shown to be reasonably worth according to the original contract price, first deducting so much as shall have been rightfully paid on said original contract by the owner or lessee, the balance to be divided between such claimants in proportion to their respective interests, to be ascertained by the court; the premises to be sold within thirty days from date of such decree, unless the judgment shall be sooner paid

§ 8 No payments to the original contractor or to his order shall be regarded as rightfully made, if made in violation of the rights and interests of the persons intended to be benefited by this act

§ 9. The lien hereby created shall continue for three months from the time of the performance of the sub-contract, or doing of the work or furnishing materials as aforesaid, except where suit shall be commenced by petition as aforesaid, and in such cases all liens shall be barred by decree entered in said case

§ 10. The act entitled " An act for the better security of mechanies erecting buildings in the State of Illinois," approved February 14, 1863, be and the same is hereby repealed. *Provided*, that the passage of this act, and the repeal of any or all former acts, shall not in any way affect pending proceedings or liens heretofore existing, but all such liens and proceedings are hereby saved, and may be enforced as now provided by law

§ 11 This act shall take effect and be in force from and after its passage.

(Approved April 5 1869)

(Session Laws of Illinois, 1869, page 255)

ACT OF 1874.

An Act to Revise the Law in Relation to Liens

(Approved March 25, 1874, in force July 1, 1874)

SECTION 1 *Be it enacted by the People of the State of Illinois, represented in the General Assembly*, That any person who shall, by contract, express or implied, or partly expressed or partly implied, with the owner of any lot or piece of land, furnish labor or materials, or services as an architect or superintendent in building, altering, repairing, or ornamenting any house or other building or appurtenance thereto on such lot, or upon any street or alley, and connected with such building or appurtenance, shall have a lien upon the whole of such tract of land or lot, and upon such house or building and appurtenance, for the amount due to him for such labor, material or services

§ 2 The lien provided for in sections one and twenty-nine of this act, shall extend to an estate in fee for life, for years, or any other estate, or any right of redemption or other interest which such owner may have in the lot or land at the time of making the contract.

§ 3. When the contract is expressed, no lien shall be created under this act, if the time stipulated for the completion of the work or furnishing materials is beyond three years from the commencement thereof, or the time of payment beyond one year from the time stipulated for the completion thereof. If the work is done or materials are furnished under an implied contract, no lien shall be had by virtue of this act, unless the work shall be done or materials be furnished within one year from the commencement of the work or delivery of the materials.

§ 4. The lien given by this act may be enforced by bill or petition in any court of record of competent jurisdiction in the county in which the land or lot, or some parts thereof, lies

§ 5. The bill or petition shall contain a brief statement of the contract on which it is founded, if expressed, or if the work is done or materials are furnished under an implied contract, the bill or petition shall so state, and shall show the amount due and unpaid, a description of the premises which are subject to the lien, and such other facts as may be necessary to a full understanding of the rights of the parties.

§ 6. Upon the filing of such bill or petition, summons shall issue and service thereof be had, as in suits in chancery.

§ 7 When any defendant resides or has gone out of the State, or on due inquiry cannot be found, or is concealed within this State, so that process cannot be served upon him, the complainant or petitioner may cause notice to be given to him in like manner and upon the same conditions as provided in suits in chancery.

§ 8 Suits instituted under the provisions of this act shall be placed upon the chancery docket, and stand for trial as other suits in chancery.

§ 9. For the purpose of bringing all parties in interest before the court, the court shall permit amendments to any part of the pleadings, and may issue process, make all orders requiring parties to appear, and requiring notice to be given, that are or may be authorized in proceedings in chancery, and shall have the same power and jurisdiction of the parties and subject ; and the rules of practice and proceedings in such cases shall be the same as in other cases in chancery, except as is otherwise provided in this act.

§ 10. Defendants shall answer the bill or petition under oath, unless the oath is waived by the complainant or petitioner, and the plaintiff shall except or reply to the answer as though the proceeding was in chancery. The answer shall be regarded as the plea of the defendant, and by replication thereto an issue or issues shall be formed, which shall be tried by the court, or by a jury under the direction of the court, as the court may direct or the parties agree.

§ 11. When the owner of the land shall have failed to perform his part of the contract, and by reason thereof the other party shall, without his own default, have been prevented from performing his part, he shall be entitled to a reasonable compensation for as much thereof as he has performed, in proportion to the price stipulated for the whole, and the court shall adjust his claim accordingly

§ 12 In proceedings under this act all persons interested in the subject-matter of the suit, or in the premises intended to be sold, may, on application to the court wherein the suit is pending, be made or become parties at any time before final judgment.

§ 13. Parties in interest, within the meaning of this act, shall include all persons who may have any legal or equitable claim to the whole or any part of the premises upon which a lien may be attempted to be enforced under the provisions of this act

§ 14 Upon questions arising between different creditors having liens under this act, no preference shall be given to him whose contract was first made.

§ 15 The court shall ascertain the amount due each creditor, and shall direct the application of the proceeds of sales to be made to each in proportion to their several amounts.

§ 16 Parties entitled to liens under this act, whose claims are not due or payable at the time of the commencement of suit by any other party, shall be permitted to become parties to the suit, and their claims shall be allowed, subject to a reduction of interest from the date of judgment to the time such claim is due or payable.

§ 17 No incumbrance upon land created before or after the making of the contract, under the provisions of this act, shall operate upon the building erected or materials furnished, until the lien in favor of the person doing the work or furnishing the materials shall have been satisfied ; and upon questions arising between previous incumbrances and creditors, the previous incumbrance shall be preferred to the extent of the value of the land at the time of making the contract, and the court shall ascertain, by jury or otherwise, as the case may require, what proportion of the proceeds of any sale shall be paid to the several parties in interest.

§ 18. Parties claiming may contest each other's rights, as well with respect to amount due, as with respect to their right to the benefit of the lien hereby created ; and upon all questions made by parties, the court shall require issues of law or fact to be formed so as to bring about a speedy decision thereof.

§ 19. Any incumbrance, whether by mortgage, judgment, or otherwise, charged and shown to be fraudulent in respect to creditors, may be set aside by the court and the premises made subject to the claim of the complainant or petitioner, freed and discharged from such fraudulent incumbrance.

§ 20. In no case shall the want of preparation for trial of one claim delay the trial in respect to others, but trials shall be had upon issues between such parties as are prepared, without reference to issues between other parties; and when one creditor shall have obtained a decree or judgment for the amount due, the court may order a sale of the premises on which the lien operates, or a part thereof, so as to satisfy the judgment. *Provided*, that the court may, for good cause shown, delay making any order of sale or distribution until the rights of all parties in interest are ascertained and settled by the court

§ 21 Whatever right or estate such owner had in the land at the time of making the contract, may be sold, and the proceeds of sale applied according to the provisions of this act

§ 22. If any part of the premises can be separated from the residue, and sold without damage to the whole, and if the value thereof is sufficient to satisfy all the claims proved in the cause, the court may order a sale of that part

§ 23 The sales shall be made in the same manner as other sales of real estate under decrees in chancery

§ 24. Upon all sales under this act, the right of redemption shall exist in favor of the same persons, and may be made in the same manner as is or may be provided for redemption of real estate from sales under judgments and executions at common law

§ 25. If, upon making sale of any premises under this act, the proceeds of such sale shall not be sufficient to pay the claims of all parties, according to their rights, the judgment shall be credited by the amount of such sale, and execution may issue in favor of any creditor whose claim is not satisfied, for the balance due, as upon a judgment in actions of debt or *assumpsit*, and in case of excess of sales over the amount of judgment, such excess shall be paid to the owner of the land, or to the person who may be entitled to the same, under the direction of the court.

§ 26 Suits may be instituted under the provisions of this act, in favor of administrators or executors, and may be maintained against the representatives in interest of those against whom the cause of action accrued ; and in suits instituted under the provisions of this act, the representatives of any party who may die pending the suit, shall be made parties.

§ 27 The cost of proceeding as between creditors claiming liens and the person against whom the lien is intended to be enforced, shall abide the event of the suit; and the costs, as between creditors aforesaid, in contests relative to each other's claim, shall be subject to the order of the court, and the same rule shall prevail in respect to costs growing out of proceedings against and between incumbrances.

§ 28. No creditor shall be allowed to enforce the lien created under the foregoing provisions, as against or to the prejudice of any other creditor or any incumbrance, unless suit be instituted to enforce such lien within six months after the last payment for labor or materials shall have become due and payable ·

§ 29. Every sub-contractor, mechanic, workman or other person, who shall hereafter, in pursuance of the purposes of the original contract between the owner of any lot or piece of ground, or his agent and the original contractor, perform any labor or furnish any materials in building, altering, repairing, beautifying or ornamenting any house or other building or appurtenance thereto, on such lot or on any street or alley, and connected with such building or appurtenances, shall have a lien for the value of such labor and materials upon such house or building and appurtenances, and upon the lot or land upon which the same stands, to the extent of the right, title and interest of such owner at the time of making the original contract for such house or the improvement; but the aggregate of all the liens hereby authorized shall not exceed the price stipulated in the original contract between such owner and the original contractor for such improvement   In no case shall the owner be compelled to pay a greater sum for or on account of such house, building or other improvement than the price or ·sum stipulated in said original contract or agreement *Provided*, if it shall appear to the court that the owner and contractor fraudulently and for the purpose of defrauding sub-contractors, fixed an unreasonably low price in the original contract for the erection or reparation of such building, then the court shall ascertain how much of a difference exists between a fair price for the labor or material used in said building or other improvements, and the sum named in said original contracts, said difference shall be considered a part of the contract and be subject to a lien; but in no case shall the original contractor's time or profits be secured by this lien, only so far as the sum named in the original contract or agreement.

§ 30. The person performing such labor, or furnishing such materials, shall cause a notice, in writing, to be served on such owner or his agent, substantially in the following form
" To   :

You are hereby notified that I have been employed by
to (here state whether you labor or furnish material, and sub-

stantially the nature of the undertaking or demand) upon your (here
state the building and where situated, in general terms) and that I
shall hold the (building, or as the case may be) and your interest in
the ground liable for the amount that is (or may become) due me
on account thereof.

(Date.)   .   (Signature)

§ 31. If there is a contract in writing between the original contractor and the sub-contractor, a copy of such sub-contract, if the
same can be obtained, shall be served with such notice and attached
thereto, which notice shall be served within forty days from the
completion of such sub-contract, or within forty days after payment
should have been made to the person performing such labor or furnishing such material.

§ 32. In all cases where the owner cannot be found in the county
in which said improvement is made, or shall not reside therein, the
person furnishing labor or materials shall file said notice in the office
of the clerk of the Circuit Court, who shall enter, in a book to be
kept for that purpose, alphabetically, the names of the owners, and
opposite thereto the names of the persons claiming liens, for which
the clerk shall receive a fee of fifty cents. A copy of said notice
shall be published in some newspaper printed in said county, for
four successive weeks after filing such notice with the clerk as aforesaid. If, however, there is no paper published in said county, then
the claimant of the lien shall post notices in four of the most public
places in the vicinity of said improvement.

§ 33. No claim of any sub-contractor, mechanic, workman or
other person, shall be a lien under section twenty-nine of this act,
except so far as the owner may be indebted to the contractor at the
time of giving such notice, as aforesaid, or such claim, or may
become indebted afterward to him as contractor.

§ 34. When the owner or his agent is notified as aforesaid, he may
retain from any money due or to become due the original contractor,
an amount sufficient to pay all demands that are or will become due
such sub-contractor, mechanic, workman or other person so notifying
him, and may pay over the same to the persons entitled thereto
In case there is not a sufficient amount due to such original contractor to pay such persons so entitled in full, the same shall be
divided and paid to such persons *pro rata*, in proportion to the
amounts due them respectively at the time of such payment   All

payments so made shall, as between such owner and contractor, be considered the same as if paid to such original contractor

§ 35. The original contractor shall, as often as requested in writing by the owner or lessee, or his agent, make out and give to him a statement of the number of persons in his employ, and subcontractors, giving their names and the rate of wages or terms of contract, and how much, if any thing, is due to them, or any of them; which statement shall be made under oath, if required

§ 36. If any contractor shall fail to furnish such statement within five days after demand made, as aforesaid, he shall forfeit to such owner the sum of fifty dollars for every such offense, which may be recovered in an action of debt before a justice of the peace.

§ 37. If the money due to the person giving such notice shall not be paid within ten days after service thereof, as aforesaid, or within ten days after the money shall become due and payable, and any money shall then be due from such owner to the original contractor, then such person may file his petition and enforce his lien in the same manner as hereinbefore provided in case of original contractors; or he may sue the owner and contractor jointly for the amount due him in any court having jurisdiction of the amount claimed to be due, and a personal judgment may be rendered therein as in other cases.

§ 38. If execution issued on a judgment obtained before a justice of the peace shall be returned not satisfied, a transcript of such judgment may be taken to the Circuit Court and spread upon the records thereof, and execution issued thereon as in other cases.

§ 39 If there are several liens, under section twenty-nine, upon the same premises, and the owner, or any person having such lien, shall fear that there is not a sufficient amount coming to the contractor to pay all of such liens, such owner, or any one or more persons having such lien, may file his or their sworn bill or petition in the Circuit Court of the proper county, stating such fact, and such other facts as may be sufficient to a full understanding of the rights of the parties. The contractor, and all persons having liens upon, or who are interested in the premises, so far as the same are known to or can be ascertained by the claimant or petitioner, upon diligent inquiry, shall be made parties Upon the hearing, the court shall find the amount coming from the owner to the contractor, and the amount due to each of the persons having liens; and in case the amount found to be coming to the contractor shall be insufficient to discharge all the liens in full, the amount so found in favor of the

30

contractor shall be divided between the persons entitled to such liens *pro rata*, in proportion to the amounts so found due to them respectively If the amount so found to be coming to the contractor shall be sufficient to pay such liens in full, the same shall be so ordered. The premises may be decreed to be sold for the payment of such liens as in other cases.

§ 40 All persons who shall be duly notified of such proceeding, and who shall fail to prove their claims, whether the same be in judgment against the owner or not, shall forever lose the benefit of and be precluded from their liens and all claims against the owner

§ 41. Upon the filing of such bill or petition, the court may, on the motion of any person interested, stay any further proceedings upon any judgment against the owner on account of such lien.

§ 42. Upon entering into a contract to do any work or furnish materials for which a lien might accrue under section one of this act, if the contractor will enter into a bond with the owner for the use of all persons who may do work or furnish materials pursuant to such contract, conditioned for the payment of all just claims for such work or materials as they become due (which bond shall be in such an amount, not less than the price agreed to be paid for the performance of such contract, and with such surety as shall be approved by the judge of the Circuit Court, or a master in chancery of said court), and shall file the same in the office of the clerk of said court, then no lien shall attach in favor of such sub-contractor, mechanic or other person

§ 43. A like bond may be made and filed, as provided in the foregoing section, at any time after the making of such contract, and shall have the effect to discharge all such liens as shall have accrued before the filing thereof, and to prevent the accruing of any such liens thereafter.

§ 44 Any person having a claim against such contractor for work done or materials furnished pursuant to such contract may put the said bond in suit for his use; or in case the same shall have been put in suit, have his damages assessed as in other suits upon penal bonds

§ 45 Should the original contractor, for any cause, fail to complete his contract, any person entitled to a lien as aforesaid may file his petition in any court of record against the owner and contractor, setting forth the nature of his claim. the amount due, as near as may be, and the names of the parties employed on such house or other improvement subject to liens; and notice of such suit shall be served on the persons therein named; and such as shall appear shall have their claims adjudicated, and decrees shall be entered against the owner and original contractor for so much as the work and materials shall be shown to be reasonably worth according to the original contract price, first deducting so much as shall have been rightfully paid on said original contract by the owner, and damages, if any, that may be found to be occasioned the owner by reason of the non-fulfillment of the original contract; the balance to be divided between such claimants in proportion to their respective interests, to be ascertained by the court. The premises may be sold as in other cases under this act.

§ 46. No payments to the original contractor or to his order shall be regarded as rightfully made, if made in violation of the rights and interests of the persons intended to be benefited by this act.

§ 47. No petition shall be filed or suit commenced to enforce the lien created by section twenty-nine, unless the same is commenced within three months from the time of the performance of the sub-contract, or doing the work or furnishing materials as aforesaid: *Provided*, if any delay in filing such petition or commencing suit is caused in consequence of the amount not being due the original contractor, the time of such delay shall not be reckoned.

§ 48. Hotel, inn and boarding-house keepers shall have a lien upon the baggage and other valuables of their guests or boarders brought into such hotel, inn or boarding-house by such guests or boarders, for the proper charges due from such guests or boarders for their accommodations, boarding and lodging, and such extras as are furnished at their request.

§ 49. Stable-keepers and any persons shall have a lien upon the horses, carriages and harness kept by them for the proper charges due for the keeping thereof, and expenses bestowed thereon at the request of the owner, or person having the possession thereof.

§ 50. Agisters and persons keeping, yarding, feeding or pasturing domestic animals, shall have a lien upon the animals agistered, kept, yarded or fed, for the proper charges due for the agistering, keeping, yarding or feeding thereof.

§ 51. Chapter sixty-five of the Revised Statutes of 1845, entitled "Liens," and an act entitled "An act to amend chapter sixty-five of the Revised Statutes of 1845, entitled 'Liens,'" approved February 18, 1861, and an act entitled "An act to amend chapter sixty-five of the Revised Statutes of 1845, entitled 'Liens,'" approved February 14, 1863, and an act entitled "An act to provide for the redemption of property sold under mechanics' lien," approved March 30, 1869, and an act entitled "An act amendatory of the mechanics' lien law of this State," approved April 5, 1869, and all other acts and parts of acts inconsistent with the provisions of this act, are hereby repealed, except as herein re-enacted: *Provided,* that this section shall not be so construed as to affect any rights existing or actions pending at the time this act shall take effect.

(Statutes of Illinois, Myers, page 216)

AMENDMENT, MAY 24, 1879—LIENS—LIMITATION.

AN ACT TO AMEND SECTION TWENTY-EIGHT (28) OF AN ACT, ENTITLED "AN ACT TO REVISE THE LAW IN RELATION TO LIENS." APPROVED MARCH 25, 1874.

(Approved May 24, 1879, in force July 1, 1879)

SECTION 1. *Be it enacted by the People of the State of Illinois, represented in the General Assembly,* That section twenty-eight (28) of an act, entitled "An act to revise the law in relation to liens," approved March 25, 1874, be and the same is hereby amended so as to read as follows:

§ 28. **Limitation.**— No creditor shall be allowed to enforce the lien created under the foregoing provisions, as against or to the prejudice of any other creditor or incumbrance or purchaser, unless suit be instituted to enforce such lien within six (6) months after the last payment for labor or materials shall have become due and payable.

(Approved May 24, 1879)

(Session Laws, 1879, page 191)

AMENDMENT, MAY 31, 1887—MECHANICS—STATEMENT OF ACCOUNT.

AN ACT TO AMEND SECTIONS FOUR AND TWENTY-EIGHT, AND ADD SECTIONS FIFTY-TWO, FIFTY-THREE AND FIFTY-FOUR TO "AN ACT TO REVISE THE LAW RELATING TO LIENS, IN FORCE JULY 1, 1874"

(In force July 1, 1887)

SECTION 1 Amends section four by requiring creditors or contractors to file statement of account before suit can be brought.

Amends section twenty-eight by requiring that the statement and claim as provided in section four shall be in four months, suit thereon shall be begun in two years

SECTION 1. *Be it enacted by the People of the State of Illinois, represented in the General Assembly,* That section four and section twenty-eight of an act, entitled "An act to revise the law relating to liens," in force July 1, 1874, be amended as follows; and that said act be further amended by adding thereto three additional sections, known as sections fifty-two, fifty-three and fifty-four, as hereinafter provided:

§ 4. Every creditor or contractor who wishes to avail himself of the provisions of this act shall file with the clerk of the Circuit Court of the county in which the building, erection or other improvement to be charged with the lien is situated, a just and true statement, or account or demand due him after allowing all credits, setting forth the time when such material was furnished or labor performed, and containing a correct description of the property to be charged with the lien, and verified by an affidavit. Any person having filed a claim for a lien as provided in this section, may bring a suit at once to enforce the same by bill or petition in any court of competent jurisdiction in the county where the claim for a lien has been filed.

§ 28. No creditor shall be allowed to enforce a lien created under the provisions of this act as against or to the prejudice of any other creditor, or incumbrance or purchaser, unless a claim for a lien shall have been filed with the clerk of the Circuit Court, as provided in section four of this act, within four months after the last payment shall have become due and payable. Suit shall be commenced within two years after filing such claim with the clerk of the Circuit Court, or the lien shall be vacated.

§ 52. Upon the written demand of the owner or his agent, or any person interested in the real estate, served on the person or his agent claiming the lien, requiring suit to be commenced to enforce the lien, suit shall be commenced within thirty days thereafter or the lien shall be forfeited.

§ 53. The clerk of the Circuit Court where such lien shall be filed shall endorse on every such claim for a lien filed, the date of filing, and make an abstract thereof in a book kept for that purpose, and properly indexed, containing the name of the person filing the lien, the amount of the lien, the date of filing, the name

of the person against whom the lien is filed, and a description of
the property charged with the lien, and for which the person filing
the lien shall pay one dollar to the clerk.

§ 54. Whenever a lien has been claimed by filing the same with
the clerk of the Circuit Court, and is afterwards paid, the person
filing the same shall acknowledge satisfaction thereof in the proper
book in such office in writing, and on neglect to do so for ten days
after the claim has been paid, he shall forfeit to the owner the sum
of twenty-five dollars.

(Approved May 31, 1887)
(Session Laws, 1887, page 219)

AMENDMENT, JUNE 16, 1887. MECHANICS — SUB-CONTRACTORS.

An Act to Amend Sections Twenty-nine (29), Thirty (30) and
Thirty-five (35), and to Repeal Sections Thirty six (36), Forty-
two (42), Forty-three (43) and Forty-four (44) of an act entitled " An Act to Revise the Law in Relation to Liens,"
Approved March 25, 1874; in force July 1, 1874.

('n force July 1, 1887)

Section 1 Amends sections 29 and 30, act of 1874, by making them conform to
the provisions of section 35 as amended by this act   Amends sec
tion 35 by requiring original contractors, when any money is due
and is to be drawn from the owner, to make sworn statements and
the owner shall retain the amount due to sub contractors for work
and materials   No liens shall accrue until statement is furnished
owner liable to sub contractor if payment is made without such
statement, penalties
  2 Repeals certain sections.

Section 1. *Be it enacted by the People of the State of Illinois,
represented in the General Assembly,* That sections twenty-nine
(29), thirty (30) and thirty-five (35), of an act entitled " An act to
revise the law in relation to liens," approved March 25, 1874, in
force July 1, 1874, be so amended as to read as follows:

§ 29. **Sub-contractors, mechanics, workmen, etc.** — Every
sub-contractor, mechanic, workmen, or other person, who shall hereafter, in pursuance of the purposes of the original contract between
the owner of any lot or piece of ground, or his agent and the
original contractor, perform any labor or furnish any materials in
building, altering, repairing, beautifying or ornamenting any house
or other building or appurtenance thereto, on such lot or on any

street or alley and connected with such building or appurtenance, shall have a lien for the value of such labor and materials upon such house or building and appurtenances, and upon the lot or land upon which the same stands, to the extent of the right, title and interest of such owner at the time of making the original contract for such house or the improvement, but the aggregate of all the liens hereby authorized, shall not exceed the price stipulated in the original contract between such owner and the original contractor for such improvements. In no case shall the owner be compelled to pay a greater sum for or on account of such house, building or other improvement than the price or sum stipulated in said original contract or agreement, unless payments be made to the original contractor, or to his order, in violation of the rights and interests of the persons intended to be benefited by section thirty-five of this act. *Provided*, if it shall appear to the court that the owner and contractor fraudulently, and for the purpose of defrauding sub-contractors, fixed an unreasonably low price in their original contract for the erection or repairing of such building, then the court shall ascertain how much of a difference exists between a fair price for the labor and material used in said building or other improvements and the sum named in said original contract. Said difference shall be considered a part of the contract, and be subject to a lien, but in no case shall the original contractor's time or profits be secured by this lien only so far as the sum named in the original contract or agreement

§ 30. **Notice -- form.**—The person performing such labor or furnishing such material shall cause a notice in writing to be served on such owner or his agent, substantially in the following form: To   : You are hereby notified that I have been employed by   to (here state whether to labor or furnish material, and substantially the nature of the undertaking or demand) upon your (here state the building, and where situated, in general terms), and that I shall hold the (building, or as the case may be) and your interest in the grounds liable for the amount that is (or may become) due me on account thereof (Date.) (Signature) *Provided*, such notice shall not be necessary where the sworn statement of the contractor provided for in section thirty-five of this act shall serve to give the owner true notice of the amount due, and to whom due.

§ 35. The original contractor shall, whenever any payment of money shall become due from the owner, or whenever he desires to draw any money from the owner, lessee or his agent on such con-

tract, make out and give to the owner, lessee or his agent, a statement, under oath, of the number, name of every sub-contractor,
mechanics or workmen in his employ, or person furnishing ma
terials, giving their names and the rate of wages or the terms
of contract, and how much, if any thing, is due or to become
due to them or any of them for work done or materials furnished, and the owner, lessee or his agent shall retain out of
any money then due or to become due to the contractor an amount
sufficient to pay all demands that are due or to become due such
sub-contractors, mechanics and workmen, or person furnishing materials, as shown by the contractor's statement, and pay the same
to them, according to their respective rights, and all payments so
made shall, as between such owner and contractor, be considered the
same as if paid to such original contractor   Until the statement
provided for in this section is made in manner and form as herein
provided, the contractor shall have no right of action or lien against
the owner on account of such contract, and any payment made by
the owner before such statement is made, or without retaining sufficient money, if that amount be due or is to become due, to pay the
sub-contractors, mechanics, workmen or persons furnishing materials,
as shown by the statement, shall be considered illegal, and made in
violation of the rights of the persons intended to be benefited by this
act, and the rights of such sub-contractors, mechanics, workmen or
persons furnishing material to a lien shall not be affected thereby.
In order that the owner, lessee or his agent may be protected, he
may, at any time during the progress of the work, demand in writing of the contractor the statement herein provided for, which shall
be made by the contractor and given to the owner, lessee or his
agent, and if such contractor fail to furnish such statement within
five days after demand made, he shall forfeit to such owner the sum
of fifty dollars ($50) for every such offense, which may be recovered
in any action of debt before any justice of the peace.

§ 2. That sections thirty-six (36), forty-two (42), forty-three (43)
and forty-four (44) of said act, and all other acts or parts of acts in
conflict therewith, be and the same are hereby repealed.

(Approved June 16, 1887)
(Session Laws, 1887, page 220.)

AMENDMENT OF 1891 — LIENS.

An Act to Amend Sections 11, 33, 34 and 35, of "An Act to Revise the Law in Relation to Liens," Approved March 25, 1874, in Force July 1, 1874, as Amended by An Act Approved June 16, 1887, and in Force July 1, 1887.

(Approved June 22, 1891, in force July 1, 1891)

SECTION 11. Quantum meruit
33 Limited to amount due contractor
Laborer's lien for twenty days
34 Owner may retain money, etc.
Laborer's preferred.
35. Contractor to make statement to owner, what to contain

SECTION 1. *Be it enacted by the People of the State of Illinois, represented in the General Assembly*, That sections eleven, thirty-three, thirty-four and thirty-five of an act entitled "An act to revise the law in relation to liens," approved March 25, 1874, in force July 1, 1874, as amended by an act approved June 16, 1887, and in force July 1, 1887, be and the same are hereby amended so as to read as follows:

§ 11. **Quantum meruit.**—When the owner of the land shall have failed to perform his part of the contract by failing to advance to the contractor moneys justly due him under the contract at the time when the same should have been paid to the contractor, or has failed to perform his part of the contract in any other manner, and by reason thereof the other party shall, without his own default, have been prevented from performing his part, he shall be entitled to a reasonable compensation for as much thereof as has been performed in proportion to the price stipulated for the whole, and the court shall adjust his claim and allow him a lien accordingly.

§ 33. **Limited to amount due contractor.**—No claim of any sub-contractor, mechanic, workman, or other person, shall be a lien under section twenty-nine of this act, except so far as the owner may be indebted to the contractor at the time of giving such notice, as aforesaid, of such claim, or may become indebted afterward to him as such contractor: *Provided*, however the claim of any person for mechanical or other labor, under section twenty-nine of this act, shall be a lien for twenty days from the last day's work performed by such person, to an amount equal to ten per cent of the proportionate value of the contract completed up to the date of said last day's work: *Provided*, such notice is served within twenty days from the day when such last day's work was performed by such person serving such notice, and the owner or his agent may retain for

31

said twenty days such ten per cent out of any money due or to become due the contractor: *And provided, further*, this ten per cent
shall not be construed as in addition to any per cent that may be
held back in pursuance of the terms of the contract between the
owner and the original contractor

§ 34. **Owner may retain money, etc.**—When the owner, or his
agent, is notified as aforesaid, he may retain, from any money due or
to become due the original contractor, an amount sufficient to pay all
demands that are or will become due such sub-contractor, mechanic,
workman, or other person so notifying him, and may pay over the
same to the persons entitled thereto   In case the amount due the
original contractor and the ten per cent in section thirty-three provided is not sufficient to pay such persons so entitled in full, he shall
first pay all claims for mechanical and other labor in full, if the
amount due the contractor and the said ten per cent is sufficient; if
not, then *pro rata;* but if more than sufficient, the balance shall be
divided and paid to such other persons, *pro rata*, in proportion to
the amounts due them respectively at the time of such payment
All payments so made shall, as between such owner and contractor,
be considered the same as if paid to such original contractor

§ 35. **Contractor to make statement to owner; what to contain.**—The original contractor shall, as often as requested, in writing, by the owner, lessee, or his agent, make out and give to such
owner, lessee, or his agent, a statement of the number of persons in
his employ, and of the sub-contractors, or other persons, furnishing
labor or material, giving their names, and how much, if any thing,
is due or to become due to each of them for work done or material
furnished, which statement shall be made under oath, if required of
him by such owner, lessee or agent, in which case the sub-contractor
shall, as often as requested, in writing, by the contractor, or his
agent, make out and give to the contractor a statement of the number of persons in his employ, or sub-contractors or other persons
furnishing material, giving their names, and how much, if any thing,
is due to each of them, which statement shall be made under oath,
if required by such contractor; and if any contractor or sub-
contractor shall fail to furnish such statement within five days after
demand, made as aforesaid, he shall forfeit to such owner or contractor the sum of fifty dollars for every offense, which may be
recovered in an action of debt before a justice of the peace

(This act is in place of sections 11, 33, 34 and 35, chapter 82, Hurd s Revised
Statutes.)

(Session Laws, 1891, page 161.)

INDEX.

32

33

34

35

36·